The Nature of God:
THE REVELATION

Channeled Messages from Your Heavenly Father, Divine Mother, and Archangel Michael

Michelle D McCann

Copyright © 2020 by Michelle D McCann

All rights reserved. This book or any portion thereof may not be reproduced or used in any manner whatsoever without the express written permission of the publisher except for the use of brief quotations in a book review.

ISBN: 978-1-7347580-0-9

Edited by Susan Robinson, Creative Power Writing

Cover design by Nevena Knezevic

www.happyselfpublisher.com

*To Steve and Aidan
for their unwavering love and support*

Table of Contents

Preface vii

Introduction xi

A Note from the Author xv

Seeing Clearly Now xxiii

PART ONE
The Nature of God: The Revelation 1

Buckle Up! Time to Meet God 3

It's All Coming In So Fast! 5

Ring! Ring! Jesus Calling 19

The Revelation 27

The Law of Attraction 37

Each of Us Is Special 45

Discerning Energy 55

Divine Mother God 69

Mother/Father God Radio 81

We Are Lights for One Another 89

Becoming Real 97

It's a Marathon 105

Putting Together the Puzzle 113

Closer to Fine 123

In the Slipstream 133

Old Fears Re-Emerge 143

Standing in the Truth 153

Patience! 161

Talk to Mama 169

The Master Key 179

Karma 185

Clear Your Vibes 197

Beautiful and Breathtaking: God's Book of Remembrance 209

The First Soul 217

One Thing at a Time 229

Just Trust 237

You Can Trust That Like a $2 Bill 247

Make Your Soul Sing 257

The Nature of God is Love, Love, Love 263

PART TWO
   The Nature of Angels: The Pathway Back to God 265

Angels: GPS to God 267

The God Squad Is Out There Watching 279

Heaven Is an Energetic Realm 285

Guardian Angels Illuminate Our Route 297

Everything Falls Into Place 307

Breaking the Trauma Chain 323

Just Ask the Angels 335

PART THREE
The Reconciliation 337

Wrap It Up with a Bow 339

The Freedom of Embracing My Truth 341

Vacation—But Not from God 349

The Divinely-Guided Life Plan 355

Stick a Fork in It: Done! 359

A Message from Michelle 361

Resources 365

Acknowledgments 375

About the Author 379

About the Book Cover 381

Preface

This message is from God, as channeled by Michelle McCann on June 14, 2019

Our story may seem confusing at first, but if you persevere, you will be rewarded with epiphanies of great clarity and joy.

I have dictated and Michelle has transcribed, and although at times the text may seem disjointed and unclear, all is as it should be. When people awaken to their divine natures and gifts, it is like learning a foreign language—everything seems jumbled and makes no sense. Michelle wrote this after she had taken many classes and read much, so she had some understanding of the spiritual realms. Still, she did not recognize the vibration of her heavenly father and divine mother. As she worked with it, she struggled to understand what was happening. In fact, she did not know or feel that it was our energy at all. She just knew she was getting "impressions" and felt called to write them down. That was us urging her to do so. Even though some of our requests sounded illogical, she listened.

I encourage you to do the same. Listen to the song of your heart, even when it doesn't seem to make sense. It is by listening to us (Father, Mother, the angels) that you find the path back to connecting with the divine.

This book's second section, "The Nature of Angels: The Pathway Back to God," is much more cohesive than Part I, as Michelle has learned to channel now with certainty.[1] Not that she wasn't channeling "correctly" before, but the information was coming in fast and she was not used to the feeling, which triggered manic episodes. We were sending energy to help her connect to the heavenly realms, but neither she nor her doctors knew that was what was happening.

---

[1] Originally, these were to be separate books. Later, Michelle was told to consolidate them into one. We retained the references to the separate books in their original channeling, so you can see the evolution of the manuscript.

When people are manic, they are connecting to divine essence. If people think they are Jesus or Buddha, it is because they are feeling the energy of the heavenly realms. It is often disconcerting because they are not used to this vibration, and it manifests in socially unacceptable or seemingly irrational behaviors. The movie *Crazywise* and the research of psycho-spiritual counselor Emma Bragdon and Sean Blackwell of Bipolar Awakenings will better explain how mental illness and spiritual connection are related.

Michelle was only "mentally ill" in the sense that she thought she was Jesus, which she was not. Rather, he had connected his energy with hers in order to heal her mind. Everyone will experience this. Some will have psychotic breaks and need the psychiatric establishment to understand that this is their reconnection with the divine, not a mix-up in their brain chemistry.

Again, I encourage psychiatric care professionals to understand this and guide individuals through their spiritual awakenings rather than treating them as if their brains are broken.

Compassionate care, free from judgment, is the key component. Medication may be required, but the idea that people need to be dosed forever is simply not true. Once they process their trauma (from this lifetime or past lives), they will be able to function normally. But having the opportunity to express their "delusions" and work through their feelings will be critical in helping them understand the meaning and purpose of their suffering and why they are here at all. They will be happier and healthier afterwards because they will have peace.

Understanding this process will also help people suffering from depression. Individuals become suicidal because they long to reconnect with me. Subconsciously, they know they are missing something integral to their essence. Emotional support and medication will ease physical and mental distress, but helping them to connect with who they truly are and through that, to reconnect with me, will eliminate the pain. This is all I will say about mental illness for now. Michelle will write (channel) more from me about this at a future point.

As you read this book, I encourage you to keep an open mind and understand that spiritual awakening is a process, often confusing and sometimes dangerous if not undertaken carefully.

> *OK, God, this is me, Michelle. "Dangerous" sounds scary.*

It is dangerous in the sense that some people may end their earthly existence. However, they will reconnect safely with me in the spiritual realms, so their souls will live on.

Is there anything we can do to make this less dangerous?

As talk show host Ellen DeGeneres says, love one another and be kind when you see your brothers and sisters floundering mentally or physically. Even if their challenges are not visible, strive to be compassionate, as all people are wrestling with something, though most don't show it today. Soon this will begin to change. The more people share their struggles openly, the more support and love they can get, both from the earthly and spiritual realms.

Is there anything else to the preface?

No, my child. This is all. Publish our book as it is written. I encourage others to read and listen with their hearts and they will begin to understand. Wishing you peace and joy and angel blessings.

Love,
God

Introduction

This message is from God, as channeled by Michelle McCann on June 10, 2019

Now is the time of revelation foretold to you in the Bible. The good news is ready to be revealed. You will all be saved from sin and condemnation. Indeed, there was never any sin and condemnation. That falsehood was perpetuated in the Bible, but it was necessary at the time.

Why couldn't we know the truth from the beginning?

Information I provided to the writers of the Bible was based in truth and has been a comfort to many throughout the ages. Now, however, it is time to set the story straight. There was no Garden of Eden, no Adam or Eve.

That story was an allegory. As Michelle has written, there is no devil, no Satan, no serpent in the garden. Eve was not "bad" for eating from the tree of the knowledge of good and evil. The scenario was simply a metaphor to explain that my children would be given the opportunity to experience contrast, the negative side of energy.

In heaven with your divine mother and me, you knew only our love. Your heart's desire was to know your magnificence separate from us. So we created a world where you could safely (although sometimes with significant struggle) learn what it was like to be "not God." Then when you returned to love, your natural inheritance, you would understand the magnificence of who you truly are. We already know this, but you did not realize it.

You are ready to learn this now. Throughout the ages you have had varied experiences, many joys and triumphs, some sorrows and tribulations, wars and famine, disease, all kinds of social ills. Now is the time for all of that to end and for our glorious children to be reunited with us in heaven.

To be clear, in the earthly realm, heaven is a state of mind, in which your will is in alignment with your mother and father God. Michelle explains this relationship later. Listen to our words and strive to live by them. This is how you will come to peace in your hearts and in your minds.

One day, we will all come together in the heavenly realm, but for now your mission is to strive to make heaven on earth. You do this by raising your vibration to one of love—never-ending, always changing, always challenging love. Choose minute by minute, hour by hour, day by day to love us and your brothers and sisters.

This reconciliation is possible through Jesus, your brother, but you do not need to be Christian to partake in his healing. Your mother and I do not prefer or show favor towards any religion over another. Having no religious affiliation is perfectly OK too. We cherish all our children equally, no matter what spiritual path they follow.

Humanity is the story of the prodigal son. No matter what wrongs you feel you have done to yourselves, to others, or to us, we will always welcome you home with a reverent embrace. Never fear your return to us. Our devotion is not conditional. You are worthy of our love despite any actions you may have taken. This type of love does not exist in the earthly realm. When we are reunited in heaven you will understand, but for now, know this truly in your heart—you can do no wrong in our eyes.

We encourage you to love and help others and take care of your body, mind, and spirit, as we know these activities will bring you joy and happiness. However, should you choose to behave in other ways, it will not take away our love for you. NOTHING you could do could ever cause that. As I told Neale Donald Walsch in *Conversations with God*, even Hitler went to heaven. He came to earth and perpetrated evils to reveal to mankind the things that can happen if we demean others who are different and let power run away with us. All are meant to be equals, God's children.

That is not to say we are to be the same. Each of us has a unique fingerprint, a soul imprint that is more intricate and elaborate than you could ever imagine. Our hope is for you to "live your fingerprint," meaning to shine your perfect light and live your soul's purpose in this lifetime. You do this, as I have said, by following your heart's desires and your body's systems. If you are tired, rest. If you are joyful, play. If you are with others, love. It is that simple, really.

Just pay attention to your process. Do not let fear get in the way. In times of doubt and anxiety when you long to retreat into your shell, turn toward others. Reveal your true feelings and your true self and you will find loving connections.

Sometimes you will encounter rejection, but that is no worse than not being who you truly are. Plus, revealing your essence means fewer slaps in the face because you connect with those who truly "get" you. Souls who have incarnated together for a similar purpose will reveal themselves as your tribe. Every person has one. Even though we are all one and connected, we bond with some souls more closely and that is OK. These are people with whom we enjoy a strong affinity and sense of safety and security. They could be family or friends—the relationship doesn't matter as long as the affection is mutual, reflecting love and respect for one another.

To achieve this, you have to take risks. You have to be seen. You have to be yourself—your funny, glorious, loving, tender, sometimes sad self. When you are your authentic self, others can be too, and you can love one another despite everyone's flaws and faults. As humans, you all have imperfections, but in heaven you are all perfect children of a perfect God. You are indeed made in God's image—perfection and pure love.

Maintain an open mind and a welcoming heart as you read these pages Michelle and I have written. If you really listen to your heart, you will know what we are saying is true. Deep inside, you have been longing for this truth—to understand the nature of the universe and of me, your God. Now, through Michelle, I am revealing myself to you.

Soon you will not need to read Michelle's writing or hear her speak because you will begin to develop your OWN relationship with me. It will be GLORIOUS! I am so excited to reconnect with each one of you, and I know that every one of you longs to reunite with me.

It starts with building a relationship with the angels, as they are the pathway back to me, guides on your route. Each person will travel a different way. Yours will be different from Michelle's, but as you work with the angels, its twists and turns will become clearer.

Michelle will channel more soon, which will provide additional information. For now, sit with this book. Rest with it. Take it in. Knowing that we will soon be one again will help calm your heart and soul.

Much love to all of you, my children. May these words bring you peace and joy.

Love,
God

A Note from the Author

December 6, 2019

The Truth Is...

Honestly, I still don't know what the truth is. I have thought a lot about this writing journey and the information I am putting out into the world and want to be completely honest and transparent about what you are about to read. Throughout the process, I worried that my writing resulted from the delusions that accompany a diagnosis of bipolar disorder with psychotic features, the label assigned to me in September 2007 when I was hospitalized for my "breakdown." Modern medicine would say I have a chemical imbalance in my brain and need to be on medication for the rest of my life to maintain my sanity. My belief is that I was experiencing a spiritual awakening triggered by traumatic events. The British Psychological Association recently addressed this:

> Hearing voices or feeling paranoid are common experiences which can often be a reaction to trauma, abuse or deprivation. Calling them symptoms of mental illness, psychosis or schizophrenia is only one way of thinking about them, with advantages and disadvantages.[2]

---

[2] Anne Cooke, ed., "Understanding Psychosis and Schizophrenia."

Michelle McCann

There are clearly conflicting ideas about the root causes of my experiences. Regardless, I have functioned normally since my diagnosis, primarily free of fanciful thoughts or behaviors. Plus, for more than two years I have diligently nurtured my spiritual abilities, taking classes to enhance my intuition, psychic skills, and ability to connect with the divine realms—in particular, God and the angels. My wonderful mentors and teachers have no mental health diagnoses, yet they connect seamlessly with the spirit realms and have told me that I can do—indeed, that I am doing—the same thing.

When I reread much of what I have channeled, I am amazed at its clarity and detail and truly the answers to the life questions I have asked for a very long time. The writing brings me peace and comfort and laughter. People with whom I shared these pages told me the readings helped them understand the nature of God and why we suffer and gave them hope for a peaceful future. In my heart, I feel like this guidance and support came from a source greater than my own thinking. Indeed, many of the ideas are ones I never came close to envisioning before.

Still, seeds of doubt swirl around me. We come to believe what we are told over and over again, and I was told that because I was mentally ill, I could not trust my own thoughts. I think of abusive relationships and how victims begin to doubt their sanity and worth after being told persistently that they are insignificant or that their feelings are wrong. For twelve years, I was labeled a person with mental illness, and letting that go has been a difficult task.

In the past year, I have come to realize that much of my "delusional thinking" was actually related to unprocessed childhood trauma and accompanying spiritual experiences in which I connected with the unseen realms. Looking through the trauma lens under the guidance of gifted therapists with the amazing trauma therapy tool Eye Movement Desensitization and Reprocessing (EMDR),[3] I have connected the dots to explain my grandiose and fearful thinking.

My actions were much like those of combat soldiers who brought home PTSD along with their duffels. Traumatized by bombs exploding in the war zone, they hear a car backfire in their quiet suburban neighborhoods and duck under a table. Although that initial traumatic situation has ended, the part of the brain where that memory is stored doesn't realize the danger is gone. The "fight, flight, or freeze" response kicks in, and the vets behave in ways that don't make sense to anyone who hasn't "been there." It may not even make sense to the veterans, themselves, until someone explains what has happened. If they are lucky (like me) and have thoughtful, supportive, and effective trauma treatment, they stop ducking under tables and the panic no longer overtakes their minds.

My trauma stems from having been raised in a very loving yet sometimes violent home. Some in my family would consider what happened normal for that day and age. Our father disciplined my siblings and me with harsh, scolding words and beat us with a belt when we "misbehaved." My brother, Duke, the first-born son and father's namesake, received the brunt of the "discipline."

My father's anger also manifested in his throwing things or kicking the dog. Our dog lost his eye when my enraged father threw a rock at him. I honestly don't think his intention was to injure the dog or us. It just happened to be the fallout from his uncontrolled anger.

I don't know much about my father's upbringing, but I understand it was not easy, and I believe he was acting out his own trauma. In many ways, he was a very loving father, providing for his family, taking us fishing, and cooking burgers

---

[3] During EMDR sessions, the patient relives a traumatic experience in small doses as a therapist directs eye movements or uses sounds or tapping to dampen the power of the trauma.

on the grill. He made sure we spent fun times with his extended family, sharing catfish fries and playing with cousins.[4]

My mother was always my safe space. My hero. Loving and kind and nurturing, my mother was our biggest cheerleader, always encouraging us and telling us how proud she was of us. We could feel the steadfastness of her immense love. Through her example, I learned to be a wonderful mother, and feeling her love, I gained confidence to know that I am a good person who deserves love. My bond with her nurtured my soul and helped me step into the TRUTH OF WHO I AM.

Despite her loving care, I did not feel safe. Her way of comforting us when we were distressed was to reassure us that everything was OK. Unable to protect us or prevent our father's violent outbursts, that was the best she could do. Her type of protection evokes the movie *Life is Beautiful*, in which Roberto Benigni's character does not want his little boy to suffer despite circumstances he cannot control. I know now that our ego, our divine mother, did the same thing for us, protecting us from what we could not bear. This experience with my earthly mother was to be a catalyst for my understanding of the ways of nature and the way of grace.

Looking back to my earthly experiences as a child, I realize I was never able to fully express my fear and turned to my teddy bear as the only one who understood how scary it was to live in that home. My biggest trauma came when my brother was four and I was six. Memories of this only recently started to return, as I had blocked them out due to the overwhelming feelings I was unable to bear. This type of disassociation is not uncommon when trauma crushes a person's ability to cope.

I was in my older sister's room playing with my dolls when Duke pulled a shoestring from Vicky's boot or roller skate. He

---

[4] In two separate sessions with mediums, my father said he was not embarrassed and wanted this story to come to light. He and all the ancestors are proud of me for ending the trauma cycle. My father was amazed at what a thoughtful and respectful young man my son, Aidan, is, given that my husband and I never used any physical discipline while raising him.

wrapped it around his neck and hung himself from her four-poster canopy bed. The details of what happened next are still not entirely clear to me. The biggest thing I remember was desperately looking for the scissors. Our babysitter was in the next room watching TV. The rest remains a blur. Years later, my mother said that the ambulance rushed Duke to the hospital. He nearly died and all the blood vessels in his face were broken so his face was blue. I recall none of this.

The story my family told was that, clad in his red cape playing Tarzan, Duke accidentally became entangled in the string. I believe he was in such pain and distress from being the "bad boy" that he was trying to find an escape. Regardless of what the "true" story is, the trauma I felt from witnessing and experiencing this event was very real. I felt responsible, that I should have protected him—or at the very least, been watching over him to make sure he didn't hurt himself, as the big sister should do. Through therapy, I now understand that as a child myself, I was not responsible for the care and protection of my little brother. I wasn't even old enough to care for and protect myself.

Through my study of, and channeled writing about, how our soul experiences awaken us to our divine natures, I understand now that all of this was planned before I was born into this family and this lifetime, just as all souls plan each incarnation on their paths to spiritual awakening. Our traumas are a deeply-rooted part of how we come to fully know ourselves and God, the source of all that is. Just as a pearl needs the continuous chafing of the sand to become radiant, we need to experience discomfort and struggle to emerge into our true state, which is one of pure grace. Our natural inheritance is love, which is also our divine nature. The purpose of our souls having human existences is for us to understand how we progress from karma to grace. With karma, the laws of cause and effect are always in play. Karma is not punishment for any wrongdoing, but the process by which we learn how the actions of each soul impact the whole. Once we move into grace, this learning is no longer required. We understand our divinity and the perfection of all the other souls ever created.

How have I come to know this? When I suffered, I looked outside myself and turned to the spirit world to make meaning of my experiences. Mentors and healers have told me I am a "sensitive," able to sense the energy of others on earth and in the spirit realms. At first I perceived these feelings as my own, not distinguishing what belonged to me and what belonged to someone else or was coming from a source in another realm. Before I began studying the ways of the spirit world, I would have considered this "woo-woo" science. Now I have learned that it is quite possible to discern external energies. It's the way you might "get a good vibe" or "get a bad vibe" when you meet someone or step into a place. I have come to understand that I often pick up those energies, both from others and the spirit world. My challenge has been learning to tease out their sources.

I finally recognize that my sensitivity is a true gift. While feeling the pain of others has been difficult, this ability to perceive has enabled me to connect with my own soul and to the collective soul, which is simply all souls combined into one. Think of the collective soul as the ocean and each individual soul as a drop of water that makes up the whole.

Recently I have been reminded about the importance of energetic boundaries, psychic protection, and grounding. In some of the channeling in this book, Archangel Michael told me that despite my impression of these ideas and practices as "hokey," they are important to cleanse and clear my energy, and I need to pay attention to them to stay sane and take care of myself.

I work every day to sort out my TRUTH. Like the veteran with PTSD, I have done some seemingly crazy things like ducking under tables when there is no current threat. Now that I understand why I acted that way, I don't feel like I was out of my mind, just that my mind was not able to process the overwhelming feelings that flooded it at the time. As I connected with the spirit realms, gleaning knowledge of the nature of God and the angels, I also worked to mitigate my response to the traumatic events. With each new effort to repair these old wounds and to grow in my understanding of energy and the spirit realms, I get stronger and clearer about what happened to me.

My hope is that this writing brings you peace, comfort, and joy, as it has me. I am sharing it despite my fear that some may discount it as manic ramblings. My wish is that if you read closely and repeatedly, as I have, the messages will resonate. They are important, and we need their vision of hope and comfort in our lives and the world today, no matter how they came into being.

With much love and wishes for angel blessings,
Michelle

Seeing Clearly Now

March 1, 2020

Michelle:
As of today, I KNOW THE TRUTH! My experiences were the beginning of God's revelation. They (Mother/Father God) started with me, but they will reveal themselves to EACH AND EVERY ONE OF YOU in the days and weeks to come. Just as the Bible says the "GOOD NEWS WILL SPREAD," now is the TIME OF GOOD NEWS!

God:
Indeed, it is being revealed that there will be PEACE ON EARTH. Michelle will be your initial guide, teaching how to connect with us, but you will find the same love, connection, and support that she experiences, should you choose to. Of course, you continue to have FREE WILL, so the choice is yours. BUT WE KNOW that, in time, EVERYONE will CHOOSE a connection (or re-connection) to us as their way of being.

God, I feel like this is you talking now.

Yes. Keep typing. This is the conclusion to the book, although it will appear at the beginning.

OK.

Now is the time foretold in the Bible—the time of famine, wars, disease, social ills, greed, deception, and turmoil. You are suffering greatly, although there is still great joy in the world. The TIME IS NOW to return to love and joy as your natural state of being. You had…

My typing has stopped.

We are going to stop here. You are not ready (and neither is the world) to hear everything we have to say. We want the world to read THIS BOOK FIRST, then *Michael and Me: Together Again*, and then a new book you will write that is yet to be revealed. By then, the world will be ready for the full story, including why Jesus lived and why he had to die on the cross. Indeed, he did die for your sins, but they are not the sins you think you know. You are not guilty in our eyes or in need of redemption. Yes, you have made mistakes in choosing not to love one another and yourselves, and us. This is only an error in judgment and not a sin worth punishing and needing redemption. The rest of the story is to unfold.

Listen to Michelle. Her words are our words. She hears us clearly now. The time has come. A new day is dawning. It is indeed darkest before the dawn, but TRUST that the DAWN IS COMING!

With love and peace and Angel Blessings,
Your Mother and Father God
(We are together as one now, reunited in Heaven. Thank you, Michelle.)

What are you thanking me for?

Remember when you felt us "grounding you" yesterday? That was Mother leaving you. You no longer need her ego as a defense. Sure, you will get scared sometimes, but you will return to us, your source, for strength and clarity. All will be well with you and with all my children once we reveal ourselves to them.

Just curious—why me first? I don't feel I have any special gifts.

No, my dear, you don't have special gifts—or I should say, your gifts are no more special than anyone else's. We chose you because you WANTED this task. It has been a hard road for you, over many lifetimes, to reach this point, and now you are ready to be in the spotlight. You are ready TO HELP OTHERS OPEN UP TO THEIR GIFTS. Everyone has them, and you will help people recognize their gifts and reveal them to one another. For that is how the world comes back together as one. Each person expresses who they truly are and shares their gifts with the world, stepping into their rightful places. There is not much more to say about this. We want EVERYONE to read what we have written, as appreciating YOUR STORY will help them understand how their own stories will unfold. TRUST. HAVE FAITH. AND LOVE. ALWAYS LOVE.

I feel like there is more . . . LOL.[5]

No, you just want to hear more, as you ALWAYS WANT TO KNOW EVERYTHING . . . LOL. Trust that it will unfold as it should. Be patient, and everyone needs to be patient too. The time will come when ALL WILL BE REVEALED. OK, Happy Ides of March!

I don't know what that means.

Look it up, Dear, and so can everyone else. Do not put it here. HAVE EVERYONE LOOK IT UP.

OK. Got it. Anything else?

That is all for now. Have a good day, folks, and look forward to this dawning spring. It will be GLORIOUS . . . the best one yet!

Thank you! Love you.

Love you too, my child.

Oh—was I the first soul?

No, that was just so everyone would understand the collective experience.

OK. Thanks for clearing that up. Anything else?

---

[5] Laughing out loud.

No, Dear. Peace and Angel Blessings. PEACE OUT, as Michael would say !

I'm BACK! Not understanding the relationship of the Ides of March. It seems confusing.

That was your thought, not ours. You still don't get everything perfectly. AND THIS IS IMPORTANT! People need to know that YOU DO NOT KNOW EVERYTHING. Your word is not gospel (PUN INTENDED). As Gospel is not gospel either. People will only know THE TRUTH by GOING INSIDE THEMSELVES FOR THE ANSWER. An answer—or THE answer—does not come from you or ANY OTHER SOURCE. Each person will connect to their own TRUTH by going within, meditating, reflecting, TRUSTING THEMSELVES.

OK. This is truly the end of this conclusion. We will write more in the coming weeks and months. STAY TUNED TO THIS BAT CHANNEL, as Michael would say.

Love to all of you, our dear, dear children.
The End (for now).
God

Part I

The Nature of God: The Revelation

By

God and Michelle McCann

Buckle Up! Time to Meet God

Get ready for us to ROCK YOUR WORLD!! That's right. We, your divine spirit team, have lots to share with you through Michelle. Buckle up!

Thank you for joining us on this journey! It is going to be a fun, amazing, and WILD RIDE! That's right. Michelle is spilling the beans on her life, her upbringing, and all the trials and tribulations it took for her to be where she is now. We want you to know that like Michelle, YOU TOO can and will have a direct connection to God and the angels, should you so choose. Know that at times the road will not be an easy one. You all have traumas to be healed before the connection will occur. Healing pain and trauma is an important step to open up to who you truly are, to embrace your God-given gifts, and to learn to connect with us on a regular basis.

We, your heavenly father, divine mother, and all the angels, which are infinite in number, look forward to getting to know you—or rather, you getting to KNOW US as you learn to connect and hear our voices. Some of you will see us (Michelle does not, other than lights that represent her guardian angel, Archangel Michael, and other angels on occasion). Your own special way of connecting with us will be revealed to you as you are ready. TRUST that this revelation will happen in DIVINE RIGHT TIMING.

Sit back, and savor this story and the insights Michelle has gleaned from connecting with us. Soon you will have similar wisdom and knowledge, which comes from knowing yourself and us. Happy Reading, and we look forward to "seeing you on the other side!"

Love,
God and all the angels

It's All Coming In So Fast!

May 20, 2019

Wow, it is all coming in so fast. All the things I want to do and say and learn—connecting motivational speaker Anne Grady with psychic Laurie Blomer about her son's past life issues . . . talking to Mike, our grass cutter, about the tree fungus, the allergy meds, the eye drops, and emailing Mt. Cuba[6] about the lily . . . watching the movie Miracles from Heaven . . . doing angelic healing for my brother Duke and my friend Christina and others . . . connecting with archangel channel Catharine Han about her Archangel Michael message . . . getting the inspiration that my current oracle deck[7] is my guardian angel deck and the cards from my friend Nicole are my Archangel Michael deck . . . the synchronicity of the cards today.

We can all channel Jesus, and it's my task to show others how to connect with the angels, God, and Jesus. Although I was never Jesus, now or in a past life, I am connecting with his energy. It's a cumulative process, like learning to read or ride a bike or snowboard. I'm an amateur really, though God says

---

[6] A beautiful botanical garden in Delaware; Michelle's home is located on the grounds.

[7] Freewheeling alternatives to Tarot cards that offer spiritual guidance and perspective.

> I'm doing better than I give myself credit for. Thanks, God!!!
>
> Pretty soon I'll be able to rattle off all I'm learning, the way I can list my skills as an email channel manager. I just reread this and realized it says I am a "channel manager." Ha! Good joke! I have been a channel manager for email[8] and now I will be a channel manager for Jesus/God as they are one in heaven. Both channel through me at the same time. They do it through writing because when I put my analytical mind to rest, I can listen and hear better.
>
> I am letting things flow. SO exciting. It makes my heart sing to write and know that it is coming from you, God. Soon, scribing the words will be unnecessary, as I will just "know" what you are saying (sometimes I do that now but am less sure about it). Additional practice will make me more certain that God is speaking and writing through me. Wow. Channeled writing. I asked to be able to do that, and God has given it to me.

Yes, my darling. I knew your deepest desire even before you asked. You wanted to connect with me and I have been helping you learn how. Both of your fathers—your birth father and I, your divine father—have been working together to teach you.

Your birth father knew your will and understood that those childhood traumas would help you recover your ability to connect with me. He agreed to be the "bad guy" to help your soul grow. Was it worth it? Yes, and I knew it would be.

Suffering enabled you to know me again in this lifetime. Although we will absolutely reconnect when this life is over, your desire was to know me now and to help others to know me. You wanted to bring peace on earth and you will, my darling.

> How can I possibly do that? I am so small. I am crying, feeling unworthy.

---

[8] A coordinator or project manager, bringing together everyone involved in creating and executing an email campaign.

You are worthy. All my children are worthy. With me here to help, you can do whatever you wish. You cannot do it alone. We are co-creators. Aligning your will to mine makes everything possible.

I believe you, but how does it actually work? Does it take time?

Yes, my child. It is in divine right timing. I know what needs to happen and the steps you must take to meet your heart's desire. Although it might not make sense now, I am never wrong. I do not make mistakes. I always know and act according to your will, which, remember, is your soul's will.

I'm getting confused.

Get out of your head and just write. There will be PEACE ON EARTH! Ego doesn't want to let you believe that you could trigger something so momentous. Indeed, you will be a spark. Many others will help and ultimately, all will be well.

Will there still be wars, famine, pain?

No, those will die away.

When?

It remains to be seen.

Does that mean I am not to know yet?

Yes. Knowing would take the fun out of the mastery of accomplishment. Go and spread my message and I will take care of the timing. Enjoy the ride. Have fun.

It has been super fun lately with all the synchronicities . . . truly like magic.

It is magic, my darling.

The trauma part kind of sucked, but I get it now.

I knew you would.

Of course you did. What about my husband, Steve, and my family? How are they going to react to me telling my story? Are they going to think it is mental illness flaring up again?

No. I am working on them. They love you and want what is best for you. Once they realize that this is your purpose, they will be fully supportive.

What do I need to do?

Nothing. Things will unfold as they should. TRUST. Do what you feel moved to do, say what you feel moved to say, and watch the magic happen!

Wow, I'm so excited, and nervous, and a little overwhelmed, to be honest. SO MUCH TO DO!!!

Please try to relax. That is the mania peeking out. Deep inside, you realize there is much to be done but don't trust that I have it all taken care of for you. If it doesn't happen now, it will happen later. There is no rush.

What about the state of the world?

Again, trust me. It looks like there is much suffering—and THERE IS—but this is the necessary evolution to reunite us. Do not despair. Take action to make things better but do not lose hope. I've got this.

Spiritual teacher and regression therapist Robert Schwartz's work about the larger purpose of individual suffering will help you and others to understand. When there is meaning in hardship, it is freeing. Yes, the misery is still there, but you know it is temporary and for a reason. People just want a reason.

For example, childbirth is painful but the outcome is worth it. A caterpillar transforms into a butterfly. And as Vietnamese Zen Buddhist spiritual leader Thich Nhat Hanh says, "No mud, no lotus." Good things emerge out of difficulty, like struggling to learn something amazing or talking to me. It wasn't without suffering, but I know you believe it was TOTALLY WORTH IT!!

I do. Yes, I do, now that I understand. Should I still be in therapy?

Yes, you will need to deal with people's negative reactions to your revelations. Some will be excited to hear them, delighted in fact, but others will hate and blame you and be nasty and mean. Do not take it personally. It is their path to live.

Will peace come during my lifetime?

That remains to be seen. Just remember, do your part now and trust that I've got this. Enjoy life. Do what makes you happy. Make a difference. Rest. Laugh. Love. Walk. Enjoy nature. Eat good food. And stand up—yes, speak up for what you think is right. Others may disagree, but you are learning my will and want to bring it to earth. It is OK to share that.

What is mental illness?

It is people connecting with the other realms. Sometimes they revisit past lives, although those are really not past. As I told Neale Donald Walsch in *Conversations with God*, time is an illusion, as everything happens simultaneously. Folks who are mentally ill are reaching into the past or future rather than living in the present moment. As is often the case with schizophrenia and bipolar disorder, they could be reliving a past life trauma or living in a future state, which creates anxiety and panic attacks. Although it might not make sense in this incarnation that someone should be anxious, the disquiet is based on something that has happened or will happen.

I'm not sure I'm getting this right.

You are tired. Time to take a break for today.

Thank you. I will. Let me know when it is time to talk again.

I will.

There you go, making me laugh again.

I know—I'm a character, aren't I? I know how much you love humor.

> I do.

That's why I gave you Steve. For many reasons, but humor is definitely one. He helps you learn to be less serious and laugh at yourself.

> I am so grateful you gave me Steve. I am starting to cry.

Yes, my darling. I knew what you needed. He was a medicine for you. His guardian angel is under Raphael—Medicine of God. His soul's purpose is to heal you.

> That seems like not enough, like he has more to do.

He does, but that was his primary wish. He is your soul twin. You will learn more about this. OK, go back to work.

> I'm back from working. I was thinking about my work as an email channel manager and relating it to this new spiritual channeling role. On occasion I get stumped in my email channel manager job, but for the most part, I know how things work and can teach other people. This new channeling will be like that. It feels so good to help others learn, and it is exciting to act as the expert, which I will be if I continue to practice.

Learning takes practice. Polyglots learn multiple languages due to their strong desire and dedication. Those who crave connection with me and focus their efforts will learn. If others choose not to, that is OK. I do not judge, as I recognize that at your core, you love me but have simply forgotten. It's no skin off my back. I know everything and do not

THE NATURE OF GOD

intervene if it is not your will. For example, if you are sick, that is your will. You may not realize it, but it is your deepest wish.

> *Are you sure, God? I can't believe I'm asking if you are SURE! You are God. How can I tell people that if bad things happen it is because they wanted them to?*

Because it is true. I know their will—their feelings, not what they think or say they want, but their desires at the deepest level. The soul level. Sometimes souls wish to suffer for a greater good. Remember childbirth—that is a choice people make every day! They want to have a child and know the upcoming labor and even the child rearing will be painful at times, but their longing is to experience parenthood.

May 21, 2019

> *I woke up this morning thinking about being born again. We were born with God in the first incarnation, when all of us were all together in heaven. God knew us but we did not register ourselves apart from him. We had such a strong desire to perceive ourselves, to truly know who we are in relation to God, that he created the world for us to understand. We are reborn into this life to remember who we truly are.*
>
> *Born again does not mean to be a Christian, although in Christ, all things are possible. We are ALL born again. OK, God. Make sure I am getting this right. I am a little tired from waking up early.*

You are a hard worker, my dear, but remember to rest. This will be a long journey, a marathon, and your body needs fuel to prevent it from burning out before the time comes. Go back to bed.

> *But I can't sleep.*

Just rest. Try not to think too much. Just try to be at peace and in calm. Write about *Miracles from Heaven* later. That movie parallels how

Michelle McCann

I feel. Yes, you understand. Night-night . . . well, morning, since it is 5:43 a.m.

May 23, 2019

>Email to my boss about starting a new mental health employee network:
>
>Good morning and hope your day is off to a good start.
>I have been thinking about my idea of starting a mental health employee network. Steve is really supportive of it as well. I think I do want to explore what would be involved and start talking to people after I talk more with you and our boss. I scheduled a 1x1 with her next Thursday afternoon, and you and I have a 1x1 next Thursday morning.
>I even got a spark of an idea for a name: Mental Health Advocacy to End Stigma (MHATES).
>Here is the link to the other networks, and there is not one for Mental Illness. I think it is part of my path to healing to become more open about my experiences, and I think that will encourage others to be too. I remember my friend Cheryl telling me that years ago, people used to keep cancer a secret, and now they talk about it more openly. My hope is that one day, people will be able to talk about mental health problems just as they do any other illness. It is vital that people have support to get through it, and that would be my aim, to help people find the support they need. The statistics say that one in five people is affected by some type of mental illness, so the impact could be significant.
>Anyway, we can talk more. Just wanted to let you know I am feeling guided to do this.

I really appreciate your support. You are a wonderful friend and manager, and I am grateful you have entered my life at this time!

Have a great day!

Michelle

Anything that's human is mentionable,
and anything that is mentionable
can be more manageable.
When we can talk about our feelings,
they become less overwhelming,
less upsetting, and less scary.

~ Fred Rogers

Mental health network ideas:

- Mr. Rogers quote—include the quote as main mantra
- Daily inspiration emails to members
- Resource website with links to the National Alliance on Mental Illness (NAMI), The Mighty (making health about people), Mad in America (rethinking psychiatric care), Emma Bragdon (bridging spiritual practices with the best in mental health care), Employee Assistance Program (EAP) resources
- Start weekly support groups in various locations
- Have a monthly virtual meeting

- Share articles on psychiatric care, therapy, different illnesses (what they are, how they are treated, and what may help)
- Information about trauma and past lives
- Optional—spirituality-based interventions with information on angels, past lives, the nature of God
- Stories from our MHATES, written and/or video interviews sharing our mental health journeys and experiences
- SHARE MY STORY video series with me interviewing participants. Might need help with editing . . .
- This will help people with and without mental illness learn about the importance of sharing their feelings.

Your story could be the key that unlocks someone else's prison. Don't be afraid to share it.

~ TobyMac

WOW! SO excited to have been inspired to do this employee network idea. It might be a great interim step for me while I move toward being fully independent as a speaker, writer, and channeler. The angels sent me the idea for the name. Even an executive in our area chimed in during a conversation we were having about our feelings and people not being open. Maybe he could sponsor it!!!

Stepping back to other things that have been happening, I realized my fear of public speaking, particularly with people in authority, has to do with my childhood trauma when Daddy used to get violent toward my brother Duke and others. I was a witness but stood by silently, afraid and not knowing what to do.

My therapist is going to do Eye Movement Desensitization and Reprocessing (EMDR) with me next week. EMDR is a technique designed to alleviate feelings of distress caused by traumatic memories. She will check first with my psychiatrist, but we both feel I'm in a good place. I told her I am channeling God/Jesus and shared some of my writing. She didn't seem alarmed. She is familiar with author and speaker Esther Hicks and her interpretation of messages from a group consciousness called Abraham.

I also pulled an amazing card from my new Archangel Michael deck: "If you have been called to write, speak, or channel, this is your sign to keep doing it"!!! WOW!!!! YES!!! Why yes, I have been called. I just need to work on getting over my fears to embrace who I truly am and share my light with the world. When my therapist heard this, she told me to keep writing!!!

I also was excited that I finished the "hook" or description of my memoir, When I Thought I Was Jesus: A Story of Mental Illness and Divine Connection. I felt moved to post it in the Hay House Online Writer's Workshop Facebook group, along with a picture of the cover photo. A member of the group said that the photo of a glass ball and a bridge resonated with her, so she asked me to share more about it. This was my reply:

Actually, I just found my book cover photo on a free photo website, but it spoke to me. During a meditation from a sarawiseman.com course on connecting to guides and angels, I had a third-eye vision of Saint Francis. He gave me a gift, a crystal ball. At the time, I did not understand the meaning.

Googling "metaphysical crystal ball," I found the term "scrying."[9] I even took a class on it! It has been an interesting journey. I realized the crystal ball is a symbol, meaning the gift of peace, both my own inner peace and me giving the gift to others.

Years back, right before my psychotic break, while listening to self-development and spiritual growth guru Wayne Dyer's "Getting in the Gap" meditation, I asked God to make me an instrument of his peace. Through some synchronistic events, I later learned that the phrase is part of the "Prayer of St. Francis." I am now at a place where I am finding the peace I was seeking. It represents his gift to me as my spirit guide. THANK YOU FOR ASKING. It helped me to remember all this. ♥

I realized the Gateway angel cards are my guardian angel deck, and the Work Your Light cards called to me as my Archangel Michael deck. My guardian angel is blue because they[10] are in Michael's hierarchy. I see four lights for Michael because he still oversees all four quadrants of the earth. Sometimes I see my guardian angel twice, which I think represents the masculine and feminine.

---

[9] Foretelling the future using a crystal ball or other reflective surface.
[10] "They" reflects the dual masculine/feminine nature of each guardian angel.

THE NATURE OF GOD

I also got inspired to select Kyle Gray oracle cards for my Archangel Raphael deck. My friend Nicole helped me learn that we can have different cards for different angels. So cool. I'm taking pictures of my decks. I still need to work on loving myself and accepting unconditional love from the divine.

May 24, 2019

Emerging into grace. . . . God and the angels are giving me ideas about the path to follow to live my dreams and fulfill my purpose.

In the meantime things are moving along at work. I'm getting support on the project I was having a hard time with—God and the angels are indeed miracle workers. I understand this course in miracles. The anxiety is decreasing and the freedom is ABOUNDING! Wow . . . amazing grace!

May 25, 2019

Stimulation leads to calmness. . . . Finding joy in doing what you came here to do leads to inner peace. . . . You are in alignment with your soul and with God. The angels are the bringers of opportunity. They comfort too, putting things in your path to help you, creating synchronicities. Because you have free will, it is up to you to listen and act. Angels can't do it for you. As guides, they can only show the way. I, God, am your co-creator. Even I can't create without you.

REALLY? God, again, are you sure?

That's right, my darling. I need you to have these glorious experiences. We are one. When you feel joy and happiness, I feel it. When you feel sad and depressed, I feel it. My wish is for you to be happy, and I have sent the angels to guide your path. But we need you to help us help you. PAY ATTENTION!!! Listen with your heart. Heed your intuition. That is how we speak to you. You can hear it if you PAY ATTENTION!!! We long for you to listen and hear us. What a joyful life you can live if you follow the guidance and take the support we offer. LISTEN. LISTEN. LISTEN.

Now is the time of revelation written about in the Bible, the time of floods and all the other tribulations that were foretold. The second coming of Christ is the reconnection of each soul to the Christ Consciousness—one by one. It is up to you, all my children, to heal the world.

I will come into your mind and heal you if you ask. I long to alleviate your suffering and pain but can't do it without permission. This is how I created you—to be free. That is the only way you—and I—could experience joy and sadness, highs and lows, love and pain. It has been an amazing ride. Now is the time to return to joy and love. Ask and it shall be given to you. Ask and you shall receive.

> *Thank you, God. I feel so blessed to be given this gift.*

I know how much this means to you. I love you.

> *I feel the love. It is so overwhelming it makes me cry. There is still a piece of me that feels undeserving.*

I know, but you ARE deserving. You are my child and have done well. Thank you for listening.

> *I'm overjoyed to connect with you in this way too.*

I have always been here, but you have not always noticed. Now you know. That was my goal the entire time—for you to know me. That is enough for now.

> *Thank you again, God.*

You are welcome, my dear.

Ring! Ring! Jesus Calling

May 26, 2019

Last night Nicole posted on our angel certification Facebook private group that she is seeing the number thirty-three and wonders what it means.[11] It seemed to me like a spirit guide sending her a message. Then I woke up this morning feeling the need to look at the clock—3:03. A bit later, again the need to look at the clock—3:36. Maybe a spirit guide has a message for me, I thought, and immediately pictured Saint Francis. I realized I am to be saying his prayer each day.

But it felt like there was more. I looked at the clock again—3:53. The Our Father prayer and then Wayne Dyer came to mind. Both appeared to be reminding me of prayers that will help me stay peaceful in my mind and in my heart. I also felt like I should give the Getting in the Gap book and CD gift to Nicole.

Other thoughts/channeled ideas filled my mind. Jesus was saying that he wants his reputation restored. It seemed a little funny that Jesus was thinking about his reputation. He made clear to me that he does not

---

[11] Numerology, like astrology, is a tool to help you learn more about yourself, which facilitates stepping into who you truly are and understanding your divine purpose. For example, the numbers associated with your name and birthdate reveal insights about your personality and path. Angels and spirit guides show us numbers to remind us that they are with us; different numbers have different meanings. There are many resources online to research the meanings of numbers.

want war or hate waged in his name. A symbol of love, Jesus represents peace, harmony, and all that is good with the human spirit and the world. Like God, he loves unconditionally—all the sinners, the criminals, the immigrants, the poor, gay people, transgender people, EVERYONE—NO EXCEPTIONS.

Jesus's call to us is to love one another as he loves us. That is all. He says if we try, we can learn to do this. Our culture conditions us to hate people who are different from us. We need to get to know those individuals, learn to celebrate our differences, and embrace one another with love.

Should I share this?

Jesus:

For now, communicate it to those with whom you feel safe. The time will come to share it with the world, but you need to take care of yourself first. You are not ready to put your whole self out there yet, telling people that you are channeling us.

God and I are different, even though we are one. I, Jesus, am the way to God. I come into people's minds and heal them, as I have done for you with the help of the angels guiding you.

Once you are healed, you will hear the voice of God more clearly. You can hear it before you are healed if you really LISTEN, but it is harder. Once you are healed, it becomes easy. Just as you are writing these words from me, Jesus, and have written words from God already, you will begin to hear us in your heart and in your mind and you can align to our will and abide by our callings. Yes, we do call you. Not like on the telephone . . . LOL.

Jesus, you have a sense of humor too.

Yes, yes, I do! I love to laugh. . . . Back to callings. People hear them in their hearts, through their hearts' desires. If they long to do something, they should do it. We talked about how humans are co-creators with God—God is the inspiration and the human is the doer. God needs individuals to take action to make the co-creation possible. With God's inspiration, we can do the seemingly impossible. Remember, when you do something that is divinely inspired, you are in alignment with God, and in him, all things are possible.

May 27, 2019

Had a lovely evening visiting with my friends Amy and Joe by the pool in their garden oasis. I described the new mental health group I'm hoping to start at work and also talked a little bit about angels. Joe said he'd had a number of experiences in which he felt someone or something guided him but hadn't necessarily attributed them to angels. I told him it was his guardian angel and that they are there to guard and protect us.

It seems even harder for me to come out of the spiritual closet than the mental health locker. When I got home I felt sad, even though it had been a lovely evening. But I couldn't share that I'm channeling Jesus and talking to God without worrying that Amy and Joe would think I was crazy and reject me.

Pulling some angel cards revealed that I am not living in the truth of who I truly am. Because I am holding back, I'm not fully in alignment yet. Repercussions of leftover childhood trauma continue to thwart me. As a child, I couldn't speak my truth, that I was scared and felt alone, because I didn't want to cause pain for Mama or give her more than she could handle. I feared I would be rejected and truly be alone. It seems it is better to ignore the truth and not be alone than to be your true self but have no one to share it with.

I hope that with EMDR and therapy this week, I can work on letting go of these old patterns that are not serving me anymore. It is time for me to stand in my light and be who I truly am, without fear. This reminds me of the author of A Course in Miracles and former presidential candidate Marianne

Williamson's statement that our deepest fear is our light, not our darkness.

Archangel channel Cristina Aroche embraces her light. Authentically herself, she declares live on Facebook, YouTube, and other networks that she is a spiritual teacher, mentor, and healer. The first time I saw that, I thought, Wow, she is pretty young to be all those things and to own them like that! I want to be those things. Now I AM those things, though a newbie who is still learning and not quite to the point where I can put myself out there. Soon, I hope I'll be ready to stand in the truth of who I am. My guardian angel once reminded me of Polonius's line in Hamlet: "To thine own self be true."

Throughout the night, I woke periodically, feeling unsettled. After saying the Our Father and St. Francis prayers, I realized I still just have some work to do. The clock flashed 4:44, my sign for abundance. It was reassurance that I am going to be just fine and live a beautiful and limitless life. I just need to give myself the time and space to continue to heal. Around 5:30 I got up without an alarm. God is working with me to ensure that early mornings are our communion time. I used to hate to get up early. Now, I sometimes feel a little tired but can't wait to talk with God and use my decks to get messages from the angels.

God, anything for me to know this morning?

I love you and you are doing a good job. Keep up the good work. Thanks for sharing about your feelings. People will need to know that even when they connect with me, there will still be moments of doubt and fear. Being human comes with the ego, always there bringing doubt. But do not hate the ego. Although it was necessary for your protection, it is no longer needed. Now that it is in your awareness, you can work through those feelings of doubt and fear when they arise.

The bees in your garden are a good analogy for this. As they buzzed around your head, you sat silently and waited for the fear to

THE NATURE OF GOD

pass. You knew that you would probably not be stung but also realized that if you were, you would survive. It might hurt for a bit, but you would be all right.

This is true in life as well. Sometimes you can be the divine child of God you truly are, and it will feel splendid to have others love you. Other times people will reject you. It does not mean you should stop being your authentic self. That is just you getting stung. You may feel some pain but you will be all right. It is worse to live in the pain of hiding your truth now that you know how glorious it feels to be aligned with me.

I created you to be you. Like the flowers that bloom, each individual is a special creation, and you honor me when you live in your truth. You know what this truth is. Listen to how you really feel and begin to express that. Heed the niggle—the thing that tells you what to say and do (that you often ignore). The niggle is me . . . and you. We are one. Each person is the expression of me in the world. I delight when you refuse to hide your gifts for fear of disapproval. Remember that the fear is just your ego. Alignment with me comes when you live in your truth. The truth shall set you free.

> I pulled a Guardian Angel card—"Believing in Magic." My reminder that being in alignment is when the magic happens. It feels spectacular!

Remember that feeling.

> Archangel Michael card: "Keepers of the Earth." Ancient ancestors stand beside me. My reminder that calling in and being open to receiving support, I am not alone.
>
> Archangel Raphael: "Change and Transition." Archangel Azrael, He Who Helps God, guides me safely through this change with phoenix-like energy to help us rise up from the ashes.
>
> Cristina Aroche sent an email with a video about feeling disconnected. This happens to everyone because we all are, and always will be, on a continuing journey. Even if we feel very connected most of the time, we all feel moments of detachment. Cristina said

> the most important thing to do when this happens is acknowledge the feelings.

You can journal about it as a great way to understand what is happening—not just the events, but the feelings that they stirred in you, what they may have triggered from past trauma, and what still needs to be healed. Also call on Archangel Raphael (Medicine of God) and all the angels to show you the next step in healing, then heed their guidance.

May 28, 2019

> Sitting outside enjoying the sound of the birds and of nature. Went to bed at 8 last night. Just felt tired and decided to listen to my body. Good thing, because I woke up early this morning. First looked at the clock at 3:03, then 3:13, 3:23, 3:31, and 3:33. With my first few glances, I was reminded how the thirty-threes are a sign from the spirit guides and thought of Saint Francis working with me.
>
> By the time the clock got to 3:33, it was like all capital letters, WE ARE HERE! The spirit guides, the angels, God, Jesus, the ancestors—our whole spirit team is working with us and cheering us on.

Just relax and trust the universe. It always knows what you need, exactly when you need it. Even if it feels like a mistake, trust that all is as it should be. Listening to your heart's desires and following your body processes help things along. Do what you feel called to do when you feel called to do it. Whether it is to write, spend time with friends, rest, drink, or eat certain foods, go do that thing.

> Lately I have been drawn to healthier foods. Most of the time I don't crave junk. The angels tell me that is because I'm raising my vibration and I want foods that match it.

Yes, foods have a vibration.

THE NATURE OF GOD

> My friend Elizabeth told a story about her relative who was all about healthy eating. One time the family went over to her house and somebody thought they'd be cute and sneak in some Oreos. Within minutes, Elizabeth's relative said, "There is low-vibrational food in my house!" She could feel it.

Our vibration rises when we do what we are called to do. That is me talking to you, showing you the way to live in alignment with my will. My will is your will. Your will is not always my will. I talked about this in *Conversations with God*. If you exert your will, I will go along because you have freedom of choice, but that doesn't mean you are in alignment with me. When you listen to the callings of your heart—the true callings, not what you think you SHOULD be doing, but what you really WANT to do—then you are following your heart and listening to me.

> Is there anything else for today?

No, my dear. You will have a busy day. Good luck in therapy this afternoon.

> Thank you.

The EMDR will help. You will shine your light freely as you release the trauma and pain. Once that is cleared, the fear will lessen. You have come so far. It won't be long now.

> Thank you and thank you to all the angels, guides, ancestors, and Jesus for working with me. I really appreciate it.

We know you do. You are filled with gratitude.

The Revelation

May 29, 2019

It is 4:42 a.m. Messages are flooding through my mind and I want to write. Steve and my psychiatrist will probably worry I'm manic because I'm not sleeping. The reality is that I went to bed at 9:30, so I got seven hours of sleep. And I can go back and rest for a bit before going to work if I need to. I just felt called to write.

So, God, the words that are coming to me, are they from you?

Yes, my child. You are starting to hear my voice and know what I'm thinking without having to transcribe it. This will become your norm, but you are still practicing. Do not be bound by time. I know the right time for you to write and to be and to do. Trust me. Listen when I call.

I'll just need to let Steve know so he doesn't worry.

I'm working with him, so he will understand. Trust me.

So what is this I was thinking about the revelation?

It was not you thinking, it was me sharing with you. The revelation is not just the knowledge that this life is a divine play, it is direction on how to act in this play to live a joyful life, the life God wants you to live. We talked before about doing what you feel called to do, when you feel called to do it. You must also say what you want to say when you want to say it. That voice you hear, those words you want to say but hold back on—so often that is my voice. Listen to it. So when you want to help that friend or reveal a part of yourself that you are afraid will be criticized, say it.

People are conditioned to hold back how they feel and what they mean so as not to hurt others or be condemned or rejected by them. But they really need to hear your truth—not mean things, but the kind thoughts and deeds that cross your mind but you usually don't say. SAY THEM. Lift each other up by sharing your divine nature. As you reveal yourself, others will do the same. This is the revelation—all of my children becoming who they truly are and loving one another.

The judgment in the Bible is not from me (as I never judge) but is the judgment that you pass on each other. Then destruction and evil come into play. There was no serpent in the garden. There is no devil. The only evil is the verdict you pass on one another and yourselves.

If you live in each moment with joy and love, the world will indeed know peace. It has to be moment by moment, as humans have a natural tendency towards evaluation. This is how you were built. But you can CHOOSE otherwise. Each time a thought of judging a brother or sister comes into your mind, recognize it. Acknowledge it and resolve to think differently. Resolve to show love and compassion for that person. If they do something that upsets you, pray for them. Have empathy for them. Try to understand that they are doing or saying such things out of pain. When you recognize this, you can commit to responding with love. You are starting to do this.

> *I feel like I am, but it sure takes practice, especially when people have such different opinions from me. Politics comes to mind, with my desire that our policies support and uplift humanity.*

I know, my dear. These are difficult conversations, but ones that need to be had. Not on Facebook, though. Yes, I am quite familiar with Facebook! It is a wonderful tool but should be used for sharing joy and promoting ideas you feel strongly about. There should be no denigration of any other person.

> *God, this feels like me talking, not you.*

It is, but our feeling is the same on this.

Are you sure it is not just me wanting my voice to be heard?

You want to be heard, but it is my voice through you. We need to add more personal discourse to the conversation so it is not just a blanket post from me. Share how you feel. Even if you are scrutinized, it is important that you speak your truth.

Again, this seems like I am promoting my agenda.

Our agendas here are one. You are trying to do what is right by your fellow humans, and that is my call to you. Facebook is the current method (one of many) of sharing ideas in today's world, so it is an important conversation.

What about people who post things that are so opposed to what I believe supports and uplifts humanity, and I get angry with them?

Remember to remain nonjudgmental. If they are posting in support of war, income inequality, or religion as the only answer, or against human rights, that is their fear surfacing. They are afraid they are not safe or that they will be lacking and not have enough if we give to others. It is not the truth of who they are. The truth is masked by the fear and worry.

Keep this in mind and practice compassion. Do not back down on sharing your truth of what is right, but do not indict or condemn. That is no better than the mistake of the person who posted the fear-based ideology. You will help people see the light.

Again, really? Me?

Yes, you along with others. You were right to support Marianne Williamson's presidential campaign. She is a bringer of truth and light.

Will she ever be president?

It remains to be seen.

So if you know all, why does it remain to be seen?

It remains to be seen by you, not by me. I know, but you are not to know at this time. You are there to live out this play to the fullest. I will share with you what you need to know when you need to know it. As in a real play, the lines of the script are given as they are needed, not before, not after, but in the right moment. Listen and you will know.

> Two other things are on my mind before I stop. First, "Revealing Radiance," the angel card.

Yes, my child. When you reveal your radiance by being who you truly are, you help others to do the same. When everyone reveals their radiance, the world will be at peace.

> Is there more to know about this?

Not at this time.

> What about the phoenix rising from the ashes? Does it mean that, moment by moment, we die and are born again?

That's right. In each moment, you make choices about your brothers and sisters. When you choose kindness, love, and compassion you are born again, like the phoenix rising from the ashes. But this is not a one-time event. It happens EVERY SINGLE MOMENT. Spiritual leader Eckhart Tolle explains this well in *The Power of Now*. There is more to his story, but this POWER OF NOW is a good reminder to live moment by moment. You will be more joyful this way. I promise.

> I feel like we are done.

Yes, for now. We will have many more conversations. Thank you for coming when I called. The time was right.

> Thank you for calling me. I feel so special.

You are special, my child. All my children are special.

> Thank you, God.

THE NATURE OF GOD

May 30, 2019

> Went to bed about 8 p.m. feeling tired and knowing I would be up early again today for my meeting with you, God.

Yes, my child. These early morning hours are our time together, when we can enjoy peace and quiet and you can clear the clutter in your mind. So much is coming in—my energy, the energy of the angels, and that of the world around you. You need to make sure to step outside and immerse in nature, walk barefoot in the grass, hug or press your palms against a tree. This contact with nature is critical to keep you grounded in earthly reality while you connect with the divine realms. I know it feels good to link with me, and we are always linked, but I also want you to maintain your worldly life. It is important that you make time to take care of yourself and be with other people to preserve your sanity.

Others will not think it strange if you do these things. OK, maybe some who do not know you will think that, but you will know the truth, and as long as you are grounded in the truth of your soul and what you need to do, you will be fine.

> I woke up after 2, so maybe six hours of sleep. I knew I needed more, so I took half a Benadryl around 3. Although I worried it would carry over and make me too tired to get up this morning, I feel OK. And I was glad to have the sleep, for I had an amazing dream.
>
> We were in a library with a man and his little boy. Steve had found some books he thought I would be interested in. One was about young children. I told the man I was a social worker and used to work with kids. He seemed interested and shared a bit about himself, but Steve told me to wait, as I was interrupting the man. I do get excited about what I have to say and need to remember to pause and truly listen to others.
>
> The most interesting part was that I said I was writing a book called When I Thought I was Jesus: A Story of Mental Illness and Divine Connection. The

> man asked, "Is there really a difference between mental illness and spirituality?" It was eye-opening for me.
>
> People are always trying to make meaning of their experiences, and when it comes to understanding life and why we are here, most people turn to the spiritual world for an answer. They are intertwined. But if someone experiences a crisis of meaning or making sense of their suffering, we say they go insane. Madness. For some people, maybe it is not a psychotic illness but some level of depression. There is so much pain in the world today.

There always has been, but this is a critical juncture, and people get that. They feel powerless and don't comprehend what is happening. You are to help them.

> Again, me?

Yes, you. You have been diligent in your studies and your connection to the angels and to me, and all these things are what qualify you now to share and help others. Many are called to do this—your spiritual teachers on your journey, for example. And you will lead others to become healers. We are all healers, but some will realize it before others and help others find the path of connection.

> I still don't know what to do about my family. We are back to the childhood pattern of not talking about the painful events and acting like all is OK. I don't want to hurt them by bringing this to light, but I need to share my story. Advice, God?

Just let it unfold. I am working with them, as I am with you. All will be well. Mama may not accept your story, but she will not reject you. Although she may be upset and prefer you not air the dirty laundry, she loves you and wants a relationship with you. Your sister feels the same. It is hard for them to face the truth, as they are not on the same path as you. But do what you need to do and trust that it will all work out how it is supposed to.

Do not be afraid. When you were a little girl, you needed your mother, so you had to pretend to make everything OK. Now that you are an adult, you desire a bond with her, but not at the expense of your connection with me and your calling for what you are meant to do in the world. It is larger than just your relationship with your mother.

Thank you. That is helpful.

Of course, my child. I am always here to help you.

What about today? I present my ideas to my managers about the MHATES program at work.

Just be your honest self and know that they may feel concern for you and others at what you are asking them to do. That is OK. You can reassure them that you are in a good place and although they are uncomfortable, you are not. You have come to a setting of peace with what was your illness.

You were mentally ill, but not any longer now that you know the truth. You will need to take medication until you are fully grounded and the thoughts are not rushing in as much. I will let you know when it is safe to reduce as you have in the past with your doctor's supervision.

Thank you for sending me my psychiatrist. He is amazing and a gift to me.

Yes, indeed. He is one of the best psychiatrists out there. I knew he would help you.

I have a presentation at work today with some of my peers and more senior leadership.

You feel positive about that, if a little nervous because you know the topic intimately. You understand why, as a child, you were so afraid to speak up and why you froze when you didn't know how to keep your brother safe from your father's rage.

This is not a life-threatening situation, so you do not need to fear. If the trauma bubbles up, remember the bees. The likelihood is they won't sting, and if they do, you can handle it. Rest assured that you are guided, protected, and loved. I am always with you, as are the angels. Call on us. We are here for you.

> Anything else for today?

No, that is enough. Thank you, my child. Smile.

> Thank you, God. I love you.

I love you too.

5 p.m.

> Met with my psychiatrist this morning and told him about my proposal for the MHATES employee network at work. He seemed positive but said that people may not want their names associated with a diagnosis, not only for fear of losing their jobs as my therapist projected but because of negative ramifications like being declined for insurance and such. He suggested they could submit their stories anonymously. Although we could allow this, it sort of defeats the purpose of making it more open. Not sure. . . . What do you think?

That is worry talking. Everyone is afraid to show who they truly are for fear of condemnation. That is what you are trying to help people with, coming to a place where they can openly share who they truly are without doubting themselves, even when others disagree or seem to intend them harm.

> My psychiatrist also talked about making sure my writing is not grandiose, as that could be indicative of being symptomatic. It made me question whether he thinks I might be bipolar again, but I feel I really know what is happening. I am talking to you, God.

You are, my dear. You know the truth. There is no need to buy anyone else's story about who you are and that you are in relationship with me. Connecting with me has been hard work and your dreams are coming true. Do not doubt. You know the truth.

THE NATURE OF GOD

> I do, but how will others see that?

Let me work on that. Just keep connecting with me, living your life, doing what inspires you, and it will all unfold as it should. Try not to worry. That hinders the flow.

> I'm trying to remember to relax, like letting water flow over my hands rather than trying to grasp it.

Exactly. That is what Wayne Dyer, your spirit guide, would say. Remember that you are my child, a child of God, and you are magnificent. I know your heart's desires, even before they are thought of or wished upon. I will help your dreams come true, if you allow it.

> I want to allow it.

You are. Keep doing what you are doing.

> OK . . . done deal!
>
> Last night I felt Archangel Michael energy surrounding my body. In the past when I perceived this, I attributed it to the Benadryl . . . but I think it was Michael.

It was. You are learning how to feel the angels. SO exciting.

> Yes, it is! It will be fun.

The Law of Attraction

May 31, 2019

Happy to have today off. It was hard getting up at what seems to be our wakeup time, 5:30. But now that I am up, it is nice to hear the birds, and although it's a little overcast, the temperature is pleasant. And I'm looking forward to connecting with you. Thanks for the nudge.

You are welcome, my dear. I knew you would be disappointed if you let yourself sleep and miss this special time, so I called to you.

I heard you and I listened. So what should we talk about today?

What would you like to talk about?

Let me think. . . . I know I am to let things unfold, but I am excited about the future. Can you tell me anything?

Please be patient. It has taken what felt like a long time for you to get here. You started this journey on retreat in October of 2017. It hasn't even been two years, less than your Master of Social Work (MSW) program. And this will be bigger and more impactful than that, so it takes some time.

> My angelic healing teacher, Karan Tumasz, wrote about this fall as a time for people's projects to come to fruition.

That is possible, but do not focus on timing and expectations. Just allow things to unfold.

> I am trying, but I do want to know.

Actually, you really don't. It is the surprises in daily life that make it exciting.

> Yes, like the surprises of healthy food and reminders for me to do things I have forgotten. I have noticed this happening.

Yes, I am already helping you to stay on track and will do that in both big and small ways. Thank you for noticing.

> I didn't at first and then realized . . . it is pretty great, thank you. The quote from my angel calendar reminded me that God takes care of the small stuff, like having food to eat, which isn't really small but seems mundane compared to the big stuff.

I am here to manage the details and let you live your life with joy.

> Please tell me about flow and the law of attraction. I get that when I follow your will and listen to your call, things happen as they should. Why do bad things keep happening with my brother? He is trying so hard and is still struggling. Is he attracting it or is it part of his path?
>
> I feel unsure of what you are trying to say. I stepped back to breathe and take in the sound of the birds.

THE NATURE OF GOD

That is good, my dear. I am reminding you to ground. It is important for you.

It seems you want me to focus on me right now and not my brother.

That is right. This time today is for us to connect about you. As for your brother, trust that all will work out as it is supposed to. Continue to send him love and support and money, and the rest will come together.

So, about money. I'm less worried about it now but still wonder if I should be budgeting more. We meet with the financial planner this morning—taking care of earthly tasks.

Taking care of earthly tasks is required. This is good. As far as money, the angels send you the 44 and 444 signs as reassurance that money will be no problem.

Do I need to wait to buy anything?

No, spend on what you desire. You are not extravagant. All will be fine. The money will come when you need it. Use the money you have and it will be replenished in divine right timing. Try not to worry.

The 44 and 444 are reassuring, but is there anything else that will help?

Just remember to stay connected and in flow with me and my will. You will be fine, more than fine—delighted and well-supported financially. You prayed for abundance of time, love, and money. That, and more, will come when you are no longer working at your full-time job. Trust that the timing will happen when it is right.

I so look forward to the freedom to set my own schedule and do the things that bring me joy and make me blissful.

I know, my dear. Just remember to be grateful for what you have now and to enjoy the moment. You like the feeling of mastery in your work and you enjoy your colleagues. Continue to do that while the rest unfolds. It will make the days go by faster and easier for you. And continue to connect with me. I would like for this to be our routine, if you are willing.

> I am willing . . . but when I am tired you may need to nudge me to remember how special this time is. I can definitely tell I'm tired today because I'm not as excited as in the past. Or is that the mania settling down?

It is.

> So I won't feel the same level of excitement?

You will, but it will be accompanied by a feeling of peace, of not needing to rush to the next thing. You will go with the flow.

> That sounds nice.

I am helping to remove the stress of time constraints for you.

> I have noticed how the timing of things is all working out. Events sometimes get moved around, but in the end, everything flows.

Yes, that is the angels and me working as your organizers. You still need to check your schedule to be where you need to be when you need to be there, but you don't have to worry about things lining up to make that happen. Do as you are called and all will resolve as it should.

> I like that feeling of things all working out easily without stress. I am thinking about Steve.

I know you are. He has seemed much calmer.

> He is not on my case as much and seems to understand my need to get up early and write.

THE NATURE OF GOD

Steve knows you are doing something special, although he doesn't know exactly what yet. Neither do you, but you do grasp that you will publish a game-changing book, speak in public, and continue to write. Your husband knows that the angels are working with you. He senses your increasing peace and calm and knows you are in a better place, which he loves for you. He is happy that you love the angels and me because he does too.

He doesn't talk about it much, but Steve is very proud of the spiritual work you are doing. He is spiritual too but doesn't share about it. Most people are, in fact, spiritual. They know or want to know that there is more to life than just the mundane. You are going to help them to see and EXPERIENCE it for themselves.

WOW! That sounds amazing.

It will be. I know you are thinking of your psychiatrist saying you are manic again if you think grandiose thoughts. He is wonderful, but he is wrong here. Know that.

Psychiatrists want more tools to help their patients. Most do want to help them and deep down, feel the system they have is not working. They see patients suffer with side effects of medications and they don't want to be "pill dolers."

That sounds funny.

Whatever . . . you know what I mean. Doctors want to help the whole person, not just prescribe a pill. They just don't know how and need someone to teach them. And as you know, the pills serve a purpose. Medication helped you to live a normal life for the most part, not stuck in an institution or disconnected from work and family. Those things are as important as the spiritual enlightenment. You are here to have an earthly experience and to connect with me when you remember. Pharmaceuticals help during the transition when people are opening up.

You mean when they are in the process of becoming their divine selves?

Exactly. That is what opening up and awakening are. It is coming into the knowledge that you are a divine being and feeling the connection with me, your source.

So, am I awakened?

You are, my dear, in the sense that you have both of these things—you know your true self and you are connected with me. That does not mean you are not human or have no faults. Work and practice keep your energy high. It is not as if once it happens, that is it. The journey continues day by day, hour by hour, minute by minute, second by second. You have to stay in the flow to stay awakened. Trust and follow my callings through the desires of your heart. Yes, you have to manage earthly responsibilities, but they will become blissful no matter your job or station in life.

Can anyone be awakened? From a streetcleaner to the president?

Yes, even him! Funny that it seems more fathomable to you for the streetcleaner to be awakened than the president.

Yes, that is exactly what I was thinking!

And you were thinking of the quote from Martin Luther King about the streetcleaner.[12] Look it up later—no rush, remember.

This has been lovely. I feel like it is time to close for now.

Yes, it is. You don't feel it yet, but it takes a lot of energy to channel. Actually, to clarify, you take IN a lot of energy when you channel, so you need to ground now. Be in nature. Connect with your angels through your cards and just relax and have some coffee.

Should I go back to bed?

Up to you, but I don't think you need to. You will get used to this morning routine and be able to go about your day.

---

[12] "If a man is called to be a street sweeper, he should sweep streets even as a Michelangelo painted, or Beethoven composed music or Shakespeare wrote poetry. He should sweep streets so well that all the hosts of heaven and earth will pause to say, 'Here lived a great street sweeper who did his job well.'" —Martin Luther King Jr.

And coffee is good? I've been thinking about clean eating.

You are eating much better, but there is no need to examine everything you put in your mouth. Eat what you feel called to eat. When your vibration is high, like yours is becoming, you are drawn to foods that nourish your body and soul. The bad stuff just falls away with ease. It is not a struggle to "eat healthy" because you will desire it. But do not worry. Let that unfold too. Don't stress about it. This will be helpful to others when they learn it. But let us end for now.

OK. Much love to you, my dear God.

Yes, much love and light to you, my darling.

Each of Us Is Special

June 1, 2019

> Good morning, God. Today is my twenty-third wedding anniversary.

Yes, I know, Dear. Congratulations.

> It has been a great ride and again, I am so grateful you brought me Steve. He has been such a blessing.

I know.

> He is wonderful in so many ways, but I wish I knew how to help him with his struggles. I feel like I need to let him work it out and just fortify and encourage him.

That is right. You can't do the work for him. Your support and your growth motivate him. Steve will be better, but for now, love and champion him and let him come to what he needs to do to make himself happy. He is content with you but does have some trauma that needs healing.

> In this lifetime or the past?

Both.

> Is it for me to know?

Not now. He is interested in past life exploration and will come to it when he is ready. Keep opening doors for him until he is ready to walk through.

> Would EMDR trauma therapy be helpful to him too?

Yes, very likely.

> So perhaps he could see my therapist?

If he chooses, she could help him.

> What about the sleep apnea test? I think he should get tested.

That is a good idea.

> I feel like it's me talking again.

It is, but we are combining now, so it is getting harder to tell.

> Is that right? Am I tired?

Yes, you are tired. Take a little break and come back when you are ready.

> Thanks. Was just thinking about feeling Archangel Michael's vibration this morning.

Yes, it was him.

> I thought so. It was about my need to feel special, and he let me know we all want to feel special, which is actually our desire to be who we truly are. God, you created us as divine beings with our own fingerprints, each one unique. You want us to leave our marks on this world by being the special individuals you created us to be—no hiding. When we come into our own

exceptionality and shine the light of who we are, we no longer strive to be in competition. We recognize the beauty within ourselves and others.

It is like the flowers. They do not compete but grow and shine gloriously as the creations I made them to be. People are drawn to some flowers more than others, and that is OK. We are not all conceived to like the same things. For example, your son Aidan finds monetary policy interesting, but it is not your cup of tea. And although you wanted to connect with me and support the uplifting of humanity, that is not for some folks either.

I designed you all to work together to build a beautiful and empathetic world. That requires contributions from everyone, all the souls I ever created—each one of a kind and special. And I love and am proud of every one of you, my creations. Even when you feel unremarkable or make mistakes ("sinning"), you are always exquisite in my eyes. There is never a time when I do not love you. I am always proud of you because even if you choose a path that is harmful to yourself or others, that is part of the journey I planned for you to live to your fullest potential.

I am never wrong. I know what each and every soul needs to live to its full potential. Sometimes that involves pain or struggle, but now that you know the reason and how much I love you and am just doing what is best for you, you will understand.

It is like the movie *Miracles from Heaven* with Jennifer Garner. You saw her character's agony as she watched her child suffer, but she stayed right by her daughter's side, doing everything she could to ease the pain and to love and support her through the treatments. That parallels my relationship with all my children. I knew you needed to go through certain struggles to reveal the truth of who you are and your unique and divine gifts.

It is like the cocoon and the butterfly—something beautiful comes from the struggle. And like childbirth, I knew the outcome would be worth the pain. I have not caused you aggravation and distress because you did anything wrong. No, my children. You are never wrong and I never criticize you. You are living the life I intended for you for a greater purpose, to truly know the glory of your spirit. Once you know, it is magnificent. So while I suffer when you suffer, as loving parents ache when they see their child in torment or battling adversity, you need to go through it to come out the other side healed.

Thank you, God. I feel much more connected now and this seems to be flowing.

Yes, my child. Sometimes it just takes time. It is OK to take a few moments to connect and ground and center. If you need to step away and relax, that is fine. I want you to take care of yourself. I am always here and remember, it will all unfold in divine right timing.

Is there anything I should do to move forward with this project?

Not at the moment, other than communing with me each morning (or other times if you feel so moved). Do not worry about promoting your work. When the time comes for that, I will reveal your next steps. Enjoy your activities with Steve and Aidan and converse with me. It will be a lovely week.

Thank you, God. Have a wonderful day.

Thank you, and have a wonderful anniversary!!! Love you.

Love you too.

June 2, 2019

Good morning. Had a nice anniversary yesterday. Did some cooking in the morning using the ingredients from our Community Supported Agriculture (CSA) box.[13] It feels good to eat farm-fresh produce and to cook with Steve and get the house organized. I feel a little tired this morning even though I went to bed at 8:30 last night, probably because I drank too much. A piece of me is stifling my feelings about how things are with Mama.

---

[13] Consumers purchase a share from a local farmer and in return receive a box of seasonal produce each week throughout the farming season.

Yes, my child. You are still sad about the situation and not being able to be open with her. It is retraumatizing, bringing back your childhood distress of needing to hide your true feelings and the fear that needed to be quelled. As you face being brave in the world, we need to work on this.

Steve got stung by a bee yesterday.

I wanted to show you that sometimes it will happen—you WILL get stung. Life will not always be free from pain, but you can tolerate it. You asked Steve to rate his discomfort on a scale of one to ten and he rated it a two—bearable. He didn't even take any medication, just sat and let it subside. This is what you will need to do.

Should I write Mama another letter and try to get her to open up more?

No. She is not at a place where she can accept what happened.

Will she ever be?

Most likely not.

What does that mean for our relationship? It feels superficial and not real, and like you said, retraumatizing because I can't be who I truly am.

But you can be. You just have to understand that you may not be happy with her reaction. Like being stung, it is unpleasant but you can handle it. Most important right now is for you to be confident in your essence and prepare to tell your story regardless of what people think.

That is so hard.

I will be here to help, and you can always call on me to ground you and keep you in the right frame of mind.

I pulled the "Anna, Grandmother of Jesus," card yesterday and felt like I was her in a past life. Is that true?

No. That is your mind playing tricks on you.

Why?

You are trying to escape reality because the pain is hard to bear. Imagining yourself as someone great (which you are) lets you feel more in control.

What about the "Age of Light" card that says I have been training for this for lifetimes?

You have, my darling. That is true. You have been a mystic, a sage, a shaman, a healer, and a normal, everyday person. As you awaken, you will call on that inner ancient wisdom. Of course, all the wisdom of all of us is inside all of us, if we kindle it. We are all one and have lived all these experiences. They are captured in God's book of remembrance, the Akashic Records. Like psychic Edgar Cayce, everyone can learn to access them and call on that stored knowledge for guidance. You are going to help people learn how to do this.

Really, that sounds so cool! But again, can I do this?

Remember, I am your co-creator and with me all things are possible. You cannot do these things alone, from your own power or will, but when you align to my will, you will see the magic unfold.

I have experienced some of this magic and it is delightful.

If you continue to commune with me, listen to my callings, and follow the guidance of the angels, you will be in the flow and in alignment.

What can I do to practice?

Just be in the present moment and PAY ATTENTION. You will see the synchronicities and feel me nudging you in the right direction.

What should I do to release my trauma so it doesn't hinder me?

Continue to work with your therapist doing EMDR, and don't forget to call on the angels for help. They will shepherd you to healing. You will recover from this trauma and it will no longer be a trigger. It won't be long now. You have come so far and are mending beautifully.

> True. Will I always have healing to do?

Yes, as long as you live in the earthly realm, there will be pain to be healed and released. Call on the angels and they will help you. Remember, Raphael is the Medicine of God. He heals all wounds. There is nothing he can't help you conquer when it comes to restoration.

> You mean things like cancer and other physical illnesses as well as emotional pain?

That is right. It is Raphael who heals all wounds.

> Not time?

Time helps. If you are working with the angels and calling on me, it goes faster and feels easier.

> I just saw 555 and 444 this morning.

We continue to send you numbers as reassurance. You can look up 555 later, as you don't remember what it means. It will help you today. 444 is your number of abundance and a reassurance that we are always here, protecting and providing for you, so you have no need to worry.

> What else do you want me to know today?

I love you, my darling, and you are doing a great job.

> I'm crying. I still feel so much hurt. I feel so small and am afraid that it may be mental illness popping up again. Sometimes I feel great and so connected, and other times I'm just not sure.

I know. We will continue to work through this. Raphael is sending you healing now. I asked him to help you.

> *I thought I had to ask?*

Usually, but I know that your heart's desire is to be healed and you have given me permission to help you, so in this case, I can request on your behalf.

> *Please, yes, God—request what I need!*

I will . . . LOL.

> *Are you trying to make me laugh with the "will" double meaning again??? You are funny.*

Yes, laughter is truly the best medicine. Remember that when you feel down or need help. It is good to cry the feelings out, and then let go and laugh once that is done. Your dear friend and social work mentor Lydia taught you that—cry, release, and then re-center on joy. This is indeed the path to healing. Lydia's work with discharging emotions will help others too. She might like to write or speak about it. You can let her know that she helps people with those skills all the time, and if she wanted to do more with that, it would be welcomed.

> *What should I do about my sister Shannon? She is planning to come this summer and I'm not sure how it will go.*

Up to you. Lately Shannon has been more open to understanding what you are going through, and you can help her to process some of the trauma and pain she has blocked out.

> *I feel that is why she is so afraid of presenting what she knows to others in her job . . . the same feeling I had of "not knowing" when Daddy hurt Duke and Mama failed to protect us.*

I'm not sure if she will connect that, but you can try.

THE NATURE OF GOD

You're not sure?

Well, I want you to sort out what you want to do and how to approach it. Because you would like to have a close relationship with her, it is worth trying. Just remember, she may not be ready and that may be hard to face. But you will be OK whatever you decide to do.

I think I'm ready to take a break now. I love being with you, but it does drain me.

Yes, it does. It is good that you are paying attention to how you feel and honoring that. This is enough for today. Enjoy your time at the beach with Steve and Aidan.

Have a wonderful day, God.

You too, my dear. Love you.

Love you.

I'm back. Was just thinking about lying in bed this morning feeling vibrations from the angels and you. Raphael felt gentle but gave me a burning sensation like the phoenix rising from the ashes. Michael felt very strong—hard to describe. You felt like a vibration and music without a song. Butterfly wings flapping came to mind. Was that you?

Yes, my darling. You are starting to feel us. That will happen more often the more you connect. Eventually it will happen during the day. You are just quieter and more still at night lying in bed, so that is why we come to you then. As you continue to grow, you will feel our presence all the time.

I have a hard time feeling my guardian angel.

Michelle McCann

It is not as important that you feel them because you know they are there all the time.

> *Jim and Johnetta are kind of funny names for my guardian angel.*

That is who they are. I named them and I rather like their names.

> *They are nice.*

It is Jim and Johnetta and they are just what you need. When I create each soul, I assign just the right guardian angel to provide the help that will be needed for this earthly experience, this course in miracles. Trust that they will help with whatever you need. Call on them.

> *OK. Thank you!*

Discerning Energy

June 3, 2019

Good morning, God.

What would you like to talk about today?

Sitting outside in Millsboro on our patio, I'm enjoying the trees and the birds' songs. I love these mornings in nature with you. Thank you for providing weather that has allowed for this.

Yes, my dear. I have organized the weather to allow you this time. This won't always be possible, but for now, you need to be in nature when you talk to me. It helps keep you grounded while you take in all this loving energy.

It's interesting—I don't FEEL the energy.

In the future you will know when you need to ground, but because you don't feel it yet, make sure you commune regularly with nature. It will be vital for you to stay grounded to continue to do our work. If you don't, you will become manic again from all the energy.

What do I need to understand about the energy and how to recognize it?

Pay attention to how you feel. It is good to be excited but not feel overwhelmed that everything has to happen NOW, which happens when you are manic. If you start feeling overly anxious or excited, find ways to relax and ground. This will be an enjoyable journey if you don't overdo it. That is why I planned for you to have this vacation now. You need frequent breaks while you are getting adjusted to our new routine.

When you go back to work, you can continue getting up early and writing and talking/communing with me. Going to bed earlier helps make sure you get enough sleep. Soon you will no longer have the responsibilities of work, as you will just be working with me. But for now, staying in your job keeps you grounded.

When will that be?

Leave the timing up to me. You will know when it is time. Do your best to stay in the moment. Enjoy these mornings with me, enjoy your work and this exciting new project there, enjoy time with Steve and with Aidan and his girlfriend. It is going to be a lovely summer with fun at the beach, good times at Mt. Cuba, lots of friends, love, and laughter—all the things you prayed and hoped for. You will have an abundance of love, time, and money.

What about sharing what I am writing?

When you feel so moved, please do. You can share with close friends who might be open to reading. Eventually Steve will be receptive, but not yet. Your therapist may be interested to read more as things progress. Talk with her in therapy about how things are going for you and ways to stay grounded. She is used to helping people center in the here and now through her experience and work with EMDR. Those techniques will be helpful to you.

She is wonderful.

Yes, she is. I sent her to help you. You were ready and the time was right.

What about the more spiritually-focused therapist I saw before my current therapist?

She is on her own path that is not related to you. She was helpful to you for the time you needed her, to learn about connecting to other realms. Now she has other work to do.

Ah, is it the ancestral work?

Exactly. Healing the ancestral wounds in our psyches is very important.

Will I help her by telling people about her?

Yes, people will begin to understand that ancestral pain is carried through generations. This will be scientifically based, so people will begin to believe and understand the connections.

Do I need to do ancestral healing work?

No, you have done the work already. By bringing the truth of the family trauma to light, not keeping it secret anymore, you have broken the cords and balanced the karma.

Tell me more about karma.

Karma is cause and effect. For every action, there is an equal and opposite reaction. It is not punishment, but the balancing out of energy. Negative energy needs a positive balance.

Does positive energy need a negative balance?

No, only the negative needs to be transmuted.

I'm not sure I understand this.

It is not important now. You will understand when the time comes. Just know that karma is not punishment, and make sure others know that too. God does not punish. The natural law is that if there is a negative action, there needs to be an equal and opposite positive reaction. The law of attraction applies here.

This makes me think of The Secret *by Rhonda Byrne and of Esther Hicks and Abraham.*

They helped people understand the law of attraction, but you are going to show them HOW to stay in alignment with me and my will for the positive attraction to occur.

I'm going to do that?

Yes, and I'm going to help—always remember that. You are not doing this by yourself. So maybe instead of saying "I" am going to do that, start saying "we" are going to do that. That way you don't feel the pressure or too glorified. You are magnificent as my child, but you also want to stay humble. Remember that you are special but no more so than my other children. I love you all for the equally beautiful gifts you bring to share with the world and with me.

> *I always wanted to be special.*

You did, my child. That is why I selected you for this task. Your heart's desire was to be known as a healer, to help other people on a grand scale.

> *I feel like that makes me sort of—I'm not sure of the word—shallow, maybe? That I wanted to be so big?*

Not at all, because your heart was in the right place. You wanted to do GOOD and be a helper, and you were willing to do this on a grand scale if that was required. Once you recognized what your soul's plan would look like, it felt so GOOD to be known and to be a helper that you agreed to be a star.

Some people, like Steve, want to do things in the background. He is the wind beneath your wings, happy to be there. Though he doesn't want the spotlight, he wants to do his part to heal the world and knows that his support can help you do this.

> *Wow. That seems the opposite of selfish. . . . What is that? I can't think of the word . . . oh, SELFLESS.*

Yes, it is. Steve is working through his own traumas, but his nature is to be selfless. He was willing to go through significant pain and put his life on the line to save Donna when she needed a liver transplant.[14] He was so courageous to be a living liver donor at a time when that was a new procedure. And there's his work as a firefighter—his way of helping others is to be a hero.

---

[14] Donna, the mother of our "little brother" mentee through Big Brothers Big Sisters, was dying of a disease that affects the liver.

Like the greeting card I gave him!

Yes, he is a hero, a quiet one who does his work in silence.

WOW . . . in that puzzle on Facebook, Steve's words were BEE, SILENT, POWER.

Indeed, he is powerful, but not in the way people think. Without putting on airs, he allows people to be who they truly are. This helps people be themselves around him.

Like me.

Yes, Dear, like you.

In that same puzzle, I got CREATIVE, MAGICAL, SUCCESSFUL.

That is right. I put that there for you to see. You will be, and are, all of those things. Creativity and magic will lead to your grand success. Do not fear. When the time comes you will be ready. You will meet so many wonderful people, both great and small, but all wonderful as my children. They will enhance your experience of life.

You love people, seeing the good in them and delighting when you can bask in their light. It connects you to me in a different way, through my children. Steve doesn't have this same pull. It is OK for you to do some of these things on your own. He will join you at times, but remember that he needs his quiet time. That will enhance, not detract from, your love for each other.

I have noticed it has been great lately. We seem to be flowing more.

Yes, he still has traumas to work through, but you are accepting him for who he is, which is what he needs. Try not to be critical, as this is a trigger for him. Loving, nonjudgmental support will help Steve's healing.

Can I do more to help him, as he has helped me so much?!

Yes, you can help him learn about the angels.

That sounds good. This was great! I'm excited, but grounded! Thinking maybe it's time to take a break.

I agree.

Thank you for this time together and for this beautiful weather and for your creation. It is stunning and breathtaking.

Why, thank you, my dear. I think I did a pretty good job, myself.

June 4, 2019

Hi and good morning. I felt your vibration briefly this morning, and then for a short time I felt Michael and Raphael. What came from Michael is that he is to give us strength to fight battles—not like in a war, but struggles with our own egos and to keep from judging others.

Judgment is the evil Michael is fighting against (that we are all fighting against). We need his strength to help us be brave. His sword is not for hurting anyone, but rather for cutting the cords that keep us tied to others energetically in a negative pattern. He cuts away the "clutter" (the judgment) and helps us see ourselves and others for who we/they truly are, divine children of God. Once we do this, all evil will die away.

With Raphael, I felt the burning in my feet again and realized his "medicine" or healing is the burning away of the past, the letting go of what no longer serves us so we can be in the presence of God, fully in his loving embrace.

People can connect with God clearly when they are not holding onto grievances against themselves and others.

THE NATURE OF GOD

> I feel like I trust what is happening about 90 percent and like this is a mental illness again about 10 percent. Actually, maybe more like 99 percent/1 percent. A little nagging part of me still says I am experiencing delusional thoughts, like when I thought I was Jesus and it felt so real. Is this just another figment of my imagination? God, what can you say to help me with this?

I know this is difficult to believe because of what you have been through. Both your childhood and your treatment as a result of your mental illness have been traumatic. Then, you did not have clarity about what was happening. But now you realize that you thought you were Jesus because you were channeling him and uniting with the Christ Consciousness.

All who suffer from psychotic episodes are connecting in this way, which is why often they believe they are Jesus—they feel his vibration. It can be very confusing because it is not an energy they have felt before. Although it has always been there, they (and you) never actually bonded with it. During your breakdown, you were vulnerable, and this opened you up to the experience of Jesus and God.

> It seems like people are vulnerable all the time, God, so why me? Why then?

You were truly vulnerable, fully! Most people will share some parts of themselves, but you were put into a situation in which it all came back—the shame, the feeling of being alone and afraid. When your co-worker videotaped you and you froze while trying to do the parenting intervention you were learning, it reminded you of your childhood, but also of the part in all of us that was in the Garden of Eden when I . . .

> I'm not sure what to write here.

Take some deep breaths and reconnect.

> This is hard. I'm crying. I'm remembering the Garden of Eden (the feeling, not the image) and first

> *being disconnected from you. It was so HARD to feel alone and separated from your love.*

This is why you felt like Eve. You connected with that story, although it is not actually true. There was no Adam and Eve and no serpent, no garden. It was when I created the earth, all humans souls at the same time, and you separated from me energetically. I was always with you, but in spirit, not in feeling.

> *Is that right? Feeling?*

That is right. You could no longer feel me like you did when we were energetically together as one.

> *So how did we separate?*

I cut the cord and released you to become human.

> *But we weren't all born at the same time.*

No, your souls were born in "heaven" with me. That is what heaven is—being with me energetically. When the time was right, each of you sojourned on the earthly plane and in other realms and worlds to experience what is was like to be separated from me. Then when we reconnected, you recognized the contrast. Suffering was required for you to understand the opposite of love, which is fear. The whole world was created by me for you to face dissimilitude. This let you differentiate joy and pain, happiness and sorrow, up and down, left and right, connection and disconnection, truth and lie, and so on.

You and I have exposed ourselves to all of these things over many lifetimes. Now is the time for this chapter to close. You selected this incarnation to let people know this is the time of revelation. Through you and others, I will teach what everyone needs to know to come together with me in the earthly realms. When humans die, they always rejoin me, but I am ready for you to reunite with me while living an earthly existence. I have seen enough suffering, you all have felt enough suffering, and it is time to come back to joy, to love.

As Marianne Williamson said, it is *A Return to Love,* the end of the ego's rule and the return of the love of brothers and sisters in Christ. Again, regardless of what religion you practice, we are all one and all connected.

THE NATURE OF GOD

So, why Christ?

He was the first to experience the non-duality, heaven and earth. Christ reconciled us to come back together.

Why him?

He was the soul chosen for this purpose, the first and the last. Whether people believe in him or not, Jesus is ushering everyone back into reunion with me. One at a time, he is coming into their hearts and healing them.

> *I am thinking there is something about him and his sheep but I forget . . . yes, like a shepherd herding his flock. He will leave none behind. I guess this takes a while . . . LOL?*

Yes, my darling, but it is time for the truth to be revealed, both for individuals to be who they truly are and for me to tell the full story.

You mean about Adam and Eve?

That's right. That is a story I created to begin the world, but as I explained above, it didn't actually happen that way. The allegory was to help people understand the difference between good and evil. People had to believe they had done something wrong, eaten from the tree of the knowledge of good and evil. But that never actually happened.

I gave you the GIFT of knowledge of Good and Evil, good being the love of God and your brothers and sisters and evil being the judgment of yourself and others. Experiencing this evil or judgment is how you came to know what it was like to not have my love, if just for a moment. In reality, you have always had my love but needed to think and feel otherwise to truly experience the contrast, the NOT HAVING it. Now you can fully appreciate what it means to feel the love of God.

My book of remembrance, the Akashic records, records energetically every thought, word, and deed, so we always have an imprint of these experiences. When you reconnect with me fully in the spirit realm, the book of remembrance reminds you how glorious it truly is. You experienced the magnificence before the descent into humanhood, but you did not fully understand. Only I did, as I knew what it was like to love you, but you did not know what it was like to love me. Now that you know the love of God fully, you understand.

I'm confused. Do I know the love of God?

Yes, my darling. Every time you cry when you feel me, that is you remembering the separation. You are crying less now. That is because you are feeling me energetically. It heals your wounds, the traumas of the lifetimes you have lived, the biggest of all being the separation from me. Releasing yourself from fault, you feel my love more fully now.

It does feel wonderful to connect with you, but yesterday I was feeling sad again.

As long as you are in the human body, in an earthly experience, you cannot always feel me. It would be too much. You would be manic all the time and not able to live a normal life. So that you can ground and live in the earthly realm, I release my energy from you from time to time. Understand that is not a lack of love but a means of protection. Your ego needs to be grounded in earthly reality or you would be in an institution or homeless.

So, that is what bipolar mania is? A connection to God?

Yes. When folks with mania feel that surge of energy, they are connecting with me and my energy. It is like an explosion, as it vibrates at such a high frequency.

Why do some people connect to you in this way and not others?

The experience is part of their soul plan. They wanted to connect with me in the earthly realms, as you did, and they were willing to suffer the ensuing ridicule and difficulties. Now that I am working with you to understand, these will disappear. I will disconnect and help you ground when you need it. Just pay attention to the callings and you will be fine.

What if I don't hear the call?

If at first you miss, I will call again until you hear. Be not afraid, my child. I know how to call so you will hear, just as I know how to call all my children. Choosing whether to listen is up to them. But my summons is clear. Once you let people know I appeal to EVERYONE, ALL THE TIME, they will begin to listen more closely and heed my call. This will help the world move toward peace.

> *There it is again, this feeling of how am I supposed to bring peace. But now I am remembering that it is US who will bring peace, not me. Thank you, God. That helps. I am so excited to see this next chapter unfold.*

The time is near, but not quite yet.

> *I need to resolve things with Mama first, don't I?*

You need to let her see your deepest self. She can choose how to respond, but it is time for you to stop hiding. It is time to heal this wound and to share your truth, your pain, without fear of rejection. Should you choose to move forward, you will need to be open about all of this.

> *So there are still some choices for me to make?*

Yes, my child. You and our mission here need to come first even if it means upsetting Mama.

> *I need to tell her that I am going to write and speak about my experiences with my family, as it is necessary for my healing as well as the healing of others. I can't hold back anymore to protect her. I did that my whole life, especially as a child. Now I need to speak my truth and be who I truly am and let her decide how to react.*

That is right.

> *Wow, that was a lot of writing in a very short time.*

It is flowing quickly.

I think it is time for a break, even though I would like to write more.

You can come back soon. Take a break and disconnect from my energy for a bit to ground. This is how it will be as we continue.

I was just thinking that I didn't see the angel lights as much yesterday.

You don't need to see them to reassure you.

I still like to see them though.

We can make that happen.

I think I will want to see them forever. It is like a rainbow, always a special treat.

Good to know.

I'm back. I took a break and messaged my friend Christina. Thank you for bringing her back to me!

You are welcome, my darling. You two had such fun together. I knew you would love reconnecting with her.

And my friend Julie—I feel so good helping her. She is grieving so.

Yes, I sent you to help her. You are indeed an answer to her prayer.

Wow, so special to be the answer to someone's prayer.

You will be the answer to many people's prayers, and you should be proud of the gifts of love and compassion that you bring. These are your superpowers!

Cool . . . I have superpowers . . . LOL.

Yes, LOVE and COMPASSION. Practice these and you will soar, my child.

Divine Mother God

June 5, 2019
3:33 a.m.

Good morning, God. I felt you calling me to write even though it is only 3 in the morning. As it is dark outside, I am at the kitchen table. I feel like you are ready to tell me about my mother, my divine mother. She is our ego, isn't she?

Yes, my child. She came before you to create the heavens and the earth. I have always been in the energetic realm, but she separated from me to create the universe. That is why you refer to "Mother Earth." I am not the creator of all things, she is.

Why does the Bible refer to you as Father, while there is no mention of the mother part of you? Sure, we say, "Mother Earth," but there is no reference, at least not a familiar one, to her being divine.

She is my other half, my soul twin. Each soul has two parts, masculine and feminine. They travel together through each incarnation, not always as husband and wife, but as mother and child, friends, relatives.

You said before that Steve is my soul twin.

Yes, that is right. You have traveled together through your lifetimes to come to know me and each other.

Michelle McCann

> Can you tell me more about our divine mother?

The first to disconnect from me, she had to initiate the separation, as I couldn't bear it. She created the ego to help the other souls cope with the distress. Three a.m., the hour of separation, is the worst trauma each soul has ever endured. It is my saddest time, when I had to separate from all my creation.

> So, you created us as souls, and our divine mother created the universe in which we live?

Yes. Now she lives as your ego. It was her idea to create the ego for protection. It was too hard to look at the parts of you that were "bad" when you were separated from us. She couldn't endure the trauma you felt. Rather, she could but didn't want you to endure it. So she created this device to protect you from retraumatization when you might feel rejected.

You know about this from your social work training. Although the first trauma has ended, if it hasn't been processed and brought into your awareness, other events can trigger the misery all over again. The original "sin" was in the past, but you feel it again each time someone spurns you or you feel unwanted.

That is why you fear being spurned by your birth mother now. She will not abandon you. She loves you, but both she and you are being retraumatized by the hour of separation. As much as you fear her rejection, she fears the same from you. That is why she accused you of thinking she's a bad mother. Even though you told her that was not true, feelings left over from the original loss and separation make her believe she must have failed.

> It seems it is now time for our divine mother to be known.

That is correct, my child.

> I wrote about this before. Let me look. . . . Here it is from March 30, 2019: "My mother's suffering was hardest to bear. It's why at times I resonated with Mary. I felt her mother love but also her pain. Mother wanted to be joined with Father again. Mother is our

THE NATURE OF GOD

ego, what we perceive as the dark side. She longs to be revealed."

Tell me more about what this means. I remember it came out of me but I didn't really understand it.

Yes, I know. It was time for it to be written, but not time for it to be fully revealed.

So, I see the word "revealed" again.

Yes, this is the revelation—the release of your mother from her prison. In your mind all these years, thousands of years, she has protected you from your own pain. She has kept you from having to feel traumatized over and over again, as my children reject each other as part of the human experience. This was needed for you to know us, but now the time has come for it to end. Your divine mother wants to be brought into the light. People do this by honoring themselves and their truth. When they become who they truly are and show the parts they fear will be rejected, the ego will no longer be needed. Your mother will be in the dark until she is no longer needed by her children. The time has come.

I wrote once that the revelation is that this world is a divine play.

That is only part of the story. The rest is that Mother is waiting to be revealed. It will happen one person at a time through her son Jesus coming into the minds of her children and healing them.

How does he do that?

Like he did with you. He knows when the time is right, when each of my children is ready to be known—to be released from the prison of their minds. Remember, do not reject your mind, as it serves a purpose. Your mother was right in protecting you from the pain of feeling bad and alone. That would have been too much to bear. Fear and rejection from your childhood reared their heads and retraumatized you. But Jesus came into your mind and healed it.

Michelle McCann

> It started in 2007. Why is it taking so long (now 2019) for me to heal?

Because the trauma was so great, the original sin (which is just another term for the original separation) takes time to heal. Yes, time does heal all wounds.

> I thought I wrote before that it was love, not time, that heals all wounds.

Both are involved. This is part of why we created time—to help you to heal. It is a process of rediscovery. Once you remember who you truly are—a divine child of God, both Mother and Father God, of spirit and of ego—you can be healed. The angels are your pilots. They steered you to Karan to teach you to work with them. And they brought you to empath and spiritual teacher Sara Wiseman, psychic and channel Laurie Blomer, Cristina Aroche, and all your other teachers and therapists and psychiatrists. As they do with each individual, the angels knew what you needed to heal and who could help you achieve it.

You (we) will work to help people connect with the angels in order to find the path back to God. With each interaction they will learn to set aside their egos and still love themselves and one another. It is important that all my children learn to do both—love themselves and each other. One without the other is insufficient. For us all to heal, the circle of love must be complete. As I have said, we are all one. When one suffers, even if it is for lack of love for themselves, we all suffer.

The time has come for all of us to heal. Even Mother and I felt the pain, Mother more than I. I have borne the suffering of your earthly experiences, which feel enormous but are quite small in comparison to the original "sin," the hour of separation. Mother bore the pain of that, as all mothers today bear the pain of childbirth. It is a pain she was willing to endure because she wanted to see you grow into your true self. She had to convince me to allow it.

> I'm thinking of the movie Tree of Life—or actually, just the trailer I saw.

That is right. Your mother is the way of nature, in which there are laws of cause and effect. Humans had to learn that their actions impact others. So the whole of creation has this built in—"For every action, there is an equal and opposite reaction." Scientists know it as Newton's

Third Law of Motion. Others call it karma. Karma was required for you to learn the ways of the world and how to not hurt each other.

My way is the way of grace, to forgive all wrongs when they happen. This is not to say that your mother doesn't forgive you. Of course she does. She just requires that you learn from your mistakes. Your birth mother always said that too.

Part of the mission of this life on earth is to learn that you can make mistakes and still be OK. You will still be loved. No matter what you do, it can be worked through. It may cause pain and suffering but in the end it all evens out—"Even Steven," as your twin soul would say. So again, karma is not to CAUSE suffering but is a natural result of making a mistake. It resets the equilibrium. The time has come for karma to end and for us to move into grace as our way of being.

> *Yes, I have been seeing and hearing about AMAZING GRACE.*

The angels put this healing in your path to help you learn that by the grace of God (both your father and your mother), you can be free of judgment and pain when you make mistakes.

> *In this world, there is still judgment and pain.*

Only if you allow it, my child. Now that you know the grace of God, you can choose to feel differently when you THINK you are being disparaged or feel pain in the human realm. There is NO JUDGMENT from heaven or from your divine mother and father. As I have said before, we love you no matter what.

> *Just took a break to go to the bathroom. . . . Still have earthly needs . . . LOL. This is so serious, yet I feel you want to be playful too.*

Yes. There are times to be serious, but it is important that no one takes things too seriously. In the end, all will be well. Even if people must suffer in the earthly realms to heal the biggest wound—the hour of separation or the original "sin"—they will be reunited with their soul family and divine mother and father in heaven.

Tell me more about heaven.

It is not a physical place. It is an energetic realm of the highest vibrating frequency.

Yes, last night it occurred to me that I see the angels as lights, but I see what I realized were ancestors as sort of gray/black. At one time, I was worried they were negative entities, but it didn't feel like that to me.

The ancestors are in a different realm, divine but not yet heaven. Although they are not beings of light, they are more evolved than humans on earth. Once all of the ancestral karma is healed, they will be released into heaven. They understand this and are joyful and at peace, so do not worry about them. When they help you, they expedite the return of all souls to the heavenly realm.

Is that something that can happen here—heaven on earth?

Yes, my child. Earth can vibrate in the same realm as heaven if all beings are enlightened, and by enlightened, I mean no longer making mistakes.

But how do we as humans no longer make mistakes?

By choosing to think differently. It is not an original negative thought that causes a hurtful reaction, it is negative ACTION. If you think something bad about someone but do not act on it by withholding love, there is no adverse reaction. Thoughts will continue to come into your mind, negative thoughts included, but as long as you act in alignment with God's will, which is always LOVE, you will be fine. You will begin to vibrate at the realm of the heavens. That is what brings heaven to earth, people vibrating at a higher energetic level, the vibration of LOVE. That is heaven—pure, unadulterated—

THE NATURE OF GOD

> LOL . . . I don't know what "unadulterated" means. I'll have to look it up.

—LOVE.

> OK, I looked. It's another word for "pure and undiluted." Gotcha!
>
> I do not feel tired, but maybe I need to take a break to ground. I want to talk about mother speaking to us in song and you in stillness.

Your mother works with people to make music, movies, TV shows, and other media and arts. What you thought were messages from me were actually facilitated by her. She inspires the arts and loves them, as you do. Since we are all connected, the inspiration for music is one another. We feel what others need to hear. All the songs you heard that had meaning to you were your brothers and sisters "knowing" at a subconscious level that someone needed to hear what they were singing. They don't realize this, but this is how it works.

> Sarah McLachlan and the "Prayer of St. Francis" . . .

Yes. McLachlan was inspired to write that song.

> For me?

Yes, for you and for others too. In the same way, other songs may touch you but their principal purpose is to heal someone else. You can tell people to listen for the meanings in songs and glean their messages.

Also encourage them to be still, in silence, to connect with me— "Be still, and know that I am God." I can come into people's hearts and minds when they are quiet. That is the holy spirit at work.

> Is there more to know about this?

Not at this time. It is time for you to go back to bed now. You have worked hard this morning. Thanks for heeding my call.

> I was a little afraid Steve would give me a hard time for getting up at 3 a.m., but I trusted you.

Yes, you will need to continue to do that. Now off to bed.

Love you, Mother and Father God.

Love you too, our darling.

7:09 a.m.

I didn't really sleep but I rested and feel refreshed.

Yes, Dear, sometimes you will just need to rest to restore your energy. Remember, even though you don't fully feel it, it takes a lot of energy to connect to this realm. Vibrating at such a high speed drains your human body. You will tune into this more as we continue. Indeed, you are already paying attention—you stayed in bed to rest today even though you wanted to connect with me and write some more. That was a good choice. If you are ever in doubt, ask Steve. He will help you stay grounded. He knows what you need.

Next, you are interested in negative energies.

Yes, I felt Raphael healing me, burning away my fear of negative energies/entities from the divine realms.

There is no such thing as negative energy in the divine realms. That is an earthly creation and idea. Movie scenarios of people being possessed are human imagination at work. When real people believe demons inhabit them, it is simply their minds devising coping mechanisms to deal with trauma. Although the invading entities feel external or "other," they are products of their own minds.

Why does it feel external?

Because there is a split.

I'm not following.

Let's not get into all the detail about this. Just know that there is no negative energy or entity in the divine realms, so you can feel safe

THE NATURE OF GOD

connecting with ancestors, divine beings, spirit guides, angels, me, your divine mother—anyone you choose.

> *As I lay in bed this morning, I felt like I connected with my ancestors. I thought about my grandparents, Ninnin and Bigdaddy; and Daddy and his relatives like Aunt Hilda, Uncle Prentice, Bobby, Gerald, and Aunt Pam; and then I thought of Uncle Ernest and Aunt Cheri, who are actually cousins, but older like an aunt and uncle.*

Yes, my child. They are all cheering you on and are so proud of the legacy you are bringing forth.

> *Now I'm thinking about Ninnin's siblings and the great-grandparents I never knew but have heard about, especially on Mama's side.*

They are all here—again, cheering you on. Call on them to help you, along with the angels, your mother, and me.

> *It feels strange to call on my divine mother when I have felt so disconnected from her.*

All my children are disconnected from their mother, as this needed to be so during the separation, but now is the time for reunification. Call on her. She desires a relationship with you.

> *How do I hear her?*

Through music, remember—and art, and the sea, and the trees, and the wind, and the birds, and the animals. All aspects of the earthly realm are of your mother. That is why you need to ground, to balance the feminine earthly energy with the fatherly heavenly energy. She is the negative energy (not in the sense of bad, but the counterbalance to my positive energy). For humans to be balanced, they need both heavenly and earthly vibrations. Your bipolar disorder came about because you were out of balance—connecting to me, but not to your mother.

You are thinking about the scales of your astrological sign.

> Yes, I've been told I am "Libra sun, Libra moon, Libra ascendant, all air."

That is right. Because you were made to connect to the heavenly realms, you needed to be all air. Others will be able to connect, but not as easily as you. You were created when the stars and planets aligned to bring forth the being who would guide earth back into alignment.

> Wow, that sounds pretty grandiose.

It is, but not because you are manic. It is true and you are magnificent, as are all my children. All were created in a time and space for when and where the planet needed their special gifts. You (we) are to help them uncover those gifts through astrology, music, art, nature, being still, and connecting with their mother and me. Some will write as you are doing, and others will paint, sing, or work in business but with consciousness of the greater good. We all have things we are drawn to and are passionate about, and as long as we do them with love and love ourselves and one another, everyone will enjoy abundance. Even a street sweeper can live abundantly if we take care of one another.

This world produces enough to provide for everyone, and my loving and creative children can find ways to make that happen. There need be no poverty or deprivation. If those with means take care of those without, then all can do what pleases them and makes them happy.

Should a mother choose to stay home with her child and not work outside the home, no one will denigrate her. The community will recognize and support her valuable contribution. Women who feel drawn to make other contributions to the world in addition to their motherhood will also be supported by the community, which will provide loving care for their children so they can pursue those additional dreams.

There is no right or wrong way for folks to pursue their hearts' desires. Men can work or choose to take care of their children. Some of that has started to occur, but in the future it will be more frequent. Once we strip away the expectation that men must provide financially, fathers can choose to be with their children if that is their hearts' desire. They will be supported by their wives and by their communities.

> What about same sex couples?

Same goes for them. I have no judgment against same-sex couples. Love is love, and I want my children to be happy loving whoever makes them happy. In the divine realm, there is only masculine and feminine, but the earthly realm encompasses a spectrum of sexuality and gender, and there is NOTHING wrong with that. Some people have incarnated to feel what it's like to be a man inside a woman's body or vice versa. That is of my creation and is not abominable.

I can't spell that . . . LOL.

I give my children the experiences their souls desire and all my creation is perfect. I encourage you to accept and love each other's most basic selves. Recognize what makes each happy and support them joyfully. Be kind to one another (yes, I gave Ellen DeGeneres that line). Love her, as I do all my children. She makes people laugh but also makes them feel good about themselves and others. That is her gift and I'm delighted she is sharing it. Actor Portia de Rossi is her soul twin, supporting her in her dreams.

Soul twins complement each other energetically, one masculine and one feminine. Physical gender is irrelevant. For example, Portia and Ellen are both female, but Ellen's soul contains the masculine energy, going forth in the world, and Portia is the feminine, buoying Ellen in her pursuits. With you and Steve, you embody the masculine energy and Steve the feminine.

Sometimes those energies influence souls' actions, such as Steve enjoying cooking and gardening, considered more feminine by your culture, and Ellen preferring short hair and typically male clothing, which is perceived as more masculine.

The bottom line is, it really doesn't matter. As long as my children are expressing who they truly are, they are living their dreams and we are all happy. That is the goal. No need to deprecate masculine or feminine—or male or female, black or white, or Asian or native American, for that matter. We are to love one another for our differences and our strengths. As you learned in your social work practice, we all have strengths. When we help each other to see these, rather than what divides us, we can be productive members of society and support one another.

I think it is time to wrap up for today.

Enjoy your day, my darling.

Michelle McCann

> *You too. Can I call you "Dad" or "Pops"? "Father" seems so formal now . . . LOL.*

Whatever you like. I love endearments.

> *Let me think about it! A nickname for you.*

Mother/Father God Radio

June 6, 2019

Good morning. It was a little harder getting up today. I stayed up later to visit with my son and his girlfriend. Now that I am outside hearing Mother's birds and the sounds of nature, I feel OK.

Yes, my child. This is your mother. As you recall my creation and remember what it is like to feel your father's energy, it will be easier to get up in the morning.

I do enjoy this time once I get started. So, Mother, is your energy at the same vibrational frequency as Father's?

No, because I am of the earth. One day when we are joined again, it will be the same.

When will this happen?

It remains to be seen.

I knew you were going to say that. You and Dad (still need a nickname) are on the same page with not letting the cat out of the bag, so to speak . . . LOL.

That's right. Your father and I are of one mind. I have a sense of humor too—just look at some of nature's quirky creatures and trees and flowers. It was fun to make so many unique and different things.

> Yes, Mother, you are VERY creative. I love your creation. Well, except for the things that can hurt me, like bugs and snakes that bite and bees that sting.

Those are all for good reason. Trust that I knew what I was doing, as your father was infallible in creating you—all of you, all of our children.

> Were you involved in bringing us forth?

No, that was Father's role. He created all the souls, and I created the earth and the other planets prior to earth.

> That reminds me. After my "awakening," I wrote that Father was OK whether the earth blew up or thrived—that this is a divine play, and he will be proud of us no matter the outcome.

At the time, you needed to hear that. You were not ready to hear that there would be peace on earth.

> HA! I'm still not sure I am ready to believe this.

You are ready now. To keep you safe though, you still have to work with your ego (me). In your dream last night, Marianne Williamson won the presidency, but that evoked nastiness and backlash. Remember that this fear is in your psyche. We will give you dreams to help you know what you are afraid of. This will bring it into your conscious mind. Once you are aware, anything is possible. You can connect with Father and me and return to love, your natural inheritance.

> So now I know I can do that with my writing, but how do I do it at other times?

Meditate and breathe in your father's essence, and step out in nature and connect with me. We are always here for you.

> Sometimes it is still hard.

THE NATURE OF GOD

I know, Dear, but I promise it will get easier. Just as you are writing on this page and it just comes to you, so it will be in daily life, every moment. We will be with you and you will know it.

> That sounds wonderful.

It will be, but you must be patient. Remember the article about the teenaged ice skater. She is in high school but has worked hard to hone her skill since she was three. This is your skill—connecting with spirit, Father and me, your ancestors, other spirit guides and fairies, and all other spiritual beings.

> "My skill"—how amazing.

Your father and I know this is your dream. And you have to work to make your dreams come true.

> Should I continue to take classes?

You can, although that is not required. Now that you are connected to us and to the angels (oh yes, you will be channeling them too), you do not need any more formal lessons. Someday you will teach, but not yet.

> Tell me more about channeling. How does it actually work?

Dad and I lower our vibration to match yours, as if you have tuned a radio to a station you want to listen to. We are at a high frequency, one you would not find on a typical radio.

> LOL . . . Wouldn't it be great if we had Mother/Father God Radio, and you could broadcast what you need us to know? "This is Mother, broadcasting on WMFG radio . . ."

Well, it will be like that! We won't be talking directly on the radio, but others will share our messages. The word will get out!!!!

> What are your messages, Mother?

To take care of me! Please! Preserve my creation. Do not build and build and build and ruin all that I have designed for your pleasure and enjoyment. Yes, some construction to make things comfortable for yourselves is good, and some of your creation is beautiful, but it has become excessive. Building just to build is marring my landscapes. People will be sad once they cannot get them back. Although you can always restore nature—for example, by planting trees and flowers—it is a slow process. Conserving it in the first place is much easier.

Is climate change real?

Yes, my child. Your brothers and sisters (and sometimes you) are doing incredible harm by being so wasteful with all the plastic, fossil fuels, overrun consumerism, and PACKAGING—so much PACKAGING of merchandise. Buyers need to stand up and insist that it stop, and manufacturers need to do more to lessen the impact of their products. You have started with a simple thing, declining plastic bags, and explaining that it is to help the environment.

We need more of that, people educating one another. It is not necessary to point fingers and say that what others do is wrong. Instead, help them lovingly to do the right thing. At your core, and at the core of all our children, is the divine essence, the soul that comes from heaven. People KNOW the right thing to do—they just need to be reminded sometimes.

Tell me more about you being of the earth and our ego. I'm still a little confused.

I am in and around you, both at the same time. Father is inside you as the holy spirit. I take care of creation by sharing my energy with her. Following her cycles, which are driven by my energy, she rejuvenates each day. She wakes with the sun and goes to bed with the moon. Just as you do, she needs her rest. Darkness allows her to rejuvenate. Providing the light of the sun takes a lot of energy.

But wait—the sun is separate from the Earth?

Yes, but their energy is connected. They work in tandem to bring beauty to the world that you see each day. The moon governs the oceans and waters, and the sun governs the plants and trees. Both impact the human body. Their unique energies restore and replenish you each day. That is why it is good to be in nature.

THE NATURE OF GOD

Tell me more.

Immersion in nature helps people feel calm and centered, and connecting with spirit helps people feel joyous and alive. Well, we both do that.

So you both inspire us? Nature and spirit?

That is right, my darling. Some people have more earth in their chart, so they feel the call of nature. These are people who love to garden and to sew—

To sew?

—At the moment, it is not important how these relate. But those with earth FEEL their connection to me more easily. With your chart being all air, you naturally feel more of a connection with your father, although now that you are spending more time in nature you are discovering your deeper attachment to me as well.

What about the ego?

That is your mind, inside you.

OK, pause for a moment. It is starting to rain. I want to be outside, but I don't want the computer to get wet.

You will be fine, my dear. It is only the wind blowing last night's rain off the trees. We have taken care of the weather for you to write during this time.

It seems a little self-absorbed for me to think this weather is for me.

But it is! Everyone can enjoy it, but we did make this time to work with you.

Back to the ego.

Michelle McCann

I am in your mind, that voice that tells you "No!" to keep you safe from revealing yourself and feeling rejection. Some people shut you out because it is too hard for them to connect and be who they truly are. You need not concern yourself with the negative judgment of others—that is only their pain talking. As Jesus said, "Forgive them, for they know not what they do."

Shine your light, and it will help others to do the same. I will still be here in your mind, warning you to be careful. But you know me now and understand that I am not here to hurt you. Neither are your brothers and sisters, although it will still feel like that at times. Remember to send them love and pray for them. We hear your prayers and will work on the hearts of those for whom you have prayed.

Both you and Father?

Yes, both of us hear your prayers and intervene when we can. As you know, we can't interfere with your free will, so sometimes there is nothing we can do to change events or outcomes, but we can always abide and be present. People feel our energy even though it may not be in their awareness. Embracing our energy is healing. So, yes, prayers do work.

But aren't we always connected to your energy?

Yes, in the sense that it is always inside you. When you vibrate at a higher frequency, as you are now, you connect to more of our energy. Father's energy revs you up and mine grounds you at the same time.

I was just thinking, do you love us unconditionally as Father does?

Of course. I love you as much as Father. His love is never-ending while mine is unconditional and educational. I make you learn from your mistakes through natural and logical consequences. As much as you dislike adverse effects for negative actions, the truth is your soul craves understanding. It wants to know itself fully and cannot do that without making mistakes and changing your behavior as a result. My laws of karma help you to know yourself and understand the impact of your actions on others and the world around you. So, yes, my child, I love you more than you can comprehend in this earthly realm.

Just because I "discipline" you does not mean I don't love you. In fact, the opposite is true. I love you so much I am willing to be the "bad guy" to help you achieve your heart and soul's desires. For thousands of years, I have been hidden in your mind. Well, not out of sight in my creation, but invisible to your awareness.

> *I am thinking about parents who abuse their children. I'm not suggesting that you abuse us, but I don't want people to take things the wrong way and think it is OK to hit or spank a child.*

No, that is definitely not OK and not what I mean—which I know you know. This is a good point to clarify. I gently show people how to approach situations in ways that do not harm others or themselves. I am never cruel, hateful, spiteful, or violent.

> *Sometimes it does seem like you are violent with tornadoes, floods, hurricanes, hail, volcanoes, etc.*

That is not me—that is you. All of the upheaval is of human origin. Before people incarnated on earth, these types of events did not occur.

> *I thought these disasters have happened for thousands of years.*

Only since the inception of humankind.

> *I did come inside because I was getting drops of water on my computer.*

That is fine. You would have been all right outside, but you can finish typing inside and then go back out to select your angel cards for the day. This is a nice routine you have. It has been almost an hour that you have been writing.

> *Wow, it is amazing how the time goes by and I don't realize it!*

Yes, when you live your dream, you don't notice time passing because you are so engrossed in the task at hand. That is when you know you are carrying out your soul's purpose, as you are now. Your life will be magical, my darling, as will the lives of all my children as soon as they learn to reconnect with Father and me. This is happening for you sooner, but as you know, this doesn't make you better than anyone else. You are just a different variety of flower, a very colorful one that wants to be in the spotlight.

> *Wow. Really?*

Yes, you want to shine your beautiful light for all to see. That is why you like the colorful birds. You are drawn to beauty and beautiful things. That is a Libra trait.

> *It makes me feel peaceful and in awe at the same time to see things of beauty, whether in nature or made by humans. But I'm getting tired.*

Yes, my child. Take a break. Sit outside again. It will not rain on you now.

> *Thank you, Mother.*

You are welcome.

We Are Lights for One Another

June 7, 2019

> I had to force myself to stay in bed. Around 4 I woke up and wanted to write but knew I had to work today and would need my rest.

Yes, that is good, my child. You are keeping yourself grounded and not rushing things.

> I was thinking about Saint Francis being the first and me being the last soul and us being twin flames. Can you tell me more about this?

Yes, my child. Saint Francis has been reconciled with us, Mother and Father, because he has led you back to us.

> I thought he was a spirit guide for me.

He is and was, and now he is in heaven. Steve was right with his comment yesterday. When you saw the Saint Francis statue at your friend's house and she offered to give it to you, Steve said "Saint Francis will be in heaven," referring to how you call the beautiful gardens of Mt. Cuba heaven. You knew as soon as he spoke. He may not realize it, but he brought it into your awareness.

> So what is this twin flame?

Your souls have the same purpose, to bring peace. Saint Francis created the prayer to bring you back to your plan. He came before you to light the way and be the flame. So it is with all people. One soul will act as a beacon for the next soul's mission. The assignment of the first is to be the light, and the task of the second is to complete the circle.

What do you mean by circle?

The alpha and omega. As I have said, I am the alpha and omega, and so are my children. Each of you is the beginning and end.

I am not following. Am I not to understand this now?

It is not important to understand all the details now. Just know that you and Saint Francis are connected. He will continue to light your path. Order the prayer you want for your wall and look at it every day to remind you of your purpose.

It seems it would be for all people.

It is, but it was also designed to help you remember me.

So other people have things designed to help them remember you and to know you like I do now?

That is right. The angels will lead each person to their light, the soul that came before them and prepared the way.

"Twin flames" is not exactly the right term, as each of you is a flame for the next, lighting the way. The "twin" is the person that goes before you, but there are others that follow.

What else is there for me to know today?

You are all lights for one another. Some shine more brightly to you to help you follow your path or your bliss. Following your bliss is what I want for each of my children. When you do this, you are in alignment with my will, and you will be at peace and live in joy.

Even with all the "bad" things happening in the world?

That is right. Those will die away and you will begin to understand that such events are only temporary until all my children, my sheep, are led back to me. It will not take long now.

Really? How long is "not long"? Sometimes our ideas of time seem very different!

I am working in terms of centuries and you have only your lifetime as a reference. But it will take less time than it took you to complete graduate school.

Wait—what will take less time than that? For the world to be healed?

No, for your word to get out into the world to begin the healing process. It will spread quickly.

I was just thinking, how will I build my platform?

Please don't go into it with that thinking. A platform is a means to an end, but you want to go into this project with a heart for helping. Do not worry about trying to MAKE it a success—it will happen naturally due to your authenticity and integrity. Just be sincere, caring, and kind, and try to help people with their pain. Sharing their stories will help them and others (and you in the process). It will give meaning to what you do while you wait for the transition.

This is a gift from me to you to help you be more patient with the process. People find joy in doing something meaningful, and this will be that for you, until you are living your ultimate purpose. Of course, as it said in *What Color is Your Parachute* by Richard Nelson Bolles, you want to live hour by hour, minute by minute, doing the will of God. Be kind to your neighbor and the strangers you meet. Even when people cut you off on the highway, let them merge into your lane—you know, all the little things—as the little things are the big things that make up your daily life and CAN make it joyous.

As you take interest in the people you meet, you see this more and more. Not all contacts need to lead to long-term relationships. Just spread the joy and light for the moment you are together. That makes an impression and triggers happiness.

I want to write more but feel like I should stop now.

Yes, let's stop for now. You go back to bed and rest for your busy day at work. It will be fun to catch up with everybody and there will be many tasks to accomplish. Focus your energy on that for today. This will be here when you get back. WE, Mother and I, will be here when you get back to help you with your next steps.

Thank you! I am so excited!

I know you are, Dear. But go back to bed.

Thanks. Love you.

Love you too.

1:21 p.m.

More questions! Why did I think I was Jesus?

You were channeling him and feeling his energy with all the history imprinted in it. He was coming into your mind to heal you. It took some time for you to understand that you were merging with his energy and that it was not your own. Others will experience this as Jesus comes into their minds to heal them. Not everyone will be mentally ill as you were, but they will need to understand that they may think they are Jesus or having Jesus experiences as his energy heals them.

I am referring to Jesus when I say, "No one comes to the father but through me." Jesus will come into every mind and heal them, whether or not they believe in Christ or are Christian. Again—very important to clarify—no one needs to be of the Christian religion. I do not favor any religion over another, nor no religion over having a religion. Christ is just the method of reunification of the human and the spirit. He was of both worlds and is the only person who has or ever will be of both worlds.

Now go have your gluten-free beer!

Yes, I was feeling ready to relax. So God has nothing against drinking?

Of course not. As long as it is not causing difficulty for my children, I have nothing against it. Some people have unhealed traumas, and then drinking becomes an addiction. Not that I label them as bad for

THE NATURE OF GOD

having an addiction, but I know it does not serve their soul purpose well.

For you, it is not an addiction—it is fun. You enjoy the flavors and the social interactions, and there is nothing wrong with that. Again, the evangelical Christians have put their own interpretation on what I judge.

> *It sounds like you are angry with them!*

No, I do not get angry. I just find it important to clarify the truth. There is no judgment in the truth. It is what it is.

> *Thank you!*
> *We move my son, Aidan, into his house tomorrow.*

The move will go smoothly, and Aidan will have a good year and a great life. You are setting a strong foundation for him to have a wonderful, prosperous, and joyous future. He will be very proud of you and grateful for all you have done and will do for him.

> *That is awesome! He is such a great boy.*

I know he is wonderful. You have done a good job as his mother.

> *Thank you!*
> *About Angel number 411, what vital information do I need to know right now?*

Nothing to know. Not to worry. We've got this. Your spiritual team is working overtime to move things forward in the direction of your dreams. Your dreams are coming TRUE!!!

June 8, 2019

> *It is 5 a.m. I woke at 3:31, thinking of 3:33, and then noticed the clock again at 4. I seem to recall that 3 to 4 a.m. is the hour of separation. I'm not sure what this means.*

The hour of separation is when Jesus descended into hell and was disconnected from his heavenly energy. Then he became human. Although he grew up with a human body, he was of a heavenly energy, except during his hour of separation. That is when he thought I had forsaken him. Of course I had not, but he had to feel, as all his brothers and sisters have felt, that I left him and rejected him. This was required for the reconciliation.

I woke up thinking about the masculine and feminine, the yin and yang.

That is right, my dear. You all have both masculine and feminine as part of your souls' twin creation, but there is some masculine within the feminine and some feminine within the masculine. This is depicted in the yin and yang and in the "Starting Fresh" angel card you have been getting lately.

Humans embody this duality. Their twin souls balance their masculine and feminine sides. This is not to disparage or neglect those who are gay or transgender. Though they also have twin souls with masculine and feminine balance, they inhabit the human body in a different way from their masculine and feminine energies.

Heterosexual humans may also express their gender energy fluidly. Some females may have more outward masculine energy, meaning they want to go forth into the world and create, be seen, be bold—like you. A woman in this lifetime, your primary energy is masculine, one of being in the spotlight. Although Steve is male, his energy is feminine, as he prefers to be in the background, the "Wind Beneath [Your] Wings."

That song sung by Bette Midler describes the twin soul relationship perfectly—one of grandeur and one behind the scenes supporting the person in the spotlight. Neither is better nor worse nor more or less important than the other. It is important to remember this. Individuals who are not in the spotlight should know that I value their contributions and love them as much as their flashier counterparts. Their souls desired supporting, rather than lead, roles.

The play needs all the characters, supporting roles included. There would be no production if all were not accounted for. I want to stress this again—EACH PERSON, from the streetsweeper to the President of the United States, has a very important role to play in my divine plan, even if it doesn't seem so. Just as each individual has a unique fingerprint, you each have a singular imprint on the collective soul, the

THE NATURE OF GOD

soul that is us all combined, reunified, back together in the heavenly vibration. We will make beautiful music when we are reunited.

Tell me more about this reunification.

It is not time yet for that. I just wanted you to understand what is coming and how each of us will play a critical role in making it happen. Although you are the bringer of the news, your role is no more important than anyone else's. You are here to help them be who they truly are so their lights—their unique lights—can shine.

It takes all of us to renew the heavenly energy—NO EXCEPTIONS. Yes, tell the liberals we even need President Trump. When he makes decisions that do not benefit mankind, it is right to stand up against them, but it is not right to be hateful towards him any more than it is right for evangelical Christians to be hateful to Muslims, Jews, and gays.

Hate is never the answer or the approach. It can be difficult to love thy neighbor as thyself, but that is my will for you. "My will be done on earth as it is in heaven."

Steve just told me that Pope Francis is changing the Lord's Prayer to remove "Lead us not into temptation."

That is right, my child. He is correct that it was mistranslated. I never lead you into temptation but rather you fall into the temptation to judge your brothers and sisters. This is the descent into hell, the separation from me and my will. The more you choose to love one another—liberals, conservatives, straight, gay, Christian, Muslim, Jew, all religions—you will be living according to my will. I beg you to please do this.

You are begging us, God?

Yes. I gave you free will, so it is your choice. But you will be happier, and I will be happier through you, should you choose love over fear and hate. There will come a time when you will all choose to live by my will and we will be reunified in the heavenly energy, but in the meantime, I encourage you all to live your daily lives striving to choose love and live by my will. If you listen to your heart, it will tell you what to do, and when, and with whom. Trust your instincts. Listen to your heart.

> Anything more for today?

No, I think that is enough. You will have a busy day with the move, so you should go back to bed for a bit and rest. It will be a nice, but busy, weekend.

> What about work? I'm starting to feel like I'm ready for my next step and don't want to do the things I am being asked to do.

No worries. Continue to bless your work for what it is giving you now (and has given you), and the time will come soon when you can step away. It is not time yet. Please be patient.

> Thank you and love you.

Love you too, my darling.

Becoming Real

June 9, 2019

Thanks for waking me up. I was a little tired, as I drank a little too much yesterday. It was a good day moving Aidan in, and then Steve and I wanted to relax afterwards.

Yes, Dear, when you drink too much it disrupts your sleep, you have a dry mouth, and you get a slight headache. Although you don't do it often, be mindful, as you don't like how it makes you feel.

The quotation from The Velveteen Rabbit by Margery Williams about becoming "REAL" is on my daily angel calendar.[15]

That is what I want to talk about today.

---

[15] "Real isn't how you are made," said the Skin Horse. "It's a thing that happens to you. When a child loves you for a long, long time, not just to play with, but REALLY loves you, then you become Real."
"Does it hurt?" asked the Rabbit.
"Sometimes," said the Skin Horse, for he was always truthful. "When you are Real you don't mind being hurt."
"Does it happen all at once, like being wound up," he asked, "or bit by bit?"
"It doesn't happen all at once," said the Skin Horse. "You become. It takes a long time. That's why it doesn't happen often to people who break easily, or have sharp edges, or who have to be carefully kept. Generally, by the time you are Real, most of your hair has been loved off, and your eyes drop out and you get loose in the joints and very shabby. But these things don't matter at all, because once you are Real you can't be ugly, except to people who don't understand."
—Margery Williams, *The Velveteen Rabbit*

Michelle McCann

> *What would you like to say about it?*

That writing was inspired by me. I created each of my children to be magnificent, but that magnificence can only be realized if they are REAL, who they truly are. Research professor Brené Brown says most people feel unworthy of love and belonging, but everyone deserves those things. As my children become their true selves, they will attract their "tribes," as your psychic development teacher Laurie and others say, and others who love them can be drawn to them.

It is when people pretend to be something they are not that they feel disconnected and unloved. This is why there is so much depression. Trauma or wounds from past relationships keep people from being able to truly express who they are. You are to teach them to take RISKS and to show others their sincere feelings and true hearts. This is how they find love.

You have experienced this. The more you have followed your heart to do the things your soul desires—to learn about me, for example, and how to connect with me, which is your true calling—you found people to bond with and who love you for yourself. Steve has loved you from the first time you met because he could see your warm and gentle spirit, and you loved his quiet strength. And he loved that little flowered dress you were wearing . . .

> *I remember that dress. Yes, it had pretty flowers!*

A good representation of your spirit, pretty flowers.

> *Awww . . . thank you.* ☺

Of course, my child, you are lovely like flowers, as are all my children. I do love it when you wear flowers, as it reminds me of the children I have created to be perfectly in my image.

> *Tell me more about what it means that we are made in your image.*

It means you are made to love. That is my vibration, my energy—pure, unadulterated love. You were created in heaven with that same pure love energy as your mother and me and now your brother Jesus. And you will return to pure love.

THE NATURE OF GOD

Marianne Williamson named her book *A Return to Love*. I inspired that title, just as I inspired your title. It will grab people's attention and they will be interested to hear more.

> *I love the title you gave me.*

Well, thank you for listening!

> *I also love how the writing just flows when you "talk" to me. I can't wait until I hear your voice—or rather, know your will and your intentions for me—all the time, not just when I'm writing.*

You are starting to "hear" more, and this will become more frequent. I just don't want to do too much too soon because I don't want you to be confused and think that "hearing voices" means your illness has returned. But if you have a question or want to connect with me, just take a break from what you are doing, breathe in and out, and ask me in your mind. I will answer. You will hear me. I promise.

> *That sounds good.*

This will be good practice for you as you learn to tune in to me.

> *What else would you like to talk about today?*

I would like to talk a little more about love—to clarify that it is not romantic love that I mean, although this is certainly of my creation and I delight when you find it. I mean love for me and for one another—again, NO EXCEPTIONS. You were created to love unconditionally.

It is hard in the earthly realm because humans make mistakes, but you must remember that is their fear of disconnection talking, not who they truly are. When you all start to remember that you are divine children of a loving God, you will begin to forgive and accept people for who and where they are. You can disagree with someone's actions without faulting the person as an individual. Approach with love, letting them know they are worthy and loveable but that their approach is not Christ-like.

> *Here's where it gets tricky. When people talk about Christ, they are ingrained to think of the*

> evangelical Christians who have done so much to harm others.

You are here to help change that perception. The reality is that Christ loved ALL people as he loved me and himself. He treated them with kindness, generosity, respect, and love and did not do things to hurt or disrespect others' free will. It is time for his reputation to be restored and for people to love him again. He is here in heaven waiting for the love of his brothers and sisters.

> Really, he is waiting for their love?

Not waiting exactly, but wanting people to know who he truly is and was and not take actions in his name that do not suit his will—which is my will, the will to love one another as I have loved you.

I have made my key points for today. Go rest. You are tired from your busy day of moving yesterday and will have a lovely day with Aidan again today, helping him get settled. You are so proud of him.

> Yes, I am. So happy he is happy. I feel like talking more, but I think you are right that I should go rest.

You have a busy week ahead, so we will not have long writing sessions. We do want to continue each day, as I have much to share with you, but we will take our time so as not to wear you out and so you can keep your energy up. You will be excited to talk with your friends this week and share with your tribe what you are up to!

> Yes, I can't wait to tell people who will be open to this.

That's right. You need to get your footing first before you go out into the world with this. You will, just not yet.

> Time to rest. Love you.

Love you. 😊

THE NATURE OF GOD

8:23 a.m.

> Archangel Michael visited me this morning! Although I felt his energy before, I didn't "hear" or "know" anything specific. This time I got messages. My knowing was that I am to start a new book with him tomorrow morning called The Nature of Angels: Channeled Messages from Archangel Michael. He is in the heavenly realms with God and has messages to share with the world and wants me to be his scribe. I am a good scribe, he says. Thank you, Michael! It sounds exciting!

Yes, indeed, it will be FAB-YOU-LOUS!!!

> You are a character!

I know. That is good, isn't it?

> Yes! I love it and I love you.

Thank you, Dear. Have a good day. Pay your bills and take care of your earthly needs now.

> Off I go.

June 10, 2019

> It's 4 a.m. I knew you were going to wake me up today at this hour. That's the time of reconciliation, isn't it, God?

Yes, my child. It is time to begin the process of healing the world through reunion with your divine mother and me. This morning we are going to write the introduction to our book *The Nature of God: The Revelation: Channeled Messages from Your Heavenly Father and Your Divine Mother*.

> Where do we start?

Just start typing.

[See Introduction]

> Wow! I just reread the introduction. Thank you. Now I'm not sure what to put into the rest of the book . . . LOL.

You will put in all the channeled writing you have done. Lois, the Happy Self-Publisher, will help you sort it out and self-publish through Amazon. You will pay her substantially for this, but it will be worth it in the long run to go this route. Trust me.

> I do trust you and I will wait for things to be revealed.

Time to work with Michael now.

> I felt him calming me this morning about 3:30 or so.

Yes, your energy was high in preparation for this step today, and I sent him to help ground you. Going forward, call on him when you feel you need to ground. He will come and help you.

> Thank you, God.

Thank you, my daughter. Have a lovely day and a nice "conversation" with Michael!

12:30 p.m.

> Waves of sadness wash over me as I think about going public with my writing and fear ridicule and rejection by the ones I love. I feel that this writing may not actually be as real as I think, but rather a retraumatization of being rejected by both my earthly

THE NATURE OF GOD

> *mother during childhood and my divine mother. Mother, can you help?*

Yes, my child. It is true. I rejected you, turned away from you. It was hard for me to bear, but I knew I had to do it if you were to fulfill your soul's desire to truly know yourself.

> *How do I heal this wound? It still is so scary, and I feel so ashamed.*

My child, you have nothing to be ashamed of. You did nothing wrong. I had to do the "harder right." You've heard that expression. The right thing—to let you think I rejected you and did not love you—was the hardest thing I have ever had to do. I'm so sorry, my darling, darling, child, my sweet innocent child.

> *I feel your pain. As a mother, I can't imagine how hard it must have been to turn away and act as if you did not love me.*

Yes, imagine with Aidan. He is such a sweet, sweet, boy, an innocent child, as you were. But now that you know the truth, I can be released from my prison of always hurting you, always making you feel not good enough, rejected, and ashamed.

If you let me come into the light, you will know I have always loved you and will always love you. As it is with your heavenly father, you can do no wrong in my eyes. It was only a pretense I had to keep up in order for you to grow. All of my children needed that, but now the growing pains are over. You are ready to reveal your true self and know that you are loved, NO MATTER WHAT.

> *What about my family? I fear they may reject me.*

That is always possible, my child, as humans have free will to do as they choose, but truly I tell you—a false love is not worth giving up on your divine nature. You are a divine being, a child of love, of God, and you need to express yourself in the world to live the fullest experience, even if at times you are rejected by others.

> *What makes it easier?*

Knowing. The knowledge and the truth shall set you free—free to be who you are. That will put you in the flow of the universe and bring you an abundance of love and of joy. You may have to wait for the right timing, but it will come. It is guaranteed as long as you live a life of truth.

Thank you. This is helpful, although I'm still scared about rejection.

It takes practice, my dear, as with any skill. The more you practice shining your light, the easier it will become and the less fear you will have. Trust in the universe and your divine mother and father to guide you, along with the angels. You will find your way. It is sure.

Is there anything else for me to know at this time?

No, that is enough for now. Your lunch break is almost over and you have work to do in the earthly realm. That will help ground you. Stay focused this afternoon, and try not to think too much more about this today. It needs to be in bits and pieces, or the remembering of the trauma is too great. We will talk more and it will become clearer to you. Go, do as you need to do, and know that I love you.

Thank you.

It's a Marathon

June 11, 2019

It is 5 a.m. I slept much better last night, although I am a little tired this morning.

You will be fine today, as you got enough sleep.

My friend Tammy and I had dinner last night. It was nice to see her and be able to talk openly about what I'm writing. She shared that she wrote her book so others wouldn't feel crazy if they were "opening." Maybe I should read it?

Yes, you should. It will help you.

I feel like Tammy and I may work on a project in the future.

No, but you will keep in touch to support each other. She will be delighted to see your success. Tammy knew your mental illness was actually a connection to the divine but that you needed to figure that out in your own timing.

I do worry when I get things wrong.

Not to worry. You are still fine-tuning your intuitive skills and sometimes miss things. You will continue to get some things "wrong," but the key points of the message you are to deliver, you understand and get just fine.

> *Should I write about the Eve Consciousness idea I have been thinking about?*

No, not at this time.

> *What is important now?*

Talk to Michael. He will help you work on your strength and your next book. This one is nearly complete.

> *Should I talk to Michael now?*

Yes. He will help you.

> *Thank you!*

Afternoon

> *Hi, just wanted to talk. I'm excited about my conversation with Lois today but not sure about how to proceed, as well as whether I should slow down, whether I'm being a little manic, and what to say to Steve.*

Yes, you were being a little manic, but you are calming down again. Start the process but don't hurry. I know you want to leave your bank job and start your new life, but I encourage you to have patience. You have waited this long, and you don't want to ruin anything by rushing things before you are ready.

> *So I need more time?*

Yes, my darling, you do. Continue weekly therapy for now, until you are ready to let your light shine. You still have some healing to do. Start the publishing process with Lois.

It is OK to tell Steve. He may bellyache a little bit, but he will be fine with it and support you. Just remind him that he wanted a new patio, even though it was expensive, and that this is your dream. Reassure him that the finances are in good shape and he will trust you. Also promise to discuss this in therapy to make sure you are not biting off more than you can chew. Your therapist will help you be ready. You will do some EMDR around your mothers, divine and earthly, and this will help you shine your light without fear of rejection or pain or loss.

Follow the example of Marianne Williamson. She shines her light without fear and has stepped into who she truly is. Cristina Aroche is another good example. Both know they are inherently worthy, so feelings of unworthiness are rare for them now. You still have some of this to "clean up," as your friend and former social work supervisor Lydia would say.

What should I do about the employee network idea?

Let your managers know that you have many irons in the fire and want to wait a bit. Thank them for listening and offering their help, and explain that being open about things is very healing for you. They will appreciate that and understand your desire to wait. You can even explain that this happens with mania sometimes—you get so excited about something you dive into the deep end and have to slow down so as not to overwhelm yourself.

What about the writing? I was originally thinking it would be good to go as is, but looking back, I notice some random conversations that may need some editing.

It will need some editing, but not as much as you might think. Let Lois connect you with an editor and tell her it will be a little more than proofreading. Most of what you have written will stay.

Should I just trust the editor?

For the most part, but you can always check in with me if something doesn't feel right. Together, we will make sure the right information gets published out into the world.

OK . . . it is 4:44, my sign of abundance.

Yes, my child, abundance is yours, already and to be continued—an abundance of love, time, and money, just as you requested. 😊

Michelle McCann

June 12, 2019

> *I talked to Lois yesterday, as you know, and am preparing to publish our book. I'm still not exactly sure what needs editing and what to keep in.*

Yes, my child. Most of the channeling, even your personal questions, you will leave in for people to understand fully how the process worked. A few pieces may need to be kept private, but otherwise the writing is as it should be.

> *Should I do the editing or have someone else do it?*

You should edit first and then have someone else look it over. You know best what should be included and what to take out.

> *So should I send the manuscript to Lois?*

You can, but let her know you are making the edits. Tell Steve today about the money. I know you are scared he will be upset, but I promise he will be OK. He might take a tone like he does sometimes but will acquiesce when you tell him this is important to you.

> *LOL . . . I didn't know how to spell that word!*

Yes, I put that in for fun to make you look it up . . .

> *Ha, yeah, don't want me being a smarty pants, right?*

That's right . . . ha!

> *I felt Michael merging some of his energy with me this morning. I was very tired, as I had been awake and was distracted.*

This will get easier as time goes on, but it is part of the transition to this new vibrational level of energy. You may be a little tired in the short run, but soon you will adjust, as Michael's merging energy will provide strength and stamina.

Off you go.

Anything else?

Nope. Just get to work. 😊

Got it!

Lunchtime

Thank you for letting me rest this morning. I needed that.

I know you did, my darling. You have been on fire, working so hard to get my message out into the world. It is time for you to slow down and take care of yourself too.

I am a little nervous—well, not exactly nervous, but feeling a little hesitant about the editing. I am not sure what to take out or leave in.

Work with your therapist before you do too much editing so you don't take out anything important. Most of what you have written is crucial, even if at times it seems disjointed. You can even write a section of the book about your process in learning to channel. Communicate to readers that you were essentially having a conversation with me and using me for support. Let them know that the chaotic, sometimes disordered writing has been retained to help them realize that I can truly support them too, once they connect with me. That is critically important. A preface could explain the process and what led up to the writing. Talk a bit about the history of your illness and the classes you took. I can help you write it. You have most of what you need and can channel the rest from me.

Should I have a section of resources?

YES!

That's what I thought. And what about my website? Did I ask this already?

Yes, but it is OK. Make some edits and include that as a resource in the book as well.

When should I do all this?

Have Lois assign you an editor so you don't feel like you are doing it all by yourself. You will gel with the editor and enjoy having someone to talk things through with.

Should I tell Steve at dinner tonight?

Then or after, whenever the time feels right. Just tell him you really want to do this and that you know he wants to make you happy. Promise you won't buy any more big-ticket items for a while. 😊

I just want to keep talking.

I know, my darling, but you should probably focus on work for a bit. This was a nice little lunch break. We will talk again tomorrow morning. You will get more rest tonight and feel better tomorrow. And talking with your therapist will help.

Thank you for always being here for me. I really appreciate it.

I know you do. Just think—pretty soon, you will be talking with other people who can talk to me too. It will be so fun for you!

Who will be first?

It remains to be seen. 😊

You love to say that, don't you?

I really do! I love to see you be surprised . . . the joy you feel when something exciting happens. It's GLORIOUS! Kind of like how you feel when Aidan achieves something or is so happy. It makes your heart sing and swell with pride.

Putting Together the Puzzle

June 13, 2019

Good morning. It is 5:15 a.m. I thought I would sleep in until 6 today . . . LOL, but I rested well from about 9 last night until 4 this morning. Though I am still not totally awake or overly energetic like in previous days, I feel pretty good.

Yes, my darling, you needed some rest and will continue to need your rest on this journey. Remember, it is a long haul—a marathon, if you will. We will be doing this your whole life, so don't feel like you have to rush and do everything at once. Together we will accomplish our mission in divine right timing. I would like to continue to have our communion time in the early morning, as that is when you are most focused and have the solitude to concentrate on me and our relationship. Some days you may need your rest and that is OK, but as long as you feel moved, please make this time for me.

I think I can do that. I have been naturally waking up, ready to talk with you already . . . no alarm.

I know. I always wake you when the time is right.

Yes, it is interesting to trust that you will do that and I don't even need to worry about it.

That is as it is with everything in your life. You do not need to worry. Just trust that I will take care of your needs before you even have to ask. As I have said many times before, I know your heart's desire and will help you to achieve it.

> *I think I should take a break from my writing with Michael, at least for today. I just feel like we should be together.*

That is right. I feel the same way. Michael will visit you tomorrow and you will continue writing with him. You are going to love what he has to say and will learn more about the angels, which will be exciting! You have learned a great deal in your angel class, but there is much more Michael has to teach you.

> *That sounds great. Therapy went well yesterday.*

I knew it would.

> *Of course you did.*

I am working with your therapist to help her know what you need.

> *Yes, I talked about my rejection from my divine mother and needing to process that pain and trauma. She seemed to think it was a little strange but just went with it.*

She did think it a bit odd but has learned through her years of experience to trust that clients know what they need.

> *I think it did help. I'm feeling less anxious about putting myself out there in the world, even if some people may not like what I have to say. Even my therapist noted that the book introduction was very Christian-oriented. Of course it isn't, but maybe the focus on Christ and the revelation of the Bible reference makes people think it so.*

This will be an important distinction to make for people, my darling. Just because Christ is the redeemer does not minimize or invalidate any other religion. All religions have their place and bring something unique and different to the table, kind of like people. They are all good, as long as they focus on love and supporting one another.

> Ah! I just remembered the puzzle idea.

Yes, my child, I just reminded you. 😊

> That is awesome.

Our reconciliation, our coming back together in heaven, is like a puzzle in which each soul is a piece. The puzzle will not be complete until each shape is in its rightful place, meaning that all individuals need to shine their light and be who they truly are in order for the puzzle to come together. Although some pieces may seem more important at first, like the edges to frame it out or a colorful section that goes together, ultimately they just help complete the picture. In the end, no piece is more important than another, because the puzzle is ONLY COMPLETE when ALL THE PIECES ARE TOGETHER!

> Wow! That is a great analogy!

Thanks, I thought so. 😊

> So I get the sense that religions are kind of the same—pieces of the puzzle that we put together to come to the final solution.

That is right. I didn't just give the world Christianity, I gave it many choices of religions as a way back to me. Each has its place and helps different people on their journeys. This business where religions say their way is the only way is bullshit.

> Really, God? You say "bullshit"?

In this instance, yes. It is critically important that my children understand I DO NOT want them fighting with one another in my name or for a particular religion. That is all hogwash.

> These are funny terms you are using.

Well, I want people to pay attention so my point gets across. There are many paths back to me, your God, and I want each person to take the path that feels good and right to them. It is not up to anyone to tell another how they should find their way. That's a job for the angels and me.

People need to stay in their places, meaning they need to focus on themselves and their own paths, not on what other people are doing spiritually. Please do not malign each other's paths, as I have designed them to be perfect for each soul. I know what they need and will ensure that they receive it. OK, rant over.

LOL . . . God has rants.

Indeed I do. I don't get angry, but I do get very vocal about how my children need to behave. Not that I think less of those who choose differently, but I do guide them to be the best person they can be and to live in love and in the truth of who they really are.

Wow, that is fabulous. Thank you! I feel more energized now. I love when you/we write things that I know will help the world to understand you and your nature and in turn, our own selves.

We will be doing lots of this. And we don't need to do any more right now. That is enough for today. You can go back to bed.

Really?

Yes, my child. Try to rest. You have a long day ahead with driving to meet your friend for dinner. Share your writing, and she will be excited for you and provide some excellent insights. She is very intuitive and intelligent and thoughtful. I know you know this, but I want her to read it here too, just so she remembers that I (God) know this about her.

Thank you for telling her, God. I really do admire her quiet strength and her way of being so funny and yet so insightful.

You two have a strong connection of mutual respect.

Anything else to know here?

No, just enjoy being able to be open about your writing. It will be nice for you to have that positive receptivity at this time.

Talk to you later!

June 14, 2019

Good morning, God!

Good morning, my darling. How did you sleep?

I slept well, and thank you for letting me snooze a little this morning. The 5:44 wake-up call was perfect. I love seeing the numbers with 44 and 444, as they remind me that abundance is coming.

There will be more and more as time goes on, but don't forget about the abundance you have now.

Yes, I am so lucky to be financially stable and have loving friends and family. And while I still work full time, the hours are manageable, so I have time to do the things I am passionate about, like talking with you. I had a nice time with my friend last night. It was so great to hear stories of her psychic experiences. She is amazing! And it was wonderful to share what is happening with me and revel in her excitement.

She will be one of many good sources of support for you as this becomes big and you feel a little overwhelmed by it.

I got the link from Lois last night to start the journey.

Yes, you should start that today when you have time.

I am interested to see what is involved.

It will take some work but will be fun too. You will swell with pride when you see the finished product. Remember *A Course in Miracles?* That was beyond people's comfort zones at first, but now look at how many people it has helped.

That helps me.

That book took effort to interpret. Your work will help even more people because the language is easier to understand. The message is clear, and interweaving your story helps make it real so people grasp the process of bonding with me and the feelings it evokes.

Even though individuals will have different emotions on their own journeys, learning about yours will help them approach me authentically. This is important. People need to feel comfortable baring their souls, showing their true selves to me and others for this process of connection to work. This too is critical. You had to break down and process your trauma, really feel it—the memories, the pain, the sadness, all the tears and struggle. That is as it needs to be.

Again, like the butterfly and the cocoon, the mud and the lotus flower, the beauty of union comes as a result of the trauma. All is by design. This is how the contrast is understood, from the deepest despair to the greatest joy and triumph, reconnecting with me and with each other—that feeling of pure love.

I feel like we should start to work on the preface.

Let's do that later after you look at the link from Lois. Tell her you want to add a preface explaining your history of illness and that you are still learning to channel, both of which sometimes make the writing sound disjointed. It will be good for people to observe that the earlier parts reflect a less clear channel so they realize that this doesn't happen overnight, but is a process.

Whatever you say!

Yes, Dear, I always know what is right. It is good for you to trust me.

You want me to talk to Michael now, don't you?

Yes. I want him to help enhance your strength. You are going to help so many people!

THE NATURE OF GOD

Correction, GOD—WE are going to help so many people. It's not me.

You are absolutely right, my dear, WE—you and I together. I couldn't do this without you, just as I can't complete the reconciliation without the help of all your brothers and sisters. They must understand that as important as they see your work here, their role is NO LESS SIGNIFICANT. Each is part of the puzzle, and the puzzle will not be complete until they are all their true selves, as I designed them to be. They are perfect in my eyes, and as they learn to follow my will, they will begin to see their perfection. It will be GLORIOUS!

You love to say that, don't you?

Yes, I love that word—GLORIOUS! It just has such a beautiful vibration to it!
Go talk to Michael now. We will talk again later.

Thanks, God.

You are welcome, my child.

Later, after channeling with Michael

I am back from talking with Michael—had a great time and learned much! You all are giving me such important information to share with the world. WOW! It is helping me and I know it will help others immensely.

Yes, my darling, your books will be game-changers, as you like to say on earth. People will understand my true nature, their true natures, and the nature of angels, all which will help them sort out why they are on earth, what happens after death, and the long-term goal and purpose of this entire universe.

WOW! That is so big.

Yes, but it is time for the big reveal. During your psychotic episode, you sat on your porch thinking, *It will all be revealed.* That was a premonition. You knew this moment was coming, but it was in your subconscious, not yet ready to be divulged. Now is the time. And now that you know the truth, you will not have any other psychotic breaks. Continue the medication until you are strong enough to handle the criticism that will arise in reaction to this writing. I will tell you when the time is right to stop.

Continue to see your therapist for the same reason. You will need reassurance that you are healthy and to subdue that little piece of you that feels unworthy and gets triggered when people challenge you. She will provide a place to process those feelings of rejection. Although you have done much to release them, this part of you will not be truly healed until you are returned to the heavenly realm.

Will that be while I'm on earth?

No, my child. The first to be told of the revelation, you will be the last soul to be reconciled with me. This is the balance of the universe, the high of being the first, but the struggle—well, it really won't be a struggle—to commit to being the last.

You are the shepherd who will make sure all my sheep are collected to return to me. I know this feels daunting, but not to worry, I have had this mapped out since the beginning of time. The outcome is sure. There is nothing you need do, other than staying connected to me and putting my words out into the universe. The reconciliation is certain. Only the timing is not to be revealed to you yet.

Let's write the preface now. Take a break, do a few earthly things, and then come back. This will take some energy, and I want you to be grounded.

Got it! 😊

I'm back. Answered some emails, took out the recycling, finished my banana, and walked in the grass barefoot for a bit, as I have been told this is a good way to ground.

Excellent. Let's begin. Just start typing.

[See Preface]

> Thank you, God, for helping me with this.

Our words may be shocking at first, but they will bring people peace of mind and the desire to read more. We will write much. This will be your new vocation, much as it was for Wayne Dyer, whom you admire. You will spend your days in meditation and joy with writing as your divine pastime.

> I LOVE THAT! What more is there to know?

Nothing more at this time.

> Thank you, God. I love you and am grateful to you for making my dreams come true—to bring PEACE ON EARTH!

Yes, my child.

June 15, 2019

> Good morning, God.

Good morning, my darling.

> Shall we write the book description now?

No, I'd like you to talk to Michael. He has some important information to share with you.

> Should I come back when I'm done?

If you have time, but if not, not to worry. We will reconnect again soon. It is important that you be with Michael for strength and love right now.

> OK, thank you!

You are welcome, Dear.

> I had a nice session with Michael. Anything you would like me to know?

Your left wrist is hurting you. You need to buy a rest for your laptop and keyboard to prevent carpel tunnel. Do that now.

> Really? Right now?

Yes, it will be a good distraction for you. You need to ground.

> I'm back. I ordered the wrist rest and messaged two of my friends.

That is great—just what you needed to do. Now is not the time to write the book description. Just look at your angel cards and enjoy some nature, as well as your angel class. The occasion will come for the book description . . . not to worry. We will reconnect tomorrow in writing, but you will hear from me throughout the day. My voice is getting clearer for you now. Just listen and you will know it is me.

> How will I tell the difference between you and Michael?

You will know. Trust me.

> I do. 😊

Closer to Fine

June 16, 2019

>Good morning, God. It is a beautiful morning.

Thank you, my child. Good morning to you.

>I wonder about floods, tornadoes, and hurricanes and such. Do you control that?

Destructive events are a result of the damage you have done to the environment—drilling for oil, fracking, fossil fuel emissions, coal-fired power plants. . . . Even wind energy, which is better for the environment, still has some impact.

When humans disrupt the natural flow of nature, which in some cases you have to do to survive, it impacts the greater whole. Just as we are all one, the universe is one of cause and effect. Every action has an equal and opposite reaction. Altering your mother's and my magnificent world design has negative consequences. Again, this is not punishment—it is natural law, the law of cause and effect.

>Thank you for helping me to understand. I also wonder why you sometimes tell me things that don't seem to come true, like the MHATES group at work.

You are to follow the path I set before you to align to my will. I know the steps you need to make. Sometimes I may tell you one thing and the end result will be another. This is helping you do what you need to do and be where you need to be to follow your path correctly. It is a winding route with lots of adventures and there is a reason for every experience.

Know that I am not lying to you. Lying is telling an untruth, something hurtful or that is not real. What I am asking you to do is real in the sense that it is your pathway back to, and reconciliation with, your mother and me. There is no untruth in that process, even if it means confusing you sometimes about where you are headed. Follow as we lead, without reservation, and trust that we know what is best for you.

> *It reminds me of that song we love from the Indigo Girls, "Closer to Fine," particularly the line, "The less I seek my source for some definitive, The closer I am to fine."*

We inspired that. Amy and Emily do make beautiful music. Their role is to be the musical poets of your time, moving millions with the sound of their voices and the magic of their words. They have a very high vibration, as all music has a high energy and comes from us. As I have said before, we send messages both through music and in silence. It is good and a blessing to make time for both in your life. This is an encouragement for all reading this book—as you follow the pathway back to God, work with the angels, listen to music, and be in silence. All work in tandem.

> *Yesterday was pretty cool. In the morning, I looked up the song "Rainbow Connection" sung by Kermit the Frog because I saw it in a book. It led me to an interview with the composer, Paul Williams, who talked about the magic of puppeteer Jim Henson. Then several Brené Brown talks came up—one with Oprah and then her speaking to other groups, including teachers.*

Yes, my child. I arranged those for you yesterday. You needed to hear Brené's words on shame and vulnerability, as you are still in a guarded place about your writing. You fear people will think you mentally ill. Sometimes you question whether your connection to me and Michael is real. Yesterday in angel class, you said you were channeling Michael and he is so funny, and someone said, "Are you sure you are channeling Michael?" It placed a seed of doubt for you.

THE NATURE OF GOD

Yes, you do know Michael and are channeling him, and he is funny. And the stuff about him having a fiery sword is false.

As your angel teacher explains, he does "push out" cords that are negative attachments to other people. She is correct that he does not cut them, as that would leave a root. He does energetically remove them, temporarily, to allow a break from the negative energy, so people can see things from a clearer perspective. The cords do grow back, but with a transmuted energy because people see things differently. This allows for healing between people.

This is Michael's primary purpose—to heal the energy of the cord connections you have to each other. This will be critical for the reconciliation, as people will need to see each other differently for us all to be one again. Michael will help remove or transmute the energy of judgment and shame of self (the self-cord).

> I'm confused. We have energetic cords to ourselves?

Yes, my darling. These are the cords of other people as they see you. Absorbing their energy impacts how you see yourself. Michael works on these cords too, to help you see yourself through our eyes as a divinely wonderful and loveable person, not as the person faulted by your brothers and sisters.

> Do we also have a negative energetic cord related to the first separation?

No. We have repaired that.

> Why was I feeling rejection from my divine mother during my EMDR therapy session?

That is because the rejection from your brothers and sisters continues. Your divine mother did not reject you, so there was never a negative energetic cord created.

> But I thought you said you repaired that?

I misspoke.

> Do you misspeak?

The words are occasionally difficult for me. Our energy is so different that we use telepathy, not words, in the heavenly and other spiritual realms. Sometimes the translation can be confusing.

So, God gets confused?

When it comes to words, sometimes. Like laughter, words are a human creation. We in the spiritual realms feel them and understand, but we are not as skilled as you are in using them every day.

Really? We are more skilled than you are?

At creating and speaking and writing, yes, as we do not do these things in the heavenly realms. We just "are." We sit and savor the moment—relish in it, in fact.

Sounds funny to say you "sit."

OK, that is not exactly right, but we do just "be." That is what Eckhart Tolle refers to in *The Power of Now*. The heavenly and spiritual realms do not concern with past or present. We just enjoy the moments.

But isn't a moment "time" . . . LOL?!

Yes, again with the words! You are funny, my child. A good sense of humor is something you never thought of yourself as having. In fact, you were often so serious it was hard for you to laugh at yourself, which is sometimes the funniest kind of humor.

Steve taught you humor, as humor is indeed taught. You learned some from your birth family too, but you didn't really embrace it until you met Steve. He is a blessing to you.

Yes, he is. He cooked all day yesterday on Father's Day weekend, but I think he enjoyed himself.

He did. Cooking is fun for him, but he also does it to please you and Aidan. He loves to take care of and make you both happy. That is his primary purpose in this life. His work helps support that and keeps him happy too. It provides a beautiful home for you all in heaven, as your friend Joyce says. Indeed, Mt. Cuba is a bit like heaven on earth—a beautiful creation.

> I want to talk more but feel like I'm supposed to take a break.

Yes. Check Facebook for messages and pull some angel cards, then have some coffee and enjoy nature for a bit.

> No talking with Michael today?

Not today. You will continue with him soon. You are back to me for a bit.

> I'm happy to be with either or both of you!!!!

Yes, I know. Take your break and I will talk to you soon. Enjoy Father's Day with Steve and Aidan. It will be a fun day for you all.

> Thank you.

Thank you, my child.

June 17, 2019

> Good morning. Yesterday I felt sad, missing you and my birth father, although it was a nice day with Steve and Aidan. I am just ready to be with you all the time. I don't want to have to work and do other things—I just want to be with you. I am crying.

Yes, my sweet, sweet, darling child. Yesterday reminded you of what it was like to be with me. It is in your subconscious, so you don't remember exactly, but thinking of not being with me makes you sad. You are not angry—you are disappointed that it will take longer than you thought to finish this project and to be with me more. In reality, it will be a long time before we are fully reunited, and for this you need to grieve.

It is like losing loved ones in the earthly realm. You know what it feels like to be with them, and you miss them. Even though you know they are in a better place, you still miss the day-to-day interaction, their smiling faces and laughter, their touch, and so on.

So it is with me. While we were not human together, you could feel my energy in the spirit world. You recall that, although not entirely, as you don't feel the energy yet. Sometimes you feel the joy, which is related. Soon you will FEEL the vibration and know it is me without typing. I will be a more constant companion, and that will make this project and being separate from your mother and me easier.

I know you just wanted me to think the book was finished so I would connect with Tammy and Lois. Settling how the book will be published will ease my mind in that regard and for that I am grateful. At the same time, I realize I am going to be in my full-time job for a while longer while we finish this and get it out into the world. Is it going to take more time?

Yes, my child. As I said, it is a marathon, not a sprint. You have been training for this your whole life, throughout all your lives actually. The time is drawing near. Just remember this has been a LONG time coming. A few more months is but a speck of sand as it relates to time and space.

Will we need to write more and edit what has been written?

We will need to do both. Remember, Brené wrote that a plaque in her home says, "We can do hard things." All the good stuff takes hard work. That is just the way the world works. Being with me is easy and joyful, but being in the earthly realm to accomplish human tasks like writing a book takes time and effort.

Think of yourself as an "Olympian" of God communication. Perseverance and dedication will lead you to the final games. You have been practicing for years—all your lifetimes have led you to this. Your divine mother, your spirit team—the angels and ancestors—and I are all cheering for and supporting you. YOU CAN DO THIS!!!

I am feeling a little better, though still a little sad and wishing we could just move on.

I know it is hard. I have such compassion for my children who go through hard times. Though I hate to see you suffer, it is for a greater good and what your soul desires to help your brothers and sisters to be reconciled with me. Your soul wanted to be "The Reconciler." Others want to be mothers, fathers, artists or musicians, architects or doctors, and so on, but you wanted to be the one to reunite us all in heaven. That has been your mission. Deep inside, you knew you were called to do something important. Remember that your purpose is no more important than any other person's piece of the puzzle. Yours is just the first to be laid down on the table to begin revealing the completed masterpiece.

Wow. That sounds nice—our completed masterpiece.

Yes, OUR completed masterpiece—created by you, me, and all of those from the heavenly and spirit realms, along with all your brothers and sisters on earth.

What else is there for me to know today?

Nothing more from me. Go be with Michael and let him strengthen you for this journey. He has much to tell you as well. I wish you a good day. You will be busy at work, so make sure you focus on that later. There will be a moment for us when the time is right. Trust that you don't need to rush this.

OK. Thanks.

Lunch break

I had a feeling I needed to look in the cabinet, and I found a gratitude journal from 2012 and an inspirational book called Believe and Achieve.

Yes, my darling, I put them there for you some time ago, tucked away by you for you to find now.
At Widener University, you had to give a two-minute speech about your passions to incoming Master of Social Work (MSW) students. This is it, my dear—your passions. You knew then that you were zealous about relationships and how to make them healthier. "Relational empathy" is the way to do this—individuals putting themselves in other people's shoes and trying on their perspectives, as

Brené Brown talked about. When people can assume someone else's role, they find it harder to be angry because they have compassion, and compassion is needed for forgiveness.

"Forgiveness is the bridge back to God" popped up in your email, and you were divinely inspired to email it to yourself. It is only through forgiving yourselves and one another that you will truly heal and be reconnected. Starting to know me and the angels is the first step, but forgiving self and others is the key in the lock. That opens the door to our reconciliation.

Finding these books was meant to remind you of these things and prod you to write them down here now. Keeping a daily gratitude journal will help keep your spirits up when things get difficult, and the inspirational book will remind you that you can do anything you set your heart and mind to. It sometimes takes hard work and dedication, but just like connecting with the angels and me, you will find it has all been worthwhile!

> *Yes, I do. I feel like I'm still waiting for the final reconciliation.*

No, my child. You need this path and process before that happens. This is part of the journey, the vacation, this glamour ride called life that you brought into being.

> *Me? I brought this into being?*

You were the soul who desired to know yourself and to know me. The other souls agreed and wanted to do the same, but your soul was the one with the idea.

> *How did I have the idea if we didn't think before we were born?*

It's hard to explain. Souls have always had ideas even before incarnation on the earthly plane, but only on earth can the expression of those ideas become "reality"—ironically, an experience that is not reality at all, but a simulation of being disconnected from God to understand what it is like to be not God. I'm not explaining this well, but I think if you reread it, you will get the concept. YES, you were the soul who sparked the idea of creation.

THE NATURE OF GOD

Wow . . . that seems pretty grandiose.

Maybe, but it is true. It was YOUR idea.

Now I feel kind of bad that I have caused all this suffering.

You helped your brothers and sisters be born into this life so they could experience contrast. Their hearts desired that as yours did, but they did not know it until you explained it to them. All the souls ever created agreed to incarnate so they could know themselves apart from Mother and me and know us more fully. As I have said, we knew you, but you did not know us. Through the pain of being "separate" (thinking you were separate) from us, now you know who we and you truly are—pure and divine love.

What else is there to know?

There is much to know about this but not at this time. Continue to balance your life and commitments with this work with Michael and me. Soon this will be your vocation, but even then you will need to maintain equilibrium between meeting your earthly needs and grounding. It is important that you have the full human experience. That is what you came here for, to have a connection to your mother and me and the angels and to also feel the joy of earthly life—the relationships, the nature, the food, the sex—

Really?

Yes, indeed. We can talk about this later. But all the joys of living as a human are yours for the taking. Do not get so caught up with me that you forget to enjoy your earthly existence. It is, or can be, so joyful, if you allow it.

Yes, I feel so much joy most of the time.

Soon it will be all the time, as you will feel my vibration ALL THE TIME. It will be magical. Everything will flow and it will feel AMAZING. AMAZING GRACE! ☺

Thank you! I look forward to that!

Michelle McCann

Back to work, my darling. Lunch break is over.

Thank you, God. I love you.

I love you too, my darling.

In the Slipstream

June 18, 2019

> *Good morning, God. I woke up thinking of lots of things I want to talk about.*

Please do not worry, my child. We will discuss them one at a time and I will help you remember the important things. No worries about forgetting! Relax.

> *Can we start with last night? I was thinking of the song "The Queen of the Slipstream" by Van Morrison.*

One of my favorite songwriters! He listens to my voice and puts it into words. We have a special relationship too. He helps me reconnect with my children through his words and music. But I digress. Back to how this song applies to you and to all my children. As long as you live "in the slipstream," letting me take on the forces while you just glide behind, life will be magical, easy, joyous, fun, and glorious. You will be "in the flow," as people say. This is what Esther Hicks/Abraham refer to as "in the vortex." Same concept, different terminology.

I know the way, the path that will make life grand for you. You just need to heed my callings and follow my lead. This is true not just for you, but for everyone. The more they listen and follow me, the more peace and joy they will feel.

> *What more is there to know about this?*

That is enough for now. You want to talk about the playground concept from the day of your awakening.

> Yes, you told me you were OK with whatever outcome, however this play ends up, and we would all be safe even if the world blows up.

That is true, but it will not happen. You were not ready to hear that you will be the spark that brings world peace. I was allaying your fears and sharing what you needed to know at the time. As many like to say, "God never gives you more than you can bear or handle," so sometimes that means I need to tell you a story until you are ready to hear the truth.

I don't view this as lying, but rather as giving you what you need. Some may disagree and feel this is "wrong" of me. But trust me, I know what is best for you AT ALL TIMES. If it means I steer you down a crooked path, there is something for you to learn or gain by going in this direction, even for the short term. It is part of the journey needed to bring you back to me. I know how to recall each of my children.

No one is to worry that they won't figure it out. I figured it all out at the beginning of time and creation. Everyone's paths are clear. They may use their free will to make choices along that path, but the master blueprint includes guardrails to ensure EVERYONE will end up safely back in my arms. Have no fear. You are protected and will always return to me.

You are now wondering about your mother and me. This entire writing has been with both of us. For a time you thought you were speaking only with your mother or only with me, but we are one. Mother/Father God in heaven and of the earth, we are connected by the divine vibration of LOVE.

> So, you are what I think people call "gender nonconforming."

That is right!!!! Individuals who choose to be neither male or female, preferring the "they" pronoun, are actually closer to the likeness of God than any other. Your society has shamed them and it makes us very sad. Like us, they are of both genders. Well, we are not exactly two genders. We are the full spectrum from masculine to feminine and everything in between—kind of like the yin and yang. In the center of the masculine is the feminine. In the center of the feminine is the masculine. It is all intertwined and there is no need for division.

> How does this relate to the separation?

It is not related, exactly. The separation came from the creation of the mind. We have unique qualities as part of our whole being but don't really have "selves" because we don't have minds. You get the concept, I think. Our mother/father energy blends together as one entity to love and support you in whatever way you need. In return, you love and support us.

Although it doesn't feel like it right now because you still feel separate from us, we are all connected. Your journey, your joys and triumphs, sadness and fear have all been felt by us (Mother/Father God).

This type of feeling was not possible prior to creation of the mind. Thoughts led to feelings. Prior to creation we never had "feelings" as such, only the vibration of love. We didn't exactly know what they "felt" like until we created you, our children, to show us. We longed to feel the contrast as much as you did and wanted to understand our own divine natures as well.

The concept of eating from the tree of the knowledge of good and evil didn't really exist, but the idea of learning about contrast, the full range of emotions, was part of the journey we created. As we have said before, there is no devil or Satan, no evil entity trying to ensnare you into bad things. The only "evil" is when you make choices that are not of love—love for yourself, for each other, and for us. This is what brings about wars, famine, environmental crises, health issues, all the social ills.

When you CHOOSE not love, your actions have consequences. Peace will come when your goal is to ALWAYS CHOOSE LOVE. Heed our call and listen to your gut/intuition, and you will always know the "right" thing to do—which is only to say, you will then know how to CHOOSE LOVE.

What more is there to know this morning?

Nothing more at this time.

Sometimes I still feel like I get things wrong, like thinking something would happen that doesn't.

Just remember that is me, guiding you down your path.

It makes it hard to trust myself, when what I think will happen doesn't.

Michelle McCann

You are still fine-tuning your craft, my dear. It is like a snowboarder or a skier falling even though they are well-skilled. Everyone makes mistakes. That is part of being human. It is nothing to worry about. Remember that you learn from mistakes. Just dust yourself off and get back in the saddle again.

LOL . . . you guys with the expressions!

I thought you needed a laugh. 😊

Thank you!

OK . . . wrap this up and maybe go back to bed for a bit before work. Have a lovely day, Dear.

June 19, 2019

Good morning, God. I wasn't sure if you would let me sleep in this morning since I'm feeling tired from being at the class with Lois last night. Thanks for having Tammy send me the notice about it. It was great to meet Lois, and she will be wonderful to work with, I can tell. She is quite lovely and so is the woman who sat next to me. The class was about blogging, not publishing, which I didn't really realize until I got there, but I guess that is what you wanted me to learn about?

Yes, my child. You will start a blog soon and people will begin to follow you in preparation for the release of your book.
You also want to write about how you felt when you woke up this morning and what I "said" to you.

Yes, I woke up feeling tired and "said" (thought) that I was surprised you didn't let me sleep. You "told" me in the way that I "know" (not hearing voices) that it was more important for me to be with you and to center than it was for me to sleep.

We will make time for sleep, but this time with me now is priority.

Thank you, Lord, for letting me know what I need to do and when.

You are welcome, my child. Thank you for listening.

What are we to talk about now?

I know you want to talk about your blog and getting it started, but that will come soon. Now I want to talk about . . .

My typing stopped.

Yes, child, I am deciding what should be next. . . . Let's have you talk more with Michael. He will help you with next steps.

AH! That is what the angels do, help us to know our path!

That is right.

OH! One quick question—my friend wrote to me last night and asked how to "pray" to her angels. It's my understanding that people ask their angels for guidance and support and communicate with them, but for some reason, "pray" felt funny to me. Why?

People do not pray to angels—they pray to Mother/Father God. Angels are there for intercession, but this is not a prayer, really. It is asking.

How is that different from prayer?

Prayer is asking for consideration of something, for me to help you, but that assistance is not a given. When you ask the angels to guide you, as long as it is on your path, it is given. It is done. With prayer to me, the outcome is not certain because I evaluate the situation and determine the next best course.

> *What if people "ask" the angels for things that are not on their paths?*

Well, that won't happen either. But if you ask the angels to "guide me on my path," that will always happen. Not right away, as things take time, but it will happen MUCH MORE QUICKLY than if people don't ask. Again, remember, neither your angels nor we (Mother/Father God) can interrupt your free will.

> *This is helpful. I will send it to my friend.*

Go talk to Michael now.

> *Thank you, God. I love you!*

I love you too, my child, more than you'll ever know. Of course, you will know when we are reunited, but you know with my words and a little with my energy now. You felt it last night.

> *Yes, I did. Thank you.*

You are welcome. Go talk to Michael.

> *OK!!!*

June 20, 2019

> *Good morning! Feeling very tired this morning. I stayed up a little later, just until 9:30 watching the movie Michael and chatting with Steve. Five a.m. came quickly!*

Yes, my child, I know, but it was time for you to wake up. We have much to talk about today.

> *We do? I thought I would talk with Michael about his movie.*

Not now. The time was right for you to watch it, but you will talk about it later.

So what should we talk about today?

The blog you are going to write.

I got the Nature of Angels ideas to start—"Seven Things Your Guardian Angel Would Like You to Know About Them."

Yes, that is good. I like that. You also need to be doing a blog each week on *The Nature of God,* beginning with seven things God would like you to know about them.[16] Start by saying that God is male and female.

Really? Shouldn't that be in the middle or toward the end somewhere?

No, I want this to be first. The nonconforming gender children are having a really hard time right now, and I want people to understand that they are most like God, in the sense that they are both genders, or on the gender spectrum, not binary. We, Mother/Father God, are like that as well. We have masculine and feminine qualities, but they all blend together.

Hmm . . . this sounds like it could be confusing.

It will be a little because there are not words to describe things exactly, but we will write it together.

Should I start now?

No. Let's just get the ideas down and we will fill in later. I would like the first thing to be "God is neither male nor female" and talk about how that relates to those who are called "transgender." Then educate people about the term "nonconforming gender," as it is better.

What next?

---

[16] "Them" and "they" refer to Mother/Father God together.

"God loves you no matter what" should be number two. Even people you might consider evil go to heaven, and there is no such place or event as going to hell. Hell is only when you make judgments about yourselves and others.

Then you can lead into number three, which is "love thyself." Loving yourself is like loving God, as we are all connected. When you love yourself you recognize that you are worthy of love as a child of God.

Four would be "love thy neighbor as thyself." Explain how people are all God's children, brothers and sisters, and God wants you to love one another and love yourselves and love God. This is how we will bring heaven on earth. Eventually you will be reconciled with me in heaven, which is not a place, but rather an energetic state. You don't need to go into more about this—just say you will discuss it in a future blog.

Five will be "God created angels to help and protect people." Tell readers you have a separate blog about angels that they can follow and that they should know that the angels also love them unconditionally and are there to help them find their pathway back to God. At the bottom of each blog, list your book titles and note that they will be forthcoming.

What is six?

Six will be . . .

I've stopped typing.

Yes, Dear. I'm "thinking" . . . LOL.

Should we just make it five things God wants you to know about them?

That sounds good. Yes, I like it. Let's leave it at five, and we can write more after that.

Wait, shouldn't I put something about "you can have a personal relationship with God"?

Not yet. I don't think people are ready to hear that. You can tell them that you are channeling me and in fact, be sure to include the snippet about the channeled message in the blurb about the books at the bottom.

Should I work on writing these now?

Yes. Do it in separate documents, one for angels and one for God. Let's start with the God one.

Quick question . . . How will I publish these, connect them to my website, and update them and so forth?

One step at a time. I am helping you break it into manageable pieces so you don't feel overwhelmed.

That sounds good.

You like the writing part, so we'll start with that. Plus, it will be fun to have something to share with your friends, who will be your first followers. And your family—many will want to read what you are writing. It will be a way for you to start building your "platform," as you learned about from the Hay House online writer's workshop. But we are getting off track. Let's START the BLOG!!!!

OK. ☺ By the way, I realized this morning marks one month since we've been doing this together! Happy anniversary!!!!!

Yes, my darling. It is exciting. Just think about all we have accomplished in one month. This is now ninety-six pages long! You have been working hard, so it was nice for you to take a break last night. We will continue to work hard, but we will also have some fun.

New York City is coming up.

I'm giving you that for a break.

That will be nice.

You will enjoy Brooklyn.

> *Thank you.*
> *I finished the blog. WOW! That was pretty cool. I like how that came together.*

Why, thank you, Dear. I have been looking forward to blogging with you.

> *That is hilarious! God wanted to blog with me. I love it!!*

That is enough for today. Do your backups, check email, and get ready to start your day.
Have a good day.

> *You too, God. Love you.*

Love you.

Old Fears Re-Emerge

June 21, 2019

Good morning. I started to send my backups and then felt like I should talk to you! Michael and I just wrote our first angel blog.

Yes, Michael is a gem . . . so funny. He learns quickly and has witnessed the humor of humans for many lifetimes, so he is hilarious. He has heard it all!!!!

Back to serious for a moment. While I'm so VERY excited about doing the writing, I'm a little nervous to put it out into the world—not for strangers but for people who know me, especially my family like Mama. I worry she is going to think it is mental illness. I'm afraid to tell her.

That is just a trigger of an old fear, my dear. There is no need to fret. You need to release this fear before your next steps. Jane will help you set up your blogs and social media. PAY HER! It looked expensive, but it will come back to you a thousand fold. You have the money. Just do it.

I just want to make sure I'm not being manic and overspending.

You are not. As with Lois's help, this is an investment in getting your work out into the world. When people start businesses, they invest money and take risks. This is actually not a gamble because you have me at your side and know the outcome will be great. "HAVE A LITTLE FAITH

IN ME"... I played John Hiatt's song for you yesterday. It will all be fine. Soon you will reap the rewards of your outlay.

> Otherwise, I feel really good about what I have written (what you and Michael have helped me to write). It should really resonate with people. I just don't feel confident talking about it yet.

But you WILL. It is your will and my will for you to speak about this, but not yet. When you are ready, you will know. Don't feel pressured to rush that part. All in divine right timing, remember?

> OK, thank you. I will try to relax and trust. I love that song, "Have a Little Faith in Me."

Yes, you should listen to it often, even now if you like. You can YouTube it.

> LOL... you like YouTube too?

Oh, yes, it is wonderful—so much access to music and knowledge! TED Talks, educational videos, and being able to find almost any song. What a marvelous creation for the world. Just like Facebook, when used lovingly, it is a great way to connect people! I love all these human creations. Of course, the ones that destroy the earth are not my favorites, but as you know, I don't judge.

I do hope people will soon figure out ways to take care of the planet and the beautiful nature that your mother and I created for you. It is for your enjoyment, and we would hate to see you miss out on savoring this creation.

Time for you to relax. Enjoy your day and have fun with your friends Amy and Joe. You can tell them now what you are doing and they will be excited for you. Sending you love and hugs.

> LOL... that sounds like me.

Yes, I love when you say that. You are so thoughtful and open about expressing your love and appreciation for people. I LOVE THAT. Keep up the good work.

> OK!! I will. 😊 Love you.

THE NATURE OF GOD

Love you.

June 22, 2019

Good morning. I'm sitting outside enjoying the sounds of the birds and the mild breeze. It is 5:21, so I slept in just a little. You gave me the choice to sleep in today, but I wanted to connect with you.

I always give you the choice. It is always up to you. I just know how special this time is to you, so I encourage you to join me.

What would you like me to know today, God?

Just that I am so proud of you for working so hard and doing such a great job. You just need to slow down a bit. Your website is almost up, which is great, but that will take a little time. Be patient. Jane will come up with something you will like. You can provide input, but trust her to lead you in this journey.

In the meantime, next week we will write two more blogs, one from me and one from Michael. They will not be published until your website is finished, and that is OK. Do not worry about money. Worrying attracts negativity into your life. Trust that I have taken care of all this for you and you will have plenty of money when you need it. Not to worry.

Any tips on how not to worry?

Have faith. I have shown you time and time again that I am here for you and when your will is in alignment with mine, all things are possible. Think about Lois and Jane. You didn't "find" them—the angels and I put them in your path. We did the same with your teachers and healers. Trust that I will take care of you. You will have what you need to pay for professional services, be able to do fun things for you and Steve, fund the book launch, and get the website and email list up and running.

Remember how you tried to trick the angel cards to give you a different one? Even after all your shuffling and mixing, you still got the "Starting Fresh" card. This is a fresh start for you—a new career, a new relationship with the angels and me, and an abundance of time, love and money—just as you asked for. The door has been opened, and all you have to do is walk in, and by that I mean just follow our lead.

You told your friend last night about the line in the Indigo Girls' "Closer to Fine"— "The less I seek my source for some definitive, the closer I am to fine." That's exactly right. Just be in the moment. Wait for the wonder and magic to happen. Yes, you need to "do" things, but listen to your heart and know what to do and when, taking one step at a time. Don't think too much about the future or past. Instead, savor the moment and look for signs or listen for your next steps.

As you told your friend, this is how you stay in the flow. You are in it most of the time now, except when you start to worry. When the anxiety bubbles up, just remember to let go and let God. I've got this! Pull an angel card for reassurance or sit down and write to me. As you know, I will help.

What else do I need to do?

Nothing now, child. Relax. Go back to bed or just sit outside and write in your newly found gratitude journal and pray. You can do the angelic healing for your friends later. The restoration has already started, so there is no rush. And do not worry about your social work continuing education units (CEUs), as you will have plenty of time later to complete those. Put off the trauma hypnosis seminar. Order the NET CE classes to do the reading and take the tests when you have time, but no rush on those either. They aren't due for a year and a half—in a few months, you will have more time.

Will I make enough money on my blog to leave work soon?

No. It will take time, but again, don't worry about the timing or where the money will come from. I'VE GOT THIS!!! Have some coffee and pull some angel cards. Message your friends. Have a wonderful day. Love you.

Love you.

June 23, 2019

Good morning, God.

THE NATURE OF GOD

Good morning, my child. You are tired this morning.

Yes, but waking up a little since I'm outside. Walking downstairs just now and all day yesterday, I noticed my heels hurting. I know from you that it is likely something emotional causing the pain.

It is the trauma from both your birth mother and your divine mother—your "Achilles heel."

I'm not sure what that means.

That is your weak spot, where you are most vulnerable—the fear of being rejected by your earthly mother, now that you know your divine mother did not actually forsake you. Your earth mother will not spurn you either. She may disagree with you on things but will always love you.

In the meantime, go about your vocation, your writing, communing with me and the angels, and living your earthly life.

Thank you. That is helpful. What more is there to know today?

Nothing else. Go back to bed. If you have time later, we can talk then, and if not, we can talk tomorrow. Sometimes you will hear my voice in your head. That is your channeling getting stronger. Soon, you will be able to hear me all the time. I won't interrupt your conversations with others, but when you are in silence, I will chat with you often. You will know what my thoughts and feelings are on things, even though I don't exactly have thoughts and feelings. I will share my will with you and you will understand.

You are going to help with my plan to reconcile all my children back to me. Do not be afraid, for you do not have to do this alone and it won't take as long as you think. A revolution of love is on the horizon.

For you, this balance is important to keep you grounded. You need to take breaks often and be with others to help stay centered and calm. As time goes on, this will get better.

Although everyone wants and needs that joyous human connection, you will always crave it more than most because your passion is relationships. That is how you thrive, by being in relation with others. Your light shines when you are with people. Developing relationships is part of your soul's path. You transmit your light through your warmth, humor, good-naturedness, kindness, humility, and friendship—and LOVE.

Everyone will feel the love you bring, as you naturally love others. They sense that when they are around you. Even when you disagree with people, you still see them as good to their core. They know that you can find love for them even when they don't find love for themselves.

Thank you. That is helpful to understand. I am feeling more awake now.

That is because you are taking in my energy.

I still don't feel it, except that, like I said, I am more awake.

It will take a while, but one day you will be able to "feel" me. Right now you just "know" what I am saying to you when you write. Soon you will hear my "voice" when you are thinking. Feeling my energy is not your strength, so that will take a while longer. No worries though. Michael and I will tell you if you need to ground until you begin to discern this for yourself.

Should I talk to Michael now?

No, my child. You should relax. Go back to bed soon. You have a busy morning with taking the car and seeing Aidan, and you won't want to be tired for that.

Thanks, God. Have a good day.

You too, Dear.

June 24, 2019

Good morning. Boy, do I feel so much better this morning! Not nearly so tired. After a nice relaxing day, I went to bed at 8 and slept until after 4.

Yes, Dear, you needed some rest. The next couple of busy days will be better. Try to go to bed early again tonight. This is our routine for now, these early mornings. When you are writing full time as your vocation, you won't be required to get up this early, although you still may want to sometimes. There is something to be said for the peace and quiet of the morning hours, the solitude before the rest of the world wakes up. You love being outside among the birds when the weather is nice. They don't last long, these summer days, so treasure them while you can.

Of course, you can be outside when it is winter too, just not as long. Remember that. When it turns colder, you will still need to make time to be outside to commune with Mother Nature. It is important in all seasons. Just bundle up!

Got it. What would you like to talk about this morning?

One of your core wounds is not feeling safe and secure in the world. It has to do with your father's abuse but also the original separation. Your therapist may need to do EMDR for this one. More of your trauma will come out and be released and transmuted.

What does that mean, transmuted?

The negative energy will be released so that positive energy can come into your energy field. Negative energy trapped there blocks positive vibrations such as abundance, joy, and love.

I feel like I have all of these.

Yes, my child, you have released SO MUCH of the negative energy that was lodged in your energy field, but it is not completely clear yet. You still have to sort through your feelings toward your mother and your fears around money, safety, and security.

Should I still see my therapist next week?

Up to you, but I think it is a good idea. You will make progress faster if you keep up the weekly visits for now. It won't be long before you can cut them back, but just ask me and I'll let you know when you are ready to reduce them to every other week. Once you work on the pieces we discussed, things will flow even more than they have been. I know you have felt the flow when connecting with Lois, blogging, working on the website, creating business cards, and setting up email, but it will be even more magical once your energy field is clear.

> *I guess this will be important for people to understand, this idea that we all have negative energy in our energy fields and how to release it.*

Yes, this will be an important theme. And there are many ways to release negative energy (also known as trauma). People can do talk therapy, EMDR, or tapping. They can talk openly and honestly with friends about their bad experiences—more specifically, the FEELINGS attached to them. Also, they can cry or journal. There are so many tools we have given our children to expel these.

No one needs a lot of money or a wide circle of friends or support. Even one person to talk to is enough. When people share their true selves, they will attract others to help them through.

> *What more is there to know about this?*

That is enough for now.

> *Should I talk to Michael now?*

No, go ahead and take a break. I know it has only been thirty minutes, but we have done a lot of work. Do your morning ritual with the gratitude journal, prayers, and angel cards. It is a lovely morning and you should enjoy it. Cute little bird, isn't it? He is coming close to you because he feels my energy. As you get more connected with my energy, you will notice the animals coming closer to you.

> *I just thought about the bugs and snakes and such. I'm not sure I want them nearby!*

No worries, my child. When the negativity is out of your energy field, bad things like bug and snake bites won't happen.

> *Really?*

Yes, if you don't worry about things and your energy field is clear, "negative" things don't occur.

What about death?

That will be delayed. People with clear energy fields live longer. No matter how clear though, you won't live forever, as the body is not designed that way. But you will live a longer and healthier life, so it behooves people to CLEAR THEIR ENERGY!

Got it. Just thinking about children. . . . Some are so young—how can they have negative energy in their energy fields to cause sickness?

Some is from past lives and some from ancestral trauma, as these carry over in the energy field. Just as people think about DNA and genes being passed down from ancestors, so is energy. Take your break now and enjoy the sounds of nature surrounding you.

Thank you. Love you, God.

Love you, my child. Heart emoji 😊

Standing in the Truth

June 24, 2019
2 p.m.

> Once again I'm feeling really distracted. Mama texted Steve, saying she was worried about me. It is triggering old feelings of me not being able to tell or live in my truth. God, what should I do?

Talk to Duke and then to Mama. STAND UP FOR YOURSELF!!! You are an adult now. You are allowed to express how you feel, thoughtfully and lovingly, but STAND FIRM. The truth is you are connecting with me and with Michael. YOU KNOW THIS! DO NOT DOUBT YOURSELF.

Mama loves you and wants what is best for you. She finds it hard to believe that you could really be talking with me because deep down, she is not sure I exist. Though she knows there is good in the world, her past causes her to doubt that at their core everyone is good. And given the history with your father and others, she is fearful.

Please don't let that stop you from saying how you feel now. It is up to her to process her trauma and up to you to live in your truth. Talk to Duke and he will give you some reassurance before you call. You need to get your strength up. TRUST that you know what is true. Good luck, Dear. Love you.

3:03 p.m.

> I talked to Mama. I feel bad for bringing this up again and again, but I have to TELL THE TRUTH.

It is up to her to face her trauma if she is going to heal. You are actually helping her, even though it feels like you are hurting her. She wants to live in the truth. She just doesn't know how at the moment. It will take some time, as she lives in her own "reality," but she will get there.

Until she can face the music, things will be strained. You are not to worry about this. Talk to her or not (or less)—it is up to you. It will feel superficial for now. But you know the truth, and don't let the old trigger of having to hide your feelings and your truth get in the way of your happiness now. You are living the life you were intended. Savor it. Enjoy it. Don't let this bring you down. She has to work through her own stuff. You can't do it for her.

> OK . . . thank you!

June 25, 2019

> Good morning. I was rereading what I wrote yesterday about Mama. It was hard to speak my truth to her, but I feel so much better that I did.

Yes, my child. This will be your new norm—speaking your truth and feeling better for it. There is no need to hide any longer. Trust in yourself and in the angels and me to illuminate and support you. OH, and don't forget the ancestors. Not only yours but everyone's ancestors in the spirit realms are delighted at the progress you are making. Soon they will be released into the heavenly realms.

> WOW. That sounds exciting.

Yes, they are all cheering you on up here, EVERY SINGLE ONE! Yes, YOU, my dear—they are celebrating YOU. They know that you are the bringer of the reconciliation.

> I'm still not sure how exactly that is going to happen.

And you don't need to know yet, my dear. Just continue to follow the steps we put in front of you, like signing up with Lois, taking the blog class, writing in the mornings with Michael and me, and updating your website with Jane. Continue to tell friends what you are doing. Soon you will go public to everyone. I will tell you how later.

It will catch on quickly once it starts, but you need the website up and running first with the email address and email list all established. Just let Jane take care of all that for you. You won't have time once things get going.

Remember, you don't have to do things alone.

What is there for me to know now?

No more from me today. Michael has been anxiously waiting to talk with you for a few days. I needed some time with you first, but he has some things he wants to share. Write your next blog with him now. Mr. Spontaneous didn't want to wait until Thursday as we had planned.

I can imagine that about Michael.

Go talk to him and come back to me later if you like.

Thank you.

I'm back. Michael said there is more to know about my book.

Lois will find you an editor soon, and you will work with that person to figure out what to keep and what to leave out. We will continue to write each day and add to the final product, but you can start on what you have written so far.

Email Lois and tell her you are ready to work with an editor now. You will actually publish them as one book. Part I will be "The Nature of God: The Revelation" and Part II will be "The Nature of Angels: The Pathway Back to God."

Have Lois help you with the design. She can start on that now if she is willing, or she may want to wait until the editing is done. You can ask her how she wants to proceed.

> *Do I need to update the blogs to reflect the new book and part titles?*

No, when people search for one, they will find all. That will work fine. Jane will finish the website soon. She is excited to work with you.

Go ahead and take a break. Read your motivational quotes. Have a good day and good luck with your therapist. Tell her about your mother and all the exciting things that have been happening. She will be excited for you. You can send her your blogs later. No need to do that today. OK, off you go.

> *Love you.* 😊

Love you.

June 25, 2019
3 p.m. from work

> *Where do things stand with my book? Am I moving forward with it?*

Yes, you just need to talk to your therapist first. Until you process this trauma, you can't do anything without distressing yourself. It won't take long, I promise. You just need to let it out. We will proceed with your book very soon. You will work with the editor and make some minor tweaks, deciding whether to leave in the family stuff or to take it out. Other than that, there won't be much editing, other than removing some names. You can do that later. No rush.

> *I feel like we need an ending.*

We do, and I will help you work on that soon. Not to worry. One step at a time, remember— in the slipstream. Just follow my lead. No worries.

> *Thank you!*

June 26, 2019

> Good morning. Thank you for the relaxing evening last night. I so wanted to cancel plans but also wanted to see my friends, so it was nice it worked out they had to cancel. I just needed that down time.

Yes, my dear. Pay attention to what you need. If you are too tired for commitments you have made, don't be afraid to let people know. They will understand. You have to take care of yourself and rest often, at least for now. Once you get more used to the energy, it won't drain you so much, but for now you need lots of rest and lots of fluids.

> I got the feeling we are going to write the conclusion to my book this morning.

We are. Just start typing.

[Refer to the Conclusion]

> Thank you for this. Susan, the editor, emailed me. She wants me to send some pages or a chapter of the book. I'm thinking of sending Part II: "The Nature of Angels."

That would be good. Get her to see your clearer writing first before you bring in the confusing passages. You can send this to Lois too. Actually, you can combine the two and send them both to Lois, but you don't need to do this right away.

> Is the part with Michael almost done?

Yes, you will write the conclusion for that tomorrow, but go ahead and send what you have. It will be good to keep the ball rolling! I know you want to in order to have more free time sooner rather than later.

> YES! I am feeling pretty exhausted during the work week with all I am doing.

Just remember to rest and take care of yourself. Your mini-vacation to NYC will be nice. Don't bring your laptop. Just relax and enjoy time with Steve, sampling new foods and seeing new sights, and hearing from Aidan all about his adventures. Do not worry. He will be safe. It is not in his life plan for danger at this time. It is not in anyone's life plan to hurt him or his girlfriend. They will be fine and have fun.

Thank you! Let me look at "The Nature of Angels" now and see about sending it to Lois and Susan.

Great! Good luck, Dear!

Thanks!

Work break

Hi there. I was thinking of doing Pranic healing[17] but realized class would take three weekends in a row, and I feel like that is too much.

It is too much. You can do the Pranic healing later when you are not working anymore and have more time. There is no rush on this.

Thank you! My boss and I had a nice lunch outside. Our boss forwarded my proposal about starting a mental health group to the executive in our area, but now I want to put it on hold.

It is OK. You can always stop it whenever you need to. It was an important step in your healing process to admit that you had a mental illness and to become more comfortable talking about it. Now you need to get more confident talking about your spiritual path and purpose as the "reconciler." You will need to own this as part of your role to play in the revelation. Again, this is not to say that your purpose is more important that anyone else's, but it will start a whole new level of conversation about connecting directly with the divine that needs to happen now.

---

[17] A technique that harnesses the energy of the universal life force to accelerate the body's innate ability to heal itself.

Trust me, Darling, it will be soon. Once your website is up and your blogs are out there, people will pay attention. The writing is at such a high vibration that people will be drawn to it. Your friend Lori felt it. She is a higher vibrational being/person, so she connects with it easily. For others at lower vibration, it may take some time. But people WILL CONNECT. Like your friend Christina said, you'll be the next angelic teacher like Doreen Virtue before she changed course. This is going to be HUGE! You just wait and see.

> *I still feel like maybe I'm being grandiose, even though you tell me that isn't true.*

That's right, my child. So many people have tried to give you your story or decide its plot that you have started to buy into it. You know in your heart what is true, so trust that. If you are ever in doubt, talk to me, write to me, call on me. I will reassure you. Everyone needs encouragement sometimes but you more than most because you experienced the first rejection. We all have it in our psyches, but for you it was personal.

> *Personal?*

Yes, you were in human form when you suffered rejection by your mothers—both your divine and your birth mother. For others, this trauma is in their psyche. There is a difference. When you experience something in human form, the reaction is greater, the feeling is stronger. You have worked through most of this, but doubt lingers, which is understandable. There will probably always be times when something throws you off and makes you distrust, but those will become fewer and fewer as you come more fully into who you truly are.

Michael and I are working with you to help raise your vibration so your channeling becomes even clearer. To avoid you becoming manic again, we have to do it slowly. This is why you need to stay on the medication.

You can share this with your psychiatrist. Send him your blogs and tell him about the books and website. Although he may think you are a little manic now, he will come to understand in time.

> *Should I set up Facebook/Twitter/Instagram?*

Not yet. Social media will come soon. We are trying to make this easy, so we will put people in your path to do these things for you. No worries.

Patience!

June 27, 2019

> Good morning! I feel pretty excited because I think we are going to write the next blog from you, and it will be about me, right?

That's right, my child. It is time for others to understand you and for you to understand yourself through my eyes.

> WOW! I would love to hear what you have to say about me.

I know. You are going to LOVE IT. It will include your faults and make you real, but it will also let people know how special you are, just as they are special. Let's get started.

> OK. You wanted me to see that picture of myself for the blog, right?

LOL . . . that's right. Check Yahoo! email now too because you want to hear from Lois and Susan, I know.

> Nothing yet.

Just be patient and remember not to let anyone's feedback deter you from what you know you need to do, which is get this work out into the world. Let's write the blog.

That was fun. I thought there would be more about me (apparently, I love things to be about me), but it was good. I'm glad you are letting people know they can all do this!!!! I know I am supposed to tell my story so people understand that with PRACTICE and HARD WORK it is possible to connect with the divine realms. Like learning a language, indeed!

Thanks, God. I want to send these blogs and the preface info to Susan and Lois.

Yes, please do!

Done. I was just wondering. . . . Will I start making money off of my blog?

It remains to be seen.

You want me to trust how this is going to unfold for my highest good?

That's right. Do not try to figure out what will happen next. "Go with the flow" and the ride will be exciting and exhilarating with cool synchronicities and interesting people. Just TRUST! Read the book *The Universe Has Your Back* by Gabrielle Bernstein. You thought about it several times, but haven't yet. Maybe this weekend?

Gabby is the real deal. Although at times you have wondered about it, she is sincere and not in it for money or fame, but as self-preservation. Like you, she desires to know me.

What else?

There is nothing more to tell you other than to wait for the surprises! I can't wait for your website to be up! You are going to love it!

I just emailed to touch base with Jane.

Good job, Dear. Once you set your mind to something, you are good at keeping things moving. You are unstoppable (with my help 😊)!

Wow, that is exciting.

Take a break, as you need to rest. Do your gratitude journal and angel cards now or later—up to you.

I want to be outside and do that now. I enjoy this morning ritual.

That sounds good. I'm glad you are choosing this. It will be a long day with class tonight, but you can always nap this afternoon should you need it. I arranged these work-from-home days to make it easier for you to take breaks when you need them, and I'm so glad it is all coming about! Have a good day.

You too! Love you.

Love you.

11 a.m.

People keep giving me ideas of where to post my blogs, web link, and book intro when my website is up.

Pay attention and when you feel moved to share, DO! This is how you get the word out. It will spread like wildfire once you start to tell people. People can preorder your book on Amazon, although then there may be pressure of a deadline—probably better not to do that yet.

3 p.m.
Taking a little break

I've been focused on work and got a lot accomplished, so I wanted to take a little break and "talk" to you. It will be nice when I don't have to write

> to do that, but it seems the only way I can trust the answers now.

That is right, my dear, it will take some time, like learning a language—but TRUST that you ARE LEARNING. The writing practice makes the channel clearer so the "knowings" will happen more often. You have noticed a bit of improvement already and this will continue. Just BE PATIENT. You have worked SO HARD and been diligent in your learning, and your dream of communicating with me is a reality. IT IS A REALITY!

For now it has to be through writing. The writing practice is also preparation for the book you will publish to share with others. Do not worry that it seems disjointed. Be brave and PUT IT OUT THERE, just as you wrote it. Others will need to know that communication with God doesn't come without confusion.

> What about Conversations with God? Why was it different for Neale? He didn't go manic, I don't think.

No, he didn't. It was in his life plan to write the books, and I set it up to be easy for him. For most people, it will not be like that as they need to undergo a journey to appreciate the accomplishment of being able to connect with me. You are proud of how hard you worked to make this happen and others will feel the same way. For some it will be easier, but that is because their souls wanted it that way versus others who wanted the sense of accomplishment.

I give each soul what it needs to grow in the way it wants to grow and be in the world. You wanted to be an achiever—big time!!! You wanted the biggest achievement of all, to be the ultimate reconciler. It will be your work that will lead to the final reconciliation, which will not be long in coming.

> Really? It seems like it will take a long time. Earlier you told me it remains to be seen.

I'm telling you now to allay your fears. It will not be long.

> What does "long" mean in your terms?

You got me—long in my terms is different from long in your terms! I'll leave it at "it remains to be seen" and let you be surprised.

> I am going to sit outside for a bit and bring my work there.

Sounds good, Darling. Relax outside and enjoy the nice weather.

> Thank you!

June 28, 2019

> Good morning. I'm feeling a little tired from being up late with the psychic development group, but so glad I went. We had a numerology discussion that was great.

Yes, my child, I timed it perfectly for you to meet Jamie, who is a wonderful numerologist and life coach. She, too, is on an important path, and you two will reconnect in the future.

Your (our) words are what will spark the revelation, you playing your puzzle piece and encouraging others to do the same.

> Jamie seemed to know SO MUCH.

Yes, she vibrates very highly because of her numbers work and the people she surrounds herself with.

Although you don't realize it, your vibration is quite high also. Not as high as mine yet, but you are taking in all the energy quite well. Soon you will be able to discontinue the medication and yes, lose weight. But not yet. Maybe another couple of months. Do not rush it. I will tell you when.

> OK, I'll trust. Last night when we talked about it, I realized that I DO trust much more now.

Yes, you trust the angels and me more than yourself, as you held back from sharing your writing and knowledge with the group. I get it—you don't want to come across as a know-it-all, but you have a lot to share now, through this writing and all your education as well as instinctively.

As you align with my will, you are learning what to say and do in divine right timing. You are "in the flow." That is why you got a parking spot. You didn't actually ask, but you thought it and we know your will, so we arranged it for you before you even had to ask. This is how it will be. We know your heart's desires before they happen, so we can bring/give them to you.

> *What about Mama? I still feel some tension in my relationship with her.*

And you will until you let go and understand that she is not ready to process her trauma—and may never be ready. It is in your best interest to accept this. You can still talk to her and beam your truth. If you need to disconnect because it gets too hard, stand firm and do that.

It may sound harsh, but you have to take care of yourself now. In many ways, you have spent your whole life taking care of her feelings. The trauma wasn't too hard for you to cope with per se, but you knew it was too hard for HER, so you repressed it entirely. It wasn't until you were faced with a challenge from your former co-worker and did the eye movements to retrigger it all that you were forced to look at it. Even then, you were not ready—it took twelve more years for you to remember your childhood. It has taken your whole lifetime (in fact, many lifetimes) to remember who you are spiritually.

Now you know. Trust this. Do not let the fear of your "illness" diagnosis make you stand down or back away from being who you truly are.

Instead, so you feel prepared for the journey ahead, it is important that you understand your role and a bit about the history that brought you here. You must be patient while others learn what you know, as they may process information more deeply. This does not mean they are not smart. All humans are smart in different ways. For example, you have always been "book smart" but know nothing about science and mechanical things. This is not in your nature. You are more social, spiritual, kind, and thoughtful and like the mystical aspect of things.

> *I'm wondering what Jamie said about my chart and what my other signs are.*

That is not important but might be interesting for you to know. She could help you with that. You have done much with astrology. I have been nudging you to listen to your tapes from your earlier astrology readings.

> *I KNOW! I want to but haven't gotten to it yet.*

THE NATURE OF GOD

That is OK. I understand you are doing a LOT right now. But maybe today, listen to them if you find a moment.

Sounds good.

They will remind you of some things you heard before but which resonate on a new level now.

It is 5:40. Should I talk to Michael?

No, not today. He is there with you, always with you. But it is better for you to rest and relax now. You can pull an angel card or just go back to bed. You have time later to journal and do the card.

Maybe I will just check Facebook for a few minutes and go back to bed.

That sounds good, Dear. You are tired, but you will have a relaxing day and a lovely weekend.

Susan sent her editing notes.

Yes, my child. Let her do her job—she is very good. Just turn it over to her, and when she sends it back, read and see if it feels right. Also send her the "Nature of God" portion soon. Let her work on Michael's section first, as your channeling was more clear by then. We don't want you to work too hard or to worry it is not going to be right. We brought you Susan because she is the best person for the job. Trust this and trust her. Ask her to make the edits she deems appropriate if this were her book, and ask her to send you the final edited manuscript.

I talked with Susan and am letting her make the edits she recommends. She lives nearby, so it will be nice to connect with her. However, she placed doubt in my mind about whether I will be able to live off the proceeds of my book, and I started to feel alone and as if I am living in Fantasyland again.

I know. I put this in your path to help you process it. Feeling unworthy is still a sticking point for you. I am here to help you with this and will keep putting things in your path that make it bubble up. You can work with your therapist on these feelings of unworthiness and your need for financial security, as they are intertwined. Once you clear out this negative energy, abundance will be freed to come to you.

> *What is the cause of my unworthiness?*

You need to work with your therapist to uncover that. Just tell her that when anyone doubts your work in the slightest way, you question yourself. See where it leads.

> *I felt called to lie down. I felt the healing . . . thank you.*

You are welcome, my dear. You are not healed but will be soon. The last of the trauma to dispel is your feeling of unworthiness, of being unlovable. In your head you know that it is not true, but your heart needs healing. Work with your therapist on this next week with EMDR. An amazing tool of human creation, EMDR really helps people release trauma quickly.

> *Is there more to know?*

Not at the moment. Clean your lunch dishes and get ready for your beach trip this weekend. It will be fun. Have a great time! ☺

> *Thank you!*

Talk to Mama

June 29, 2019

> *Good morning. I wasn't sure if I was to get up today but felt like it once 5 a.m. rolled around.*

Yes, my dear, it is important that we do this every day, even on your vacation.

> *I thought you said not to bring the laptop.*

I changed my mind. You need this communion time right now. Your vibes are getting low.

> *I feel it. I have been more bothered by not being able to have the old food and I thought something was up.*

You have cords to your mother, so her energy is in your field, and she is really low right now. The cord pushing meditation you learned from your angel teacher will help clear it out, but your mother is going to be connected to you until she works through this a bit.

> *What can I do to help?*

Talk to her. I know you don't want to, which is bringing down your vibration too.

> *What should I say?*

Tell her you love her despite all that happened in your childhood and that she is going to suffer until she faces the truth.

I don't know if I can tell her that.

Of course, it is up to you, but things will not get better until she comes to terms with her actions.

I just don't feel like I can help her do that.

You can, my dear, with love and compassion. She feels like you don't love her anymore.

I do love her. I'm just frustrated with her at the moment. I don't know what to do.

TALK TO HER. The old wounds still protest that you can't tell her how you feel, but you are an adult now. The worst that can happen is that she gets mad at you, and she is already mad at you. Although she is hiding it, she is angry. She is trying hard to keep the past buried. It is not in her full recollection, but it is coming into her awareness, which is why she needs your forgiveness now.

Tell her you need her now, that you have worked through what happened in the past and forgive her for everything. You just want her to say she is sorry and heal the wound.

Should I talk to Steve about it?

Sure. He may not believe you or understand, but it might help you process how you are feeling about Mama now. He knows she loves you but is not perfect.

Is Mama actually ever going to face the past?

It remains to be seen, but you can try to help her should you choose to. You love her and want her to be happy, but by burying the past, she is not releasing the pain it caused all of you, Duke included. Shannon still has blocked a lot of it, so she is where you were before you started remembering everything. She is not suffering as much because she doesn't remember it.

THE NATURE OF GOD

What about Will?

Will is a funny guy. He takes things in stride and doesn't hold onto the anger. He was mad at your mother for not protecting him and gets mad at her now for her politics, but he doesn't hold grudges, so his energy field is clear. Just remember—by talking to your mother, you are helping her to get better. It doesn't feel like it, but it is true. She won't feel better until she releases the pain. Your suffering is the hardest for her, yours and Duke's. You two were the most damaged by the abuse that occurred, but it was necessary for you to be who you are now.

Explain to your mother that you all agreed ahead of time to incarnate together into this family, choosing to experience the trauma and pain so you could come to the place where you are now. It was part of a greater plan for your souls' growth.

Totally random question. . . . Will there be a place in the hotel for me to write?

You can go down to the lobby or the breakfast room or somewhere. It will all work out. Not to worry. That is the other way you can tell your vibration has gotten lower. You are worrying more about things—worrying whether you will find the right food to eat and where you can write versus trusting that this will all be taken care of for you. You are not in the flow at the moment, and negative vibration is in your energy field.

It is not only being in New York that has you discombobulated—anxiety about unfinished business with Mama is forefront in your mind. But even if she gets angry, and you don't get resolution, standing up for what you know to be true will raise your vibration again. Standing in truth is important for a high energy level.

Will Steve believe me?

It remains to be seen, but telling him will also raise your vibration. The more you keep secret, like things you are doing for the book, the lower your vibration. You don't need to tell everyone everything about your life, but purposely hiding things lowers your energy.

Now I'm worried. I don't want my vibration to be low.

Do not worry, my child. That makes things worse. Trust that Michael and I will work with you to raise your energy again. It won't take long. You are feeling optimistic now just hearing that. We will take care of you. *The Universe Has Your Back.* Yes, keep reading that book and TRUST that we know what you need.

Should I talk to Michael?

Yes, that is a great idea. He is excited. You need some fun to raise your vibration too!

4:40 p.m.

I've been thinking about my talk with Mama. She still seems distressed.

Yes, she is, but that is the way it needs to be for now. She will settle down as she comes to terms with the truth.

I have doubts that everything is going to be OK, but I guess, as with everything else, I need to turn it over to you.

Yes, I've got this. You have suffered enough. Now is the time for you to be strong and stand up for your truth. It may take time, but please be happy and do not let this concern you. If you need to take a break from talking with your mother while she sorts things out, that is OK.

What about Shannon?

That will be difficult, but it, too, is as it needs to be. Do not worry. I will help you with the struggle. It is time for you to make peace with yourself and with the world. There are only a few pieces left to put into place and the puzzle will come together. Have faith. Go be with Steve now, watch a movie, and relax. You have earned it. I am so proud of you. Good job.

That sounds like something Mama would say.

Indeed, that is why I said it. You still love her despite her shortcomings. Believe. All things are possible with me.

Is this Christ?

Yes, all things are possible in Christ. I will come into her mind and heal it, as will happen with all souls. Have faith.

Thank you.

June 30, 2019

Good morning. So many things swirl in my head, yet sort of nothing at the same time.

Yes, my child. That is the confusion about your current life circumstances. You don't know what to do, so it is overwhelming, but you are also grateful because you know the truth is going to come out.

Do I? I still have doubts but like you said, I do have faith in you. If you say it is possible, I will trust. In the meantime what do I do?

You just live your life and BE HAPPY! You have so much to be happy about—Steve and Aidan and your friends, your work (yes, your work!), your time at home and in the mornings with me. Plus you have two beautiful homes, and you are so blessed.

Indeed I am.

Remember that when you start feeling the fear come over you. I have blessed you with SO MUCH, and this is just the beginning. You will be astounded by the new blessings coming your way. Yes, my child, you are a blessed one—just the right one for this task.

For now, just sit back, relax, and enjoy the signals.

For a second there, I felt like I should be doing something else, like talking to Michael.

No, my child, this is our time together. You can be with Michael later if you like. Remember, he is always with you, as am I—it's just that you only know us to be with you when you are writing and sometimes in your thoughts.

I feel like I have been drinking too much.

Yes, you have been overindulging a little lately with the drink and the spending. All will be fine, but cut back the liquor a little if you like. It is not necessary to limit your spending, but Steve may see it as a red flag, so you may want to cut back just to ease his mind. Otherwise, no need to worry. You are just fine financially, and the additional abundance will come soon.

I feel a little distracted.

Because you are not outdoors, you are less grounded. That is OK. You could go outside, as it is only spritzing. Maybe not with the computer, but when it comes time to do your angel cards and gratitude journal (I love that for you), you can go outdoors.

What else is there to know?

Nothing at this time. Go outside with your angel cards and your coffee. Or not. You don't have to have coffee, but it may help you feel better. Your stomach is a little queasy—a banana might help.

Good idea. Yes, it may.

Take a break from me and come back later.

See you soon.

I went to the bathroom and got a banana, and I'm feeling a little better.

Good, I'm glad. You are still a little tired.

Yes, I am.

You could go back to bed.

Really? I wouldn't want to miss this time with you.

I am always here, my child. I think you need to rest.

Really?

Yes, go back to bed. If you have time later, you can write then. If not, we'll talk tomorrow. Shut down and go back to bed.

Love you.

Love you.

6:30 a.m.

I'm back and feeling better. I didn't sleep but just rested.

Yes, Michael and Raphael and I worked on you a little bit.

It's going to start raining. Is that just me?

Yes, that is your fear. Your vibration is still a little low. It was much better yesterday after you talked to Mama and let it go. You noticed the synchronicities.

I did.

This morning you are thinking about her, but your desire for a certain outcome is bringing you back down and making the channeling harder. Just TRUST. Remember to turn it all over to me. I've got this. Things will unfold as they need to, and yes, some things will trigger your old wounds, but that is for the purpose of healing them. Know that all will be OK, and when the anxiety surfaces, remember that you have nothing to fear.

You are not all alone as you were as a child. Steve may not always believe everything, which is hard for you, but he loves you and will not leave you. You can talk to me, to your therapist, to Jamie for coaching, to your other friends, and really anyone else you feel called to reach out to. Like now, you feel called to write to your friend Julie. Do that. I will be here. Come back if you have time.

Writing to Julie felt good. Now, what can I do to let this go?

Just make a choice to let it go. It is all in your mind, and you control your mind and your thoughts. If you choose to think differently about things, you get away from that place of fear of abandonment. That is what the fear is—a trigger for you. Remind yourself that you are no longer a child being abandoned by your birth or divine mother. That is all in the past.

You can work with your therapist on this fear of abandonment. Although you have done some good work on this, there is more to be done. It is tied to your feelings of unworthiness, but the bigger thing is the abandonment issues. Your therapist will help you work on that as your target.

I feel like it is time to do my gratitude journal and angel cards.

Yes, my dear. Thanks for joining me today. I'm glad you are feeling better.

Have a lovely day.

You too!

3:19 p.m.

I was just thinking about Mama. I hate to see her suffer but feel like reaching out is not good for me.

You can send her a text just to say you love her and are thinking of her. That's it. If she responds, do not engage. Continue to approach her with love. I know it is hard because you are frustrated and just want this to be over, but it is a journey you need to go through for your growth. Trust me on this. You need this.

The Master Key

July 1, 2019

I feel like I should write about my dreams.

Yes, my child, I placed them there for you.

There was a girl, a young woman I admired, who said she wasn't allowed to choose what her higher self knew. She and I had master keys to do some sort of inventory of rooms at a school, but the rules weren't clear. When someone looked up the woman's name, it wasn't right, so she changed it. This didn't follow the rules and someone else saw.

There was something about a pie shop and my website and how Jane is not normally available, but I was saying to a girl that it is my work with the angels that made her available to me, along with everything else that happens so easily for me.

Earlier in the dream, people, including a number of blacks, were outside listening to Our Voice, an African-American radio program. It was all about educating people about race relations and re-inspiring the civil rights movement.

In another part of the dream, I was by a pond and wanted to learn to swim again. I first thought about diving into the deep end, but then decided I should start in the shallow end to practice. While I stood close to the pond, a fish, dark with rainbow colors, jumped out and tucked itself under my arm, keeping me company.

At one point, someone was supposed to get his car fixed, and the repair shop said, "We have an urgent request!" A former co-worker of mine pulled in with a fancy car. I tried to solve the problem by finding a way for us to leave the car and get a ride.

I was supposed to hang by my arms from a bar, pumping myself and working on my muscles. A muscled man was there to show me what I could do if I kept at it. Then he lay down, flexing his muscles, getting ready for a massage. I worked with a woman to give another woman a massage.

At some point, someone told me I really should go vegan and once I embrace it, it will be fine. It was a matter of me learning about the different foods and taking my time to transition.

OK, God. It feels like this dream or all these dreams are important, but I'm not sure what it all means.

You can sit with it and figure it out. Or I can tell you . . . LOL.

Tell me, please. Thanks for the laugh.

First of all, the key—you have the master key to unlock others' pain. It is in your story and in your connection with the angels and me. Of this, you will write in your book. You will also need to write about your mother and your family. Your higher self wants you to do this. Do not worry about the edits—Susan will help you. You will publish the writing from after the last date you gave her, with all your feelings and family "laundry" out in the air. Even if things haven't resolved by then with your family, you need to do this.

About the car, that is right—you are a problem solver. If something gets in the way of you achieving your goals, think things through, but also call on the angels to help you. You know that they are always there and will grease the wheels for you.

> There you go with the expressions like Michael.

He is coaching me on the funny parts to say so this won't be so serious. I know it scares you, Dear, but you can choose to see things differently. Work with your therapist on this. Let her know that you have journaled about all this and feel called to publish it as such despite the disapproval of your family. Also talk about your fear of abandonment.

As Brené Brown wrote in *Daring Greatly*, "We are psychologically, emotionally, cognitively, and spiritually hardwired for connection, love, and belonging." Without that, we feel alone, abandoned, and "bad." If people can share the experiences that made them feel ashamed, their "fear of disconnection," they are no longer alone.

> Anything more about the dream?

Not at this time, Dear. Go ahead and take a break. You can come back when you are done.

> I read Susan's edits. She is really terrific. I don't want to have to make all the changes and wonder if I should just offer to pay her to do them.

Yes, that is a good idea. Just make sure you read the edits to make sure the meaning isn't lost. Some rewording is OK, but sometimes words will need to be repeated to get the point across. It may not flow as well, but being perfectly clear is more important. You can email or talk to Susan later today about this. Actually, talking to her would be best.

Send her all the writing (this edition) of "The Nature of God." There will be parts you remove, but leave the family discussion stuff in. That is part of your healing and needs to be known. We will work with your mother at the higher levels, but in the meantime, the editing can begin. By the time you are ready to publish, you will feel secure in writing your whole story. This is part of the revelation—YOUR STORY!

> Really?

Yes, my child.

> I want to go lie down for a bit.

Please do so. It has been a busy morning already. You rested well last night but still need to take care of yourself. Wishing you a wonderful day. Love you.

> Love you.

And no need to talk to Mama yet. Soon, but not now. She is processing things.

10:13 a.m.

> I'm ready to cry. I'm so scared.

That is just your old fear coming up. Mama will not abandon you. She may deny what you say at first because she doesn't want to face it. This fear is what makes her so willing to join in the hatefulness the president is putting out there. Steve may not believe you, but he understands you need to work it out on your own and with your therapist. He knows you have suffered but just doesn't know the details or extent of it.

If you like, wait to talk to Mama until after you meet with your therapist tomorrow and work on your abandonment issues. It will cause you less fear so you can be present for your mother when she needs you. She wants to be seen and known and not to have this shame surround her anymore.

July 2, 2019
6 a.m.

> We need to have a little "come to Jesus" meeting, God. You have told me some things that haven't been exactly true, and now I worry that I am off track or maybe confused.

This is as it needed to be, my darling. I had to present things a piece at a time for you to be able to process and accept them. Do not doubt yourself. In your heart, you know this to be true. You are the bringer of the light. The truth.

How do I do this?

By telling your story. Your story is the key that unlocks someone else's prison. You put this on your vision board. Then, you didn't quite know what it meant, but now you do. You will continue to doubt yourself and will need support to follow through. Working with your therapist and your spiritual coaches will help you stay grounded in reality, which is what I have told you.

Are you sure this isn't just another trick or step toward something else?

This is the end of the story. It is time for it to be told. Work with Susan for the edits, Jane for the website, and Lois to publish. This will take a little time, but it won't be long now.

What about Steve? Will he think I'm losing it?

He will find it a little far-fetched at first, but he believes in unusual things happening. As long as you are happy and connecting with him over normal day-to-day stuff, he will be fine and happy for you.

Is there anything else to know?

Not at the moment. Pull your angel cards and have your coffee outside. It is a beautiful day.

July 3, 2019

Hi, God. Good morning. It is 5 a.m. I'm still not sure what to think about all you are saying. I started to think I was experiencing psychosis again. My therapist did some EMDR related to my first psychotic episode and how traumatic that was for me. What came up was the trauma from when my brother tried to hang himself, whether intentional or accidental. In the room

> *playing with my dolls, I thought it was my fault because I wasn't watching him. I froze when I saw what happened, I think.*
>
> *It's still fuzzy, but my therapist helped me see that as a six-year-old girl, I wasn't accountable for the safety of my four-year-old brother. That was the sitter's responsibility, but she was in the other room watching TV. Not that I blame her in any way, but the relief of knowing it shouldn't have fallen on my shoulders was very helpful.*
>
> *What is there to know for today? Should I write with Michael? I thought of an idea earlier about the next blog, but now I can't remember.*

No, not now. Go back to bed. You should be able to rest more easily now that you are not as worried. All will be well.

> *That feels better. I'm feeling more awake now. Should I do anything else?*

Just check your email and pull a few angel cards if you like. Up to you.

> *We are done for today?*

Yes, Dear.

> *Thank you. Love to you both.*

Love to you.

Karma

July 4, 2019

> Happy Independence Day! I dropped Aidan and his friend off at the airport last night and they got an earlier flight!

Yes, we arranged that because we knew you were worried he would be tired.

> Will he catch an earlier flight to Ismir?

That remains to be seen.

> I am trying to take things one step at a time. With the GPS last night, Steve kept asking, "What's next?" and I said I didn't know. It was only one step at a time. Kind of like with you guys.

Not kind of, but exactly!

> I have to wait for each step to unfold and to trust you. Oh, and I forgot—a couple of days ago, I heard the song "Trouble Me" by Natalie Merchant. That was nice. I feel like I'm getting distracted.

You are, my darling, but that is OK. We have lots to talk about today, but why don't you tell us about your dreams first?

> We were in Turkey in an area by Aidan's girlfriend's family home, and there were some nice shops but her parents said maybe next time we should stay in another part of town with a Sheraton. I don't remember much else other than that we all seemed to get along.
>
> I'm excited we are all in the What's App group to be part of Aidan's adventure. Since I don't know his flight times now, I wonder when he will arrive? Anyway, I hope they will be OK.
>
> Steve and I had a nice dinner at a little French bistro and a nightcap at the hotel bar. I'm feeling a little tired but not too bad. Today we go to the Brooklyn Botanic Garden and will watch the fireworks at Brooklyn Park. We met some lovely people yesterday who gave us ideas. One was from Robinson, Illinois, so she knew the small Illinois town I grew up in. Then we met a guy by the elevator who graduated from Loyola Marymount, where Aidan's friend goes to school. All the synchronicities again . . .

You are getting back in alignment.

> I was out of alignment?

The channel is not as clear.

> I thought you said I was back in alignment?

Yes, but you overdid it with the alcohol last night and that fogs up the channel a bit. Not that we don't want you to relax and have a good time—the choice is up to you. Just know that if you drink too much, the channel is less clear.

> So, about the book?

Don't worry about that now, my dear. Let's talk about the tree of life.

THE NATURE OF GOD

Am I going to get this clearly?

I hope so. I'll let you know if you are not on track.

Where do we start?

Just start typing. The tree of life describes the way of nature and the way of grace. The way of nature is that for every action there is an equal and opposite reaction. Karma is the requirement that there be an opposite action, so when "mistakes" occur, there must be a reconciliation of the energy. In that lifetime or in a future lifetime, there has to be a "positive" offset, something to counter the negative.

Remember, we don't censure you for making mistakes, but you judge yourselves and each other, which is human nature. This triggers negative energy that requires a positive balance of people doing something that they or others deem good. That offsets the judgment that an action was bad.

So Karma is related specifically to our judgments, not something Mother created?

Well, we created this to be the case, but we do not "dole out" punishments. That is not what karma is. Karma is simply to understand how your actions affect you and others in the larger whole. Your thoughts, words, and deeds all have an impact. The more positive they are, the greater peace and happiness there will be. The more negative they are, the more turmoil, distress, and upset there will be.

To turn the world around, people need to think more kind, caring, loving, funny, thoughtful thoughts and more importantly, take positive action on those thoughts, doing kind and caring and loving things.

At the core of what causes judgment of ourselves and others is the shame that emerged from the initial core wounding. Anytime individuals feel such mortification, it triggers in their consciousness a feeling of the initial "rejection." They don't want to feel that again, so they put on masks or try to hide their emotions.

Now is the time for this to come to light, for the pain to heal—for people to "go public" about their shame and pain. And by public, I don't mean they need to tell everyone (although they could), they just need to tell SOMEONE—a therapist, a friend, a member of the clergy—someone who will be nonjudgmental.

Michelle McCann

> *What else is there to know?*

There is much!!! But this is enough for now.

> *You know of course, I'm thinking about how to get this out into the world without ending up in an institution or alone.*

It will be fine, my dear. You know we will help you. It may involve some work and you feel resistant to that, but you will be glad once you have done it—as you are with all you have accomplished so far. Take a break. Enjoy your day and the fireworks tonight. They will be spectacular!

> *Thank you. Love you.*

Love you.

July 5, 2019

> *Good morning. It is 7 a.m., the first morning in months that I haven't been up at 5. We were out late with the fireworks and grabbing a bite to eat and drink afterwards. It worked out nicely. Our bench on the promenade gave us a great view. We had to wait a couple of hours, but the night was nice if slightly humid. It was a true NYC experience. Then, of course, the traffic during our Uber ride back to the hotel was a true NYC experience as well . . . LOL.*
>
> *Steve and I were shocked that we were out until 11:38. We NEVER stay out that late, but it is good to do that once in a while. I'm in the hotel lobby and see people with coffee. I think I need some! I'll be back.*

> I'm back. Love the coffee here.
> So, I have been thinking about all we have been writing about and my confusion.

Yes, Dear, I know it has been confusing. Your vibration has been lower in NYC. There is not as much nature, so it is difficult to connect and ground there. Go to a park today and walk around if you can.

> The Brooklyn Botanic Garden was a breath of air yesterday, but being hemmed in by hordes of travelers on the subway and walking in the concrete jungle were very ungrounding.

Let's take a break from the big stuff for now. We will resume when you are back home. Just pull some angel cards and write in your journal.

> Should I write a blog or anything else?

No, it is OK to take a break. Go ahead and do that now. Power down. You don't need to worry about backing up. It will be fine.

> Thanks.

July 6, 2019

> Good morning. I went to bed early and slept well with some nice dreams. It is about 4:30 a.m. now and I feel pretty good.

That is great. Glad you are feeling better.

> I am so ready to be home today. I'm glad we did this NYC trip and got to see some friends last night,

> but I will be ready to be home and surrounded by nature again.

This trip was to show you how much you need nature in your life. It was for other reasons too, but that was the big one.

> Well, I definitely get the message! I have felt out of sorts for sure. Like I said, some of it was fun, but I could never live in a big city with so little green space. What would you like to talk about this morning?

What would you like to talk about?

> I'm not really sure. I just wish I had some understanding of next steps with the book. It seems all jumbled up now.

It has taken a detour, but that is as it should be. Do not worry about timing or the work involved. It will all come together. You will work with Susan to sort it out. Your website will be ready soon and you can start to publish your blogs.

> Where?

That remains to be seen. We will figure that out after the website is up and exactly how you want it to look. Then you can start directing people there and collecting email addresses for future blogs.

> What about that? We haven't done the blogs in a while.

Your vibration is low, so we need to wait until it is higher. People will connect better with higher vibrational pieces. What we have done so far is VERY high vibrational.

> Is there anything for me to do?

No, Dear. You just need to be back home in your routine, and we will get back to it. Read the blogs if you like. This will help increase your vibration, as it does for all who read them.

I just reread them. I LOVE THEM!

You (we) did a great job with those. Mother and I are proud of them too.

Tell me more about this. You and Mother are one?

No, not yet. We parted during the original separation. She is of the earth and I am of the heavenly realm. Initially we were one and will be again when all of our children are reconciled to us.

What does this mean exactly?

When all of our children are back in the heavenly realm.

How does that happen?

It will take time and I don't want to reveal all the details to you yet. That will be part of the adventure . . . the discovery of how the reconciliation will occur.

I am starting to cry. I have felt so disconnected lately, questioning my role and wondering whether this is all real.

I know. This doubt was necessary to help you move forward. You WILL move forward and step into your role in the divine plan, which is a great one. You will be delighted when you accomplish your goal of being an instrument of God's peace. That, indeed, was your soul's greatest desire. It WILL come true for you.

Thanks for the reassurance. Why have I felt so disconnected?

You have been drinking too much and have been out of your routine of communing with us and nature (your mother). You need her to feel connected to me (and us both).

And the meat—it is not bad, per se, for you to eat meat, but it does lower your vibration. You felt it a little last night after you had the burger. Red meat, especially, lowers energy. Seafood is not as damaging, but still has a deleterious effect. Anytime you are in the business of hurting other animals or God's creation, it lowers your vibration. Of course, the choice is up to your free will. Plus, it doesn't have to be all or nothing—each individual occurrence impacts your energy.

Striving to eat mostly plants (as you have been) helps. Since you want your vibration to stay high, we will guide you to foods that will help. We know how much you and Steve love good food, and there are lots of plant-based options to help you enjoy the eating experience and feel nourished too.

And, yes, we encourage you to be vegan and free of dairy as well. Production of dairy products exploits animals and takes away their freedom. Though they are not killed, their living conditions and the way they are treated are often atrocious. Again, we know such radical changes can be hard for you, so take your time and do what you feel is right. We will keep putting vegans in your path to help ease the transition.

What about gluten?

Your friend Kim is right that it is sprayed with glyphosate, the active ingredient in the herbicide Roundup, but it also "clogs you up." In general, grains are less digestible than plants, but rice and quinoa are better than others. You will be fine if you stick with those, along with gluten-free pastas. Feel free to enjoy them. Just remember to make the meal MOSTLY plants.

This is helpful. Thank you.

Your vibration is higher already because your mind is open to these suggestions and to you stepping into your role in the divine plan. When people become who they truly are, their vibrations will rise.

Tell me more about vibration.

The higher the vibration, the closer you feel connected to God (me, Father in the heavenly realm). It also helps you connect with Mother, but that is more by communing with her in nature.

So, vibration is our energy?

That's right. Every person is surrounded by an energy field known as an aura. This aura emits light that some people can see. When . . .

My typing is slow . . .

You don't need to know all this now, only that the energy field or aura needs to be clear to vibrate highly and allow you to feel connected to God. Have your friend Janet do an aura cleanse for you, as yours has been depleted on this trip with the meat, the drinking, and the dearth of nature.

Then why did you have me come here?

Being in NYC helped you become aware of how you feel and of the need to stay on your path of drinking less, eating less meat, and connecting more with nature. You know the difference now, and you do not like feeling disconnected from us. This was like taking a step back so you can see your path forward.

Your vacation with Shannon and Steve in a couple of weeks will be more enjoyable. Writing and being near the sea will help you feel more connected.

Being near the water raises your vibration too. This is not true for all people, but it is true for you, as it was for Edgar Cayce. You and he belong to the same soul group, and your group draws inspiration and connection from the ocean. That is why I had you get the larimar stone[18]—so you can have that sea vibration with you at all times, even when you are far away from the actual ocean.

Wow. I just feel so much better already. I feel reconnected, like we are having meaningful conversation again and it isn't so confused.

What would you like to talk about?

---

[18] A rare blue variety of pectolite found only in the Dominican Republic.

> *I was thinking about our friends we met up with last night. At the end of the evening, I shared very openly details about my writing and my history of mental illness. At first I felt fine about it, but then worried they might judge me.*

That is OK. It was nice for you to connect with them last night.

> *Let me ask about money. Am I spending too much?*

Yes, rein it in just a little. It will be fine. You don't need to have everything that strikes your fancy, like a new laptop. This one is fine 'til you are traveling more and want something smaller. The shoes are fine—you need comfortable shoes . . . LOL. Everyone does!
Smile, Dear. Trust it will be OK.

> *Will I like the website?*

You will want to make some edits and tweaks to the design, but overall it will be good.

> *What about the editing?*

I hate to tell you this, but there will be quite a bit to do there. Trust Susan and she will help you. In the meantime we will write more blogs and that will keep you sustained through the process. These will take off pretty quickly. Once the website is up and running, you can post to different places. We will cross that bridge when we come to it.

> *I have enjoyed our conversation this morning. I feel much more connected.*

Yes, it is in your energy that you will be returning home, plus you slept well last night. That all helps. Why don't you take a break and pull some cards and write in your gratitude journal? You don't have to power down yet in case you want to come back. Just take a break.

> *Will do. Just thinking, what about paying Susan to do more of the revisions?*

That is fine. Do what you can to make it easier for you. Susan is very good, and you can trust that she will help you communicate the messages you and we want known.

Clear Your Vibes

July 7, 2019

Good morning. So WONDERFUL to be outside in our backyard again, listening to the birds and feeling the breeze! I've so missed this, and connecting with you here.

For now this is your heaven, the closest thing to heaven on earth for you. Being at your home, in your yard, on the grounds of Mt. Cuba nourishes your soul.

I had some nice dreams last night. I don't remember all of them, but they reassured me that what is happening is real and spiritual.

Also, I have been reading the book recommended by Susan, *Gorilla and the Bird* by Zack McDermott. The stories of the author's manic episodes and hospitalizations are hard for me to read because they remind me so much of when I was out of touch with reality.

Yes, you were out of touch with reality, but remember—you were having a SPIRITUAL AWAKENING! Western civilization didn't know what was happening. If you had been in a village in Africa or somewhere else where they are still connected to spirit, they would have known that this was your kundalini awakening, although they wouldn't have called it that. They would have said something like "opening up to your gifts," which is actually what was happening.

Why did it take ten years?

It didn't actually take that long. You were medicated for much of it and ignored your spiritual side. It wasn't until the fall of 2017 that you started to reengage with the spiritual world, so the awakening took less than two years. That is not to say the journey you took to get here was "wrong." It was as it needed to be. Your focus was on Aidan and Steve and your work, and you needed to be "sane" for those to be priorities then. You wouldn't have wanted to miss Aidan's childhood to do this work. We knew that was more important to you at the time.

Should I keep reading this book?

No, not now. It triggers too many uncomfortable memories for you. In the meantime, read *The Universe Has Got Your Back* instead. You can come back to *Gorilla* later.

As for the dreams, I sent them all to you, especially the part about some people expressing their feelings and others hiding them based on how they were raised. All people hide some of their feelings, but some are better than others at letting them out. Actually you are pretty good at this now. Lydia and your social work training really helped you learn to express your emotions more openly and to trust that people would not react with scorn. You will continue to do this more and more, and you will help others learn how to do this too.

With the book, keep things moving by reaching out to Susan and asking her about next steps. Acknowledge that the draft is difficult to follow and that you need her help to organize it coherently. Share your feelings of vulnerability around this project and let her know you appreciate her support. You can also explain that you have learned that some parts were channeled incorrectly and that you will have some editing to do based on what you are channeling now.

Your energy is better but not fully resonant yet. We need to wait on this so you don't intertwine with all the other energies that are coursing through you.

It is so interesting you say this about the energy, as I still don't feel it.

We know, but trust us—there is a LOT of energy coming through you, not just from us, but from all of consciousness. Having practiced this in your psychic development and angelic healer courses, you have a special gift for tapping into energy, yet now you don't even know it is happening. Sometimes you feel us, like in bed yesterday when you were napping, but that is rare. Sensing the energy takes time. It comes through your psyche (your mind) first, which is why you are able to write about it. Your body hasn't caught up yet.

Is there anything I can do?

Sit in stillness and meditate more. You don't meditate much. Writing is similar to meditation, but different because you engage your mind. When you meditate, you try to quiet the mind so you can "feel" and "know." You used to do this at 6:30 each night while Steve was watching the news. We recommend you restart this practice. If it is nice, you can take a walk to the pond and meditate there, or if it is raining or too hot, sit upstairs in one of the comfy chairs you bought for meditation. Either way is OK. Nature is good, but when you meditate, you connect with spirit, so it is not required.

What else is there to know?

What else would you like to know?

Ah! I was dreaming of a pride flag last night and understanding that PRIDE is not just for LGBTQ+ but for all of us to be who we truly are.

That's right. It is definitely a symbol for the LGBTQ+ community and individuals, but all humans can take a lesson from this. People are like colors in a rainbow, each bringing unique gifts to the world, their "colors" to share, and others should not try to stifle or hide them. Everyone should TAKE PRIDE in their gifts and who they truly are to help make this planet a better place. The more people are living in the truth of who they are, the more humankind will be at peace.

I feel like I want to write to Susan.

Go ahead. Take a break and come back. Or not. Whatever you want to do is OK.

It is really nice to connect with you again. I have felt so out of sorts.

Yes, we know. We are glad you are getting back to your routine and feeling happy again.

> I just wrote to Susan and Julie. I feel so happy to be in my yard, writing and connecting. It might be nice to talk some more.

What would you like to talk about?

> I don't know. I just want to feel connected.

Then why don't you shut down and meditate for a bit?

> That's a good idea. Thanks.

Of course.

> I am going to go back to bed for a bit. It is nice out, but I'm still feeling a little tired.

Yes, do what feels right to you. If you are tired, rest.

July 8, 2019

> Good morning. Mostly pleasant dreams reassured me, but I'm not remembering them specifically. There was one I do remember about a friend's husband dying and she was in such grief. We were moving Aidan out of college. I don't remember the other two dreams.

Try to remember.

THE NATURE OF GOD

One had something to do with John 3:16. Isn't that the verse evangelical Christians cite about Christ being the only way to God?

That's right. Christians often interpret that verse to mean that Christianity is the only way to God. That is not true. The only way to God is through Christ, but you don't have to be Christian.

What would other religions say about this?

It doesn't matter what they say. I'm only telling the truth.

Can you tell me more? I feel like there is something important missing.

Yes, indeed. Religions can continue to believe and practice whatever they wish, but Christianity does not have a corner on the way to get to me. You are not a practicing Christian, yet you are connecting with me. Christ—or rather, the Christ consciousness—will come into the minds of all and "save them." People don't actually need saving from sins, only from their judgment of themselves and one another. Once they connect with the Christ consciousness, as you have, they will stop judging. Although you are still critical sometimes, especially of your mother, you try to see the best in people and put yourself in their shoes to understand their behavior.

This is harder for you with your mother because you idealize her, and it really upsets you when she does not live up to that standard, especially when it comes to politics and her support of Donald Trump but not the immigrants.

The plight of the immigrants is one that touches you deeply, as it reminds you of feeling abandoned and how hurtful people can be when they let their fear take over. Those opposed to the immigrants are afraid for their own safety and for their wallets—they fear that there won't be enough for everyone. The media reinforce the alarm, and those already afraid use that as validation for their beliefs—a vicious circle.

We are getting off track.

A little, but this is important, not just with the immigrants, but with all judgments you make of yourselves and one another. The more you remember that they are rooted in fear, mostly fear of detachment or rejection, the better off the world will be.

> *I feel like I might get confused if we talk about Jesus.*

Yes, you are still a little confused.

> *Why is this?*

Your vibration is still a little low.

> *That is frustrating because I feel like I'm doing better now that I'm back home and had an aura cleanse.*

Yes, but you are still frustrated about work and wanting the book to progress, and you are trying to force things. The more you push, the lower your vibration becomes. You need to relax into it and let things occur as they will.

> *Yes, but that is so hard. I feel like we have come so far, and things are at a bit of a standstill.*

They are. We are slowing things down to let you get back into the flow. This is as it should be to help you understand how flow works. You have not felt as joyful, partly because you were in NYC, but partly because you are not accepting what is. Focused so intently on the future, you are not being in the here and now.

Enjoy your job—don't dread it. Savor each moment, talk with friends, laugh, have fun, and let go of the need to finish this book. It will be finished when the time is right. Your fear interrupts your flow and your vibe.

> *So what do I do?*

Let go and trust. Keep reading *The Universe Has Your Back* by Gabby Bernstein and possibly reread from the beginning to take it all in. You need this reminder. And remember, you can CHOOSE to think differently. Rather than setting a plan that your book will be done by autumn, just "go with the flow." Trust it will be done when the time is right.

> *I feel like I should plan a dinner for Tuesday with a friend.*

That would be a good idea, Dear. Get out of your head and try to be happy. Any of your friends would be fun for you. Text them today and see what you can work out.

> *Well, now I'm feeling kind of bummed but will try to choose to be happier and do more things that please me. I was going to say "while I wait," but I guess the whole point is not to look at it as waiting but as additional time to enjoy the moments as they are.*

That is right. You understand. It would be helpful for you to relax. Focus on your work and your friends and just allow this to happen.

> *I wanted to keep moving with the Michael blog or the* Nature of God *blog, but I feel like that has to wait.*

It does. We want those to be VERY HIGH vibrational writings, and you aren't there right now. This is not a judgment, and please don't denigrate yourself over it. It doesn't make you bad any more than someone having cancer is bad. You just have some feelings to work through. Talk with your therapist tomorrow, and she can help you process your frustration at things slowing down.

Part of your low vibration has to do with your continued judgment of your mother. You still hyper-focus on the parts that frustrate you and gloss over the parts of her that you love. There is much to love—she is a wonderful person with a good heart. Her stance on immigrants is not in line with a Christ- or God-like approach, but in many other areas, she is loving and giving.

Think about your family and all she does for them and you. She is already planning for Aidan's birthday. And think about how much he loves her and how much she has meant in his life.

> *I'm starting to cry. Yes, it's so true. You've reminded me of how I felt about my grandparents Ninnin and*

> Bigdaddy—SO MUCH love for them! They were so wonderful. Aidan feels the same about his Nana.

He may even think more highly of her than you did of your grandparents because he thinks she is "cool"!

> Yes, he does.

Just remember this when you feel frustrated with her. Picture her with Aidan, laughing and giving him a hug and telling him how proud she is of him. REMEMBER all the wonderful things she did for you as a child, from waking you up to say "Good morning, sunshine" to hugging and comforting you when you were distressed. She was a VERY GOOD mother, but you are blocking out those parts.

> Thank you for helping me to reset my block there. You are right—my judgment was taking over and getting in the way of my love for her.

Yes, this is one of the biggest things bringing down your vibration, even more so than your frustration about work and the book taking so long. This relationship with your mother is negatively affecting your energy field. The aura cleanse helps, but it is up to you to CHOOSE differently. That is, to remember to see her as a loving and caring person who is a child of God too, rather than someone who is hurtful and mean. She may be making poor choices politically, but her heart is good.

> What else is there to know?

This was the biggest message for you today, to "clear your vibes." You keep getting this from your Michael deck. It is related to both your mother and your willingness to go with the flow. If you try to relax in both of these areas, you will start to feel better.

> Thank you. Should I go back to bed or pull my angel cards?

Up to you. Feels like the angel cards and journaling might be good, and then back to bed for a bit before work.

Sounds good. Love you.

Love you too.

July 9, 2019

Good morning. Last night I met with Jamie for a "coaching" session. She really feels like another spiritual advisor for me.

That is right, my child. She has been doing this work longer than you—not the writing, but the numerology and coaching—and she has listened and read a lot to understand the ascension process that is happening on the planet. She will help you with discernment. This is the lesson you are learning right now.

I thought so. Have I been channeling other energies besides you?

Not exactly "channeling" other energies, but when your vibration is low, other energies intertwine with mine when we connect. A clear connection is more difficult when your energy is all over the place.

I was thinking I should be doing more white light meditation to clear my energy.

That is a great idea. I suggest you do that now.

Done.

You should do this often. It doesn't take long but helps to clear your energy field. Karan is right that you need to do some cleansing rituals. I know you don't want to think of "negative" energy and the possibility of it hurting you. It won't make you manic again, but it will confuse the writing sometimes, and I know you want it to be clear. I recommend that you practice the white light several times every day.

> *So what happened exactly? I felt like I was so clear and then got so confused.*

It is easy for negative energy to enter the field when someone is open like you are. You welcome messages from the divine. The negative energy is not coming from divine sources, but rather from human ones in the collective consciousness. Human trauma and fear create a LOT of negativity. You pulled that in when you started to be afraid about money, not being able to leave your job, and your book not getting published. Remember your intent, which is to love and be loved and to do something good in the world.

Leave it up to me as to what that looks like. Yes, for you it will be writing and yes, it will have a big (in fact, global) impact. But trust that the timing and the execution are in my hands. You are my co-creator and I want to do this together, but you need to take my lead.

Follow your heart, which is the guidance from me through you. Work on nonjudgment of your mother and others who don't yet see the light of your work.

> *What about money? My family and I have been spending a lot lately, and I worry about running out of money before more comes in. Since some of what I have channeled has not been correct, I wonder if I'm wrong about that too.*

You are not wrong, my child, and you have nothing to fear in regards to money or your work life. The time will come when you can leave your job and in the meantime, it will support you financially. Do the things you are thinking of, like scheduling a session with Sara, getting a massage, and meeting with Chris for another astrological reading. Your finances will cover this. The balance will go down a bit, but you will be fine. Again, try to trust and not to worry about this.

> *Why has some of my channeling about things and people been incorrect?*

It is not that the channeling has been incorrect but rather, that you are inserting your own beliefs in with the channeling.

> *How do I avoid doing that?*

It just takes practice for you to discern what is your will and energy versus what is other energy versus what is Michael and me. With Michael, your writing has been more clear. You seem to feel his energy more easily. If you have questions you feel uncertain about, perhaps you should write with him for a while to see if that clears things up for you. In fact, do that about the money now.

Beautiful and Breathtaking: God's Book of Remembrance

July 10, 2019

> Good morning, God. I sent off the payment to Susan for the editing of the book. I feel good but nervous that I am being manic by spending so much. Also, when I look back at some of the writing, I know I was off about some things, like my friend who is a more evangelical Christian. I thought she would be supportive and she is not.

She will, my dear. Just not yet. Her challenge helped solidify what you are doing. Many will challenge you, evangelical Christians and non-Christians alike. For many in the New Age crowd, this will resonate immediately. That is where we will start. Those folks will understand and feel touched and moved by your writing. It will help them greatly, as they also feel the collective pain of the universe. The New Age crowd will help bring on the reconciliation. They have agreed and signed up for this task. As some of the first souls to be incarnated, they will also be the last to reconcile.

> Tell me more about how souls incarnate. Is it one at a time?

No, it is in soul groups. You have heard this term before. Essentially, all the souls got together and decided who would play what roles and who would need to be on earth together to meet those objectives. You incarnated initially by yourself and then your soul group joined you as the first group to incarnate. That included Steve,

Michelle McCann

Aidan, your birth family, your in-laws, and all your friends in this lifetime. Even some of the strangers you have met along the way were in your soul group. It is quite large—hundreds of people/souls. Other soul groups are larger, some smaller.

> *So, after my soul group incarnated, other soul groups incarnated one group at a time?*

That is correct. They each made their soul plans together and incarnated when the time was right. Some have been through many, many lifetimes and others not as many.

> *Is this what is meant by "old soul"?*

Yes, indeed. The more lifetimes a soul goes through the "older" it is. However, it is important to remember that all souls are the same age in the sense that, prior to earthly incarnation, they were all together in the heavenly realm at the same time. This is a little difficult to explain, so do not worry about it now. Just know that you incarnated first in the earthly realm, then your soul group joined you, and then other groups followed.

Each group and individual soul has a role to play. Like I said, you and your soul group are the reconcilers. As I have mentioned before, this included Saint Francis and Edgar Cayce. Their roles are complete and they are in heaven with me now.

> *What are some other groups?*

There are the healers, the challengers, the writers, the artists, the . . .

> *My writing has stopped.*

Yes, Dear, there are just too many to name. It is not really important to understand now.

> *What more do I need to know?*

You need to work on trusting more. Yes, some of your earlier writing was confused and disjointed, but that does not mean you are manic or losing your mind. You are consolidating the energy, processing it, and getting accustomed to it. It takes time for humans to clarify all the vibrations they absorb. You are taking in my energy, Michael's, and truly, that of the entire collective. YES—the entire collective. Then you will help transmute the negative energy.

> *Wow! So part of my role is writing, but it sounds like another part of my role is actually just healing myself and my wounds?*

That is right, my dear. The more you heal yourself, the more the collective can heal. As you reconnect with me and the divine realms and heal the trauma of the initial separation, that pain will diminish.

The realization that IT WAS NOT YOUR FAULT is HUGE! Feelings of having made a mistake, not being good enough, and being unworthy have been a huge burden on the human psyche. All souls will have to heal this wound for themselves, but your healing creates a pathway in the consciousness.

> *I like it, except that people are going to think I'm too big for my britches, thinking I'm all that!*

Some may, but you know you are human like the rest of your brothers and sisters. You make mistakes, you judge, you fail to love at times, you need to heal, and you have ups and downs—days when you feel fully connected and supported and days when you feel blue and disconnected. That is all part of the human experience. AND YOU ARE HUMAN!

Being first makes you no more special than your brothers and sisters. The specialness comes in the sense that you were first to make us parents, but just as in families, the parents love all the children, as we do you and your brothers and sisters. Whether they look up to you or not doesn't matter. You are who you are. They are who they are. The love comes from all of you reflecting your essence of love.

Just as human parents love their children for their unique qualities, so your divine mother and I love each of you for your distinctiveness. Each individual brings gifts, talents, a way of loving, a way of being, that no other soul can. It is the collective, the tapestry of the whole of humanity, that makes it so beautiful—each soul an individual thread and the tapestry the final product of the collective.

> *It sounds so AMAZING!*

It is, my darling. Just wait until it is complete. The tapestry is being woven as we speak. Every loving gesture, every hug, every bit of laughter, all the joy, the triumphs, the struggles, the sadness make A BEAUTIFUL PIECE OF ART—one that can never be duplicated.

This piece of art IS the Akashic records—the book of remembrance. Not yet complete, it houses the records of every thought, word, and deed of every soul through every incarnation and lifetime. Some people can access bits and pieces of it, but once reconciled in heaven, we will ALL see the majesty of our completed creation. You won't believe how amazing it will be!

All the struggles of humanity will have proven worthwhile when we are in heaven, sitting back (OK, we don't sit, but you get the idea 😊), sipping a martini, and reflecting with wonder at our BEAUTIFUL and BREATHTAKING piece of art. It will be grand.

In the meantime, do not fret. Do not worry about money, about how things will unfold, about how to play your role. Just live your life joyfully. Commune with us in the divine realms and it will all come together as it is supposed to. There is indeed a grand plan for how this will all come to pass. TRUST and enjoy the ride. That is all for today, Dear. Reread, feel free to share with your spiritual mentors, and enjoy this beautiful day outside! Love you.

> Love you too.

Afternoon

> Hi there. I have been thinking, is what I am writing really the revelation?

Indeed it is. What we are sharing with you is the revelation that was foretold.

> I feel a little overwhelmed. Is it really going to be a book?

YES!!! As hard as it is to look out of step, you need to show what awakening is like. This is IMPORTANT. You can't sugarcoat—

> You like that term. . . . Is this Michael?

YES!!! I am here to strengthen you to TRUST that you NEED to do this!!! Others will understand at some point that this is what awakening looks like. . . . IT IS MESSSSYYYY!!

Why does it have to be that way?

People are recovering from all the trauma they have suffered and healing is DIFFICULT! SO much pain needs processing—individually from this lifetime, from past lifetimes of the soul, and from the collective soul. THERE IS SO MUCH TRAUMA!!! We need to release it for the reconciliation to occur. Once enough souls have done the difficult work, the collective will shift. It is starting now with you and others who are awakening.

July 11, 2019

Good morning. I keep going back and forth between this belief that I was the first soul to experience the separation from God and then thinking that is not possible. I feel so confused.

Yes, Dear, I know it is confusing, but just type as you understand things and it will become clearer. Confusion comes with the awakening. It has been a long time since you connected with my energy in the earthly realm, and that makes it difficult to discern what is real and what is not, as well as what is your soul and what is the collective soul.

The past lifetimes of your soul and those of the collective are all in your psyche, and you are delving into the unconscious where they all reside. As you are very "plugged in" to the energy, you intertwine the two quite regularly and easily. Discernment is key.

So how do I do that—discern?

You just have to practice. I'm sorry—I know this is not what you want to hear. You want a quick fix, like with finishing your book, but there is no quick fix. It will take time and I ask that you please be patient.

I find myself frustrated.

It is OK to feel frustration. I know you just want to move forward and help people and to live a life you feel is meaningful and worthwhile. Remember, your life now is worthwhile. You are a mother, a wife, a friend, a daughter, a sister, and so on.

Yes, but that is not all I want to be.

Things take time. With more healing to do, you are not yet ready to be thrust out into the world. You still get upset every time you think someone may disdain your writing. Before MANY people question it, you must work on your self-beliefs. I want you to feel sure you are healthy.

Already you are thinking about what to say to your psychiatrist. It is good that you are going to tell him what is happening and assure him this is not mania, but rather, part of your spiritual awakening. But you still wonder whether he will want to increase your medication.

I feel like we are talking in circles a bit, going back and forth over the same things. I just want to move forward.

I know we are rehashing things, but that is as it needs to be. You need time to process everything.

I feel a little angry and disconnected at the moment. Almost like I want to stop for today, but I want to feel better. And I know talking to you makes me feel better.

It is OK, Darling. Go ahead and cry.

This is hard. SO HARD.

You just want to be DONE. You have worked so HARD, and you are tired. You have put in so much effort. You have written hundreds of pages and been connecting with me for months. I don't want to tell you to move past your feelings, but you already feel better thinking about what has been accomplished in only two short months!!! Imagine what can happen in two more!!!

I know you are ready for NOW, but it won't be long. It feels like it has been going on forever and will be forever before it is done. This is not true. When you publish your book, it will be GREAT. In the meantime, TRY to be happy with where you are. This helps with the flow.

It is flowing more already, as your vibration has lifted in the last few minutes. You are joyful again, just communing with me. Try to remember this is what you wanted, to commune with me. The book is just an . . .

> My typing has stopped.

Yes, I don't want to minimize the importance of the book. But, at the same time, I don't want you to get consumed by it. Taking a break last night was a good idea. You will need to work hard to finish, but you also need to practice self-care and spend time doing things that make you happy. Editing will be the hardest part of the process and it is OK to take your time. Don't pressure yourself.

> I want to ask you and the angels for help to make the editing easy, or as easy as it can be. I don't want to struggle through it. I just want to tackle it head on and feel positive about it.

We can help with that, FO SHO!

> Is that Michael?

Yes, FO SHO!!!

> I don't know how to type what you are pronouncing!

You got it, my dear. Good job! YESSS!!!! Just call on me (Michael) and I will be sure to make it FUN for you! No worries. WE GOT THIS!

> Michael, you crack me up!!! Did you want to talk to me today? Should I write in the Angels blog or work on book stuff?

NAH, not at the moment. We are good. The *Angels* is almost finished. We have PLENTY of time to get back to that. We will do a few more blogs, wrap up the book, and VOI-LA! It will be FINITO!

> You make it sound so easy, Michael. Even in all different languages . . . LOL.

> WITH ME, EVERYTHING is EASY PEASY, Kiddo! No worries at all!

What else is there for today?

> Nothing else. Just relax. Have some fun. Go back to bed for a bit if you like. Just savor the moment.

Will do. Thanks!

4 p.m.

I've been thinking about who I truly am and still wondering about this "first soul" business. Am I tapping into the collective or is that really my soul? I don't feel clear.

> It is not for you to feel clear yet. Sit with it for a little bit. What would it mean to you if it were you? What would it mean if it weren't you?

I feel like I'm in therapy! I just want you to tell me what the deal is . . . LOL!!! I don't want to have to figure it out.

> But you need to, my dear. You need to figure it out for yourself.

How do I figure it out?

> Call on the angels (especially Michael) to help you have clarity about your role in this divine play. You do have an important role, but how important and what your role is remains to be seen.

Oh, the old "remains to be seen" business again, eh?? Geez. Should I write to Michael now?

> If you like. Totally up to you.

Thanks.

The First Soul

July 12, 2019

I'm in the flow again! The website is coming together and the editing of the book has started in earnest. I'm so excited!

Yes, my dear, it is because you are embracing your essence of divine love!

I wrote with Michael after my talk with you yesterday, and he told me that I'm not confused—I was indeed the first soul. I'll try to embrace it and see how it feels. It feels pretty awesome, actually, to just know it for myself. But thinking about telling other people . . . ! I know you are going to push me to share it with the world, and I'm definitely not ready for that!

I would not push you. Challenge and encourage, for sure, but never PUSH. You always have a choice. I encourage you to share with a few people. A good start would be in therapy and with Jamie, your spiritual coach. Both will help you explore your feelings about what is happening. You will definitely need to process the idea that people will think you are grandiose, WHICH YOU ARE NOT!!!! People feel grandiose when they come to learn who they truly are, their true natures, because they are GRAND.

It feels a little like Michael here with all the caps.

It is both of us, actually—our energy combining for the moment.

> *You can do that???? Combine energy?*

Yes, when we choose to. Sometimes when we do healings on you and others, it helps to have God's vibration of love and Michael's vibration of strength together. People need both to embrace who they truly are. Society conditions people to think that they are not special—or are "egotistical" or "grandiose" if they think they are. That is simply not true. All my children are SPECIAL, and when they come to embrace that, they can do AMAZING THINGS!

It is not just about accomplishment (which is fun), but about helping others. The more each person embraces their true nature, others around them will be inspired to do the same. It's contagious. There should be a better word for that . . . LOL. It's not like a DISEASE—it's a GOOD THING!!!

> *You guys are funny—the dynamic duo!*

YES, we call ourselves that!!!! Of course, we "whispered" that to you. YES, we are self-nicknamers. It is OK to self-nickname! When you got it, you GOT IT!

> *Wow, this is fun.*

Yes, you are excited about your work but also need to take breaks and have FUN. For you, this work is FUN, but simply connecting with us is important too. Remember to continue to do this, even when it is not for publishing or for anyone other than yourself. THIS IS FOR YOU! Your connection with us helps you stay clearheaded, grounded, and above all things, loved and joyful!!!

We want you to LOVE YOUR LIFE! It is GRAND, GLORIOUS, and meant to be enjoyed. The trauma part is behind you. You still have some emotions to process, but the heavy-hitting stuff is DONE. You did the work. CONGRATULATIONS!

> *I still feel like I have work to do in trusting myself.*

You do, indeed, but it is OK. It takes a lifetime to trust and have faith that *The Universe Has Your Back* (we love that title). SO AWESOME!

> I want to type up my notes about the website for my meeting with Jane later so I don't miss any of the updates I want to make. Michael, I ask that you help guide her to make the changes so the website will be one that I (and others) LOVE!!! Help us, please. 😊

YOU GOT IT, DEAR! DONE! *KEIN PROBLEM!!!*

> You are speaking to me in German now???

You love German, right?

> I do when I understand it . . . ha! You really do know me, Michael. I love that.

THANK YOU! Have a wonderful day, Dear. Just reach out anytime you want to "talk." I am (we are) always here for you.

July 13, 2019

> Good Morning! I was so excited yesterday about the progress on my website and with the editing. Susan and Jane are doing a GREAT job! When I first woke up, I felt fine, but now I'm a little sad again because I still have doubts about my sanity. While reading my writing and working on the website or proofing, I feel normal, sane—like this is all real. I'm channeling, I'm connecting with you and Michael, and I'm going down the right path. But when I sit to reflect on this "first soul"[19] business, as I call it, it makes me

---

[19] In this entry, I talk about being the "first soul" to be separated from Mother/Father God. In later discussions with God and Michael, I felt that this was not true. An inexperienced channeler, I believe I tapped into the consciousness of the first soul. Instead of deleting entries that discuss this, I left them in the text so you can see that learning to channel, like learning any new skill, involves bumps and missteps along the way.

>feel crazy. Maybe I'm tapping into the collective and I'm getting it confused.

YOU ARE NOT, my dear. YOU ARE NOT CONFUSED!

>Wow, with the all caps, it seems like Michael, but it definitely feels like you talking, God.

It is ME TALKING!!! LISTEN TO ME!!!

>Wow, you are getting pretty emphatic.

Yes, my dear . . .

>I'm starting to cry now. Though I want to believe it's true, I don't have enough faith or confidence or I don't know what. I just feel so sad.

Yes, I know. It is that feeling of unworthiness again.

>Was that me or you?

It was both of us at the same time, Dear. We both know it is the lingering feelings of having made a HUGE mistake and being banished from your mother and me that make you feel you must be wrong. Of course you don't want to be separated from us again. That was the biggest trauma of all your lives, and you HAVE SEEN SOME TRAUMA!

From your Akashic record reading, you know that in one lifetime you were killed by lions and responsible for the death of your wife, who was the same soul as your son in this lifetime. This happened because you followed your religious beliefs, which were out of favor with those in power. That fear of persecution—maybe not the fear of death, but of being ostracized or alone again if you SPEAK YOUR TRUTH—carries over into this incarnation. It all goes back to the original separation.

>So, how do I deal with that? Can you help me?

Yes, let's write about it now. Start typing.

THE NATURE OF GOD

Michelle was the first soul in the first incarnation to be separated from Mother/Father God. She thought she made a mistake and that her punishment was being separated from us. For many lifetimes she has blamed herself, subconsciously, for the fall of humankind. She felt like she was "Eve" in the Garden of Eden and caused the turmoil for all her brothers and sisters.

This is not true, but it has been in her psyche for many lifetimes. Although not in her conscious awareness, it was just something that she believed at her core—that she was "bad." Now, as I tell her she was the first soul, she finds it hard to fathom that someone so bad could be given such a role. Her confusion, and the story that caused it, were placed in her psyche by her mother and me to facilitate the creation of the world and allow this earthly experience to be felt and experienced by all.

OK, God. That is sounding grandiose again. Am I confusing things?

No, your channeling is EXACTLY right and correct. Do not doubt.

Let's continue.

That is all there is to know at this time. You are EXACTLY who you think you are, the FIRST SOUL. Entirely human in your incarnated state, you make mistakes. You are not holy the way Jesus was, as he was fully of the spiritual realms. Although you are also of the spiritual realms, you were born through the typical human process. This makes you fallible, just as all humans are. You feel the full range of human emotions—joy, sadness, happiness, anger, annoyance and frustration, fear, grief, all of it. You have to work at not judging your brothers and sisters. And you do WORK AT IT.

You believe to your core that all people are essentially good and carry the light of God inside them. This is true and you are correct. When you see people making choices that hurt themselves or others, it doesn't make you question their goodness, per se, because you BELIEVE they are good. You just don't know what to say or how to respond in a loving way. This is what you need to learn in this lifetime—how to use your voice to be both LOVING and FIRM. You need to help others see HOW to love like you do.

I feel like I fall short in the loving department.

Actually, no, my dear, most of the time, you don't. You ALMOST ALWAYS see the worth in others and try your best to be kind and loving. When unloving thoughts intrude, you catch yourself and try to practice compassion and empathy. No, you are not perfect at it, nor will you ever be, but you are as close as anyone on earth at the moment. The Dalai Lama and Pope Francis come to mind—their mindsets are similar to yours.

Wow! I'm in the company of the Dalai Lama and the Pope, both of whom I admire greatly.

They are how you strive to be. And trust me, you are doing well.

Thank you. I think I have a lot of work to do, but you are right, I certainly do TRY to be loving!

Your intent is there, which absolutely helps. Intention is IMPORTANT. When you mean to be loving, a positive outcome is more likely. This is related to the law of attraction, but much has already been written and spoken about that. People can look to the work of Esther Hicks/Abraham and to the book *The Power of Intention* by Wayne Dyer.

What are my next steps?

You should publish today's writing as a blog.

I'm a little scared.

I know, but you are feeling stronger now. You are starting to believe and trust. I can feel it.

Again, was that you or me?

It was both of us. We both feel and know what is true.

Is there anything more to add to the blog?

I don't think so. You can send it to Susan for editing and then publish.

I'm afraid again.

Take that leap of faith, just like the post you saw yesterday. You feel scared when I tell you to jump off a cliff, but you don't see the whole picture. Behind you the ground is crumbling, and below you is a set of steps that will catch you when you fall. You don't always understand why I nudge (or sometimes strongly encourage!) you to do things, but TRUST that I ALWAYS HAVE YOUR BEST INTERESTS and HIGHEST GOOD at heart.

I do. Thank you!

Thank you, Dear.

By the way, what should the blog be called?

"The First Soul."

July 14, 2019

Good morning. Aidan landed safely in Istanbul! He is nearing the end of his Turkish adventure, and it seems like it has been amazing for him!

Yes, Dear, he has loved almost every minute of it, except the extreme heat . . . LOL!

So what would you like to talk about today?

What would YOU like to talk about today?

Hmmm . . . let me think. I'm starting to feel more accepting of this first soul business. It's just that I'm not sure I'm ready to share it with the world.

You can take your time. No rush.

So I don't have to make this my third blog?

Only if you want to. I personally think it would be a GREAT idea to discuss this "being who you truly are" business, as you call it! May as well dive in with both feet, as they say! But if you want to start in the shallow end, I will understand—no pressure from me. I just encourage you to continue to be brave and take risks. As they say, no risk, no reward!

> This is true. You know I am not much of a risktaker.

This will change. You will start to trust more and feel more comfortable taking leaps of faith into the unknown, knowing that the universe and I have your back.

> I still love that saying! You seem extra—I'm not sure—cheerful this morning?

I'm just so delighted in the progress you have made. I'm so happy that you are not crying and sad. The road bringing you here has been long.

> I'm starting to cry a little now . . . LOL!

Yes, but they are tears of joy, as you know the progress you have made. They are tears of accepting your personal truth and of moving into the life of your dreams. Not that almost every moment of your life hasn't been wonderful—because it has been a WONDERFUL LIFE, but now it will be MAGICAL. Things will just flow and come together and you won't have to work at it. You will still do your daily tasks of living and writing, but it won't FEEL like work because you will be joyous and in the flow.

> Yes, that will be NICE! I'm trying to not feel so rushed about leaving my job and letting the book, the website, the blogs, etc. come to fruition as you (and Michael and the angels) advise me.
>
> I was just thinking that I have not been referring to you as "they" and "us" when you talk.

That is OK, Dear. Mother and I are not together, exactly, so it really is me you are talking to. When we are reunited, it will be "they" and "us." For now, he/him (singular) is OK as this is your Father in

THE NATURE OF GOD

Heaven—"father" meaning the male energy/vibration of love. Thank you for clarifying.

Will I be "talking" with or channeling/writing from Mother?

Not at this time. Down the road, but it will be a while. Do not worry about this. You are not hurting her feelings by being with me. I know you were thinking you feel bad for her to be left out, and also that you want a connection with her. She is not quite ready yet but will let you know when the time is right.

It won't be TOMORROW, as you would like . . . my sometimes impatient daughter! I mean that in the most loving way.

I know. I can be impatient when it comes to moving things forward. I like things to GO!

Yes, Dear, that is your masculine energy. You have a LOT of it.

Tell me more about what you mean.

It is not important. Just know when you feel impatient that it is that masculine energy at work, and try to relax and embrace your feminine side.

This is a little confusing.

Not to worry. One day it will all make sense, but "not today, Zurg!" I'm reminded of that line from *Toy Story* that you and Steve quote sometimes. The angels and I get a kick out of how you humans love to quote lines from movies. It is SO FUNNY! We also love how you use words Aidan butchered when he was a kid, like "foffee" for "coffee" and "I borgot" for "I forgot." It is so sweet! We remember when he was little too and how fun that was for us and for you. We remember the childhoods of all the souls with great pride and joy, just as parents do.

Awww . . . that is so sweet.

It is!!!

> This has been nice. What else would you like to talk about?

What else would YOU like to talk about?

> Oh, the harder parts—Shan and Mama. How on earth am I going to tell them about writing about our abusive (and loving) childhood? Or do I not tell them at all?

You don't need to worry about this. It is all in my hands. Have fun with them. Spend time with friends and family and be joyful. It will be fun. No need to drag down the energy with your worry about how they will react to your book. As Steve said, it's not coming out RIGHT NOW, so there is time to sort all that out. AND, IT IS IN MY HANDS!

> OK, I will let my worry go (or try to) and focus on being happy with them. We do have fun together!
> What do I need to work on in therapy?

Up to you, Dear. What is most distressing to you at the moment?

> I actually don't feel distressed. The biggest thing is the fear that people will think I'm out on a limb with this "first soul" business. I am still not entirely sure whether I have channeled this accurately. Maybe it doesn't matter one way or the other, whether I was indeed the first soul or am tapping into the collective soul experience. Maybe this is meant to be a mystery, and the experience was just for insight. I just want to move forward and share these messages with the world, and I am trying to let go of the fear of judgment and of being wrong.

You know the truth. People need to see that learning to channel means you will take missteps at times. The important thing is that you are constantly analyzing your work and evaluating where it needs adjustment.

THE NATURE OF GOD

Admitting you are human can actually make readers trust you more. And those who love you will always root for you. Steve is your champion, even though he doesn't know it yet. You will have the support of your family. Knowing what you have been through and seeing what you are accomplishing, MANY friends will be happy for you. They love you for your kindness and generosity.

> I am crying . . . I'm not sure why.

It is because you still can't believe what the future has in store for you! You so desire it to be true but don't fully trust it yet.

> I was wondering if we could talk about politics this morning. I woke up thinking about Marianne Williamson.

Yes, she started a whole new level of conversation. A big shift in consciousness is happening. People want to start moving toward love. Some are still afraid, but do not let their masks of fear get you angry or upset. Just put forth positive, loving energy around helping others and taking care of yourself and one another, and that is all you need do. You already do this in conversations, on Facebook, and in your writing. This is enough. In your day-to-day interactions, just be your kind, loving, and joyful self! We LOVE that about you!

> Thank you! What else is there to know?

Nothing at the moment, Dear, other than you are DOING GREAT! KEEP UP THE GOOD WORK.

> Is Michael here with you? A lot of all caps today.

Yes, he is here, and you are channeling him with me today. Of course, caps and the comments about cartoons should have tipped you off.

> Ha! They should have. I'm not sure why it took me so long to figure out!

You were focused on the task at hand, Dear. We like that about you. You GET THE JOB DONE!!!

> Michael, that was totally YOU!

Yes, my dearie, it WAS ME! I DO LOVE ALL CAPS!!! I'm not yelling, just EMPHATIC!!! There is SO MUCH to be EMPHATIC about!!!! The world is magnificent, as are all its inhabitants. I JUST LOVE THE EARTHLY REALM!!!

> What's funny, Michael, is that last night on my walk, I thought about the movie Michael with John Travolta, and it came to me that you picked him to play you because you like to dance. Is that right?

YEPPERS. He is just a COOL GUY! I wanted to be portrayed by a COOL GUY because I am a COOL GUY! I can say this about myself. It's not bragging when you are an ANGEL—it's the TRUTH, especially when you are an angel AS COOL AS ME☺!

> Yes, Michael, you are cool. I'll give you that!

That's what I wanted to hear. Thank you!

> I'm going to take a break now. It is beautiful out. Thank you for this lovely weather. I'm really taking it in . . . basking in it.

It is for you and your brothers and sisters. We love to give you beautiful days. Every day can't be beautiful because we need rain for the plants and the earth, but even then, you can find joy in the rain. It is all about perspective.

> Thanks, I'll try to remember that! I definitely need to remember that with winter and the snow. I do love how it looks when it snows, but I miss being able to sit outside like this.

I know, but it is a much-needed hibernation period—a time to rest and rejuvenate. We can talk more about this another time. Take a break. Relax. We will talk again soon! Love you.

> Love YOU!

One Thing at a Time

July 15, 2019

> Good morning. I was texting with Aidan. It's his last day in Turkey. He flies back tomorrow. YAY! I'm sure he is probably sad for his time there to end, but I will be glad to see him!
>
> Yesterday, I picked the "Anna, Grandmother of Jesus," card from my Michael deck, and I kept picking it! At one point, I thought maybe I was Anna in a past life and felt a little manic, then realized it wasn't true. Now it feels like she is a spirit guide for me. Do I have this right?

Mostly, Dear. She is a spirit guide for you. You wondered if Steve was Anna in a past life, and on that you are wrong—but I think you pretty much knew that. You are becoming more and more discerning. When something comes to you, you sit with it a bit and see if it makes sense. And you are starting to sort out when it is right and when it is not.

> Yes, that does seem to be happening, but I always feel like I need to check in with you to make sure!

That is A-OK with us (Michael and God here). For now, you are focused on Michael and me. As we said before, the time will come when your focus will be your divine mother and that will be a book you will write, *Messages from Your Divine Mother*.

> Sounds good. I've got a LOT of writing to do, it seems!

Yes, my dear. You will be busy, but you will be free to do it in your own time and on your own terms. We would like to see you continue this 5 a.m. communion time, as you have no distractions and can focus on us. When you are free from your full-time job, you can write anytime you wish, but we would still like to maintain this routine. It will not be as draining when you can nap later in the day and relax more often. The time is drawing near.

> It is?!?!

"Near" in our view of time, maybe not in yours. OK, even in yours. It truly won't be long. You are almost ready to be in the spotlight but still need to trust yourself and believe you are OK. Your family dynamics also need attention, although that is not as much of a rush.

Edit your book and figure out what parts to adjust so as not to distress your family but still tell the truth.

We will cross that bridge when we come to it, as they say.

> There you go with the sayings again! It's so funny to me.

Yes, we love your colloquialisms.

> Not sure of spelling—need to fix! Susan just emailed with editing for the blogs. Let me take a look now . . .

YES, DEAR, DO THAT!!!

> Wow! So much moving forward. We are ON A ROLL!

Yes, now you are only worried about how to get your work out there. Do not worry. We've got you covered. It will take off quickly. Take a little time to do the website edits and to face your fears, as you told Susan. Talk to your psychiatrist and therapist about your plans. If

THE NATURE OF GOD

their fear bubbles up, don't let it hinder you, but take in what they have to say. It may help you formulate your next steps.

There is definitely a piece of you that worries about what other people think and a smaller piece that worries you are crazy sometimes. Some people may try to make you believe you are, so you need to be strong in your own convictions, in your truth, before you are ready to face the world.

You might think about starting with your psychic development group. Send them your website and let them know you are channeling. And talk to Jamie—she is going to love your work. She will encourage you to GET IT OUT THERE!

> I am going to head back to bed for a bit.

Do you really need to? It seems like you feel pretty awake.

> I do. Maybe I'll just go to bed and surf for a bit. I feel like lying down.

Go do that, then.

> Thanks and talk to you later.

TTYL! 😊

> I am pulling angel cards and got "Age of Light" from your deck, Michael. It means I have been training for this for lifetimes and I am READY! From my Raphael deck, I got "Balance," which made me realize I'm trying to rush things a bit. I'm ready to get this work out into the world, but I need to trust it will happen in divine right timing and not to force it.

That's right, Dear. You are putting pressure on yourself again. Just do what you feel moved to do and sit tight when it doesn't feel right. Work on the website first and get the emails all set up and then take your next steps. One thing at a time!!!! ONE THING! You jump in to do it all at once and you need to slow yourself down. It WILL HAPPEN! Work is not too stressful right now, so just relax into it. It will come soon enough, when you are ready.

> My guardian angel card was "Trusting Your Intuition." I love that. I need to just pay attention to what my heart is telling me and be JOYFUL.

Enjoy each moment. There will come a time when you will look back with fondness on this time of awakening and starting your new career. SO EXCITING! We are excited for you, and we know you are excited for yourself. It will be so fun to share what you are doing. You are enjoying discussing it with Susan and the few others you have already shared with. It IS some amazing work that will mean a LOT to a LOT of people. Feel proud of the effort you have put in.

It's OK to rest sometimes—like this weekend, when you had a lovely time. Make time for experiences like that. ALL WORK AND NO PLAY MAKES MICHELLE A DULL GIRL! OK, not really, you could never be dull to us. BUT we want you to HAVE FUN!

July 16, 2019

> Sorry, God! I got all absorbed in making updates for my website and the emails about it!!! I'm SO VERY EXCITED! And, I LOVE my business cards! It's all coming together.

I know, Dear. It is good that you are excited. You still need to spend a little time with me and take a break from that for a bit.

> I'm happy to. What would you like to talk about?

Well, I have something a little hard for you this morning.

> Uh-oh. Things have been going so great! I'm a little nervous to hear what this is.

It is your mother. She is not doing well.

Really? She sounded fine when I talked to her.

She is still worried about you, and you avoiding her is making her feel bad.

I don't mean to make her feel bad. I didn't think I needed to call her every day anymore.

You may not need to, but she needs you to be in touch. She is having a hard time and could use your support. A piece of you is still angry with her and that is OK, but it is time to start mending fences. Keep it light—you don't need to talk about the hard stuff. Just let her know you are thinking of her. Right now, she really does need your help.

Can I text her now?

Sure.

One sec. . . . OK, that's done. It does feel good to let her know what is happening with me. And, AIDAN IS BOARDING HIS PLANE HOME!!!! YAY!!! I can't wait to see him and hear all about his trip.

You will love all the stories and seeing the historical sites he visited and hearing about his time with his friend and girlfriend.

Yes, I am so excited!!!! Sorry, God, I'm getting distracted with writing to my friend Christina.

That is OK. It is exactly what I want you to do right now. No worries!

She is SO EXCITED for me, as are Julie and Susan. It is wonderful to feel so loved and supported. I was going to say I can't wait until the book gets out there, but actually, I'm enjoying this moment quite a bit just as it is. The delight of creating something and the joy of sharing it is glorious! WOW!

Yes, my child, this is a perfect example of the exhilaration of co-creation. This is how I intended it to be—you being who you truly are, and the flow of the universe supporting you fully.

> I'm just thinking about money again.

DO NOT WORRY ABOUT THE MONEY. It is coming soon. Think about what we have done in two months—two books almost completed, a website, business cards, a publisher, an editor, a web designer, a photographer. Connections to Julie, Christina, Jamie. It is like. . . . I don't know what it's like. . . . It's like MAGIC, THAT is what it is like.

> Is this Michael?

YES! I had to jump in to help God with the words. We are a team!

> I'm just so excited. I feel a little manic.

You are, but only in the sense that there is a lot of POSITIVE ENERGY around you. You are ALL GOOD!!!!

> I guess I should start to get ready for my day soon.

Yes, Dear. That is enough with us for today. Finish up your email and your conversation with your friend Christina, get your shower, and get ready for your day. Have a LOVELY DAY!

> Thank you, and you both too☺!

Evening of July 16th

> Just checking in. Things are coming together. I got a photographer to do some shots, and Jane is designing a logo for me. Thanks for having me mess up the website to figure that out!

SURE, NO PROBLEMO!!!

> Michael, you again?

YEPPERS, IT IS ME. I've been paving the way for all the stuff that is happening for you now—the photographer, the logo, the beginning ideas for your social media platform. No rush on this though. You have some time off coming up and should focus on your family. It's Aidan's birthday too. After vacation you can work in earnest on the social media. We will help you with it. NO WORRIES. WE GOT THIS!

People are going to be interested and pay attention—PROMISE YOU!

# Just Trust

July 17, 2019

Good morning. It's funny that today is 7/17 and the time is 7:17. I have been seeing that number some lately.

Yes, we are sending it to you. Look up its meaning now.

On her Sacred Scribes webpage, psychic and spiritual advisor Joanne Walmsley writes:

> Number 717 is made up of the vibrations and energies of number 7 and the attributes of number 1, with number 7 appearing twice, amplifying its influences. Number 7 resonates with study and learning, spiritual awakening and development, Divine and inner-wisdom, emotions and feelings, mysticism, empathic and psychic abilities, persistence of purpose and determination, and manifesting good fortune. Number 1 relates to new beginnings, creation, progress, inspiration and intuition, self-leadership and assertiveness, motivation and progress, striving forward, uniqueness and individuality, creating your own reality, positivity and activity.

> The three numbers together form a message from the angels about new beginnings and positive changes that reinforce your soul's purpose and confirm that you are on track toward becoming the divine self you are meant to be. Number 717 also nudges you to pursue additional knowledge and put it into practice to help others and further your own spiritual development.
>
> That's nice. What more is there to know?

Now that you are manifesting your dreams, do not let negative energy get in the way.

> What negative energy is getting in my way? I feel like you have more to tell me here.

Your worries about money and about your mother are making your vibe negative—not entirely pessimistic, as you are excited about all the positive things. But it would be helpful for you to let go of your worry.

> I try. It comes in and I try to reassure myself and let it go.

But, my dear, you ruminate on it quite a bit—especially the money. You don't need to stop putting aside money for Aidan's college "just in case" the savings gets low. It will be sufficient and you will have what you need.

> How do I stop this worry?

You TRUST!!!!

> Yes, I feel like I trust most things now, but there is still that lingering doubt about whether all the MAGIC could really be possible and happening to and for me.

Yes, my dear, that is part of the trusting—to KNOW it IS HAPPENING!

THE NATURE OF GOD

Is this Michael again?

It is us both—Michael to strengthen you in faith and in your truth, me to comfort and nurture you, and both of us to make you laugh. Your friend Doreen is right. Michael hasn't cornered the market on funny. I (God) am funny too.

Yes, I have definitely seen that, although it seems we have been more serious most of the time.

We have, because that is what you needed, my love and support and comfort. Now you are moving past the trauma and grief and moving into joy, so you will get more humor from me, like now—CUT IT OUT . . . LOL!

My worrying? Just cut it out?

YEP, KNOCK IT OFF! JUST DON'T DO IT!

Ha, like Nike but NOT.

You get the picture. Just trust and know you will be taken care of. Buy what you need to get your business started and to make you happy, and it will come back to you tenfold. You are doing something to make the world a better place, both by living your truth and by contributing your creation (this writing). It will make a difference and have an impact.

You have seen it already with the blogs you have shared with some of your friends. Our words moved them to reflect and think deeply and to feel comfort. This is your role—to help others understand my nature and that of the angels—and YES, of YOU, Michael. I (God) know you want them to understand YOU.

I will do my best to capture your essences and to help the world to know you.

That would be GRAND, my dahhlling!!!

I just looked back and reread the 717 number description. What positive affirmation should I say?

> Something as simple as "I have enough money for what I need and want"?

That is good. Say that every day. Add it to your prayers book where you also have some manifestation items. Writing it down and looking at it daily is almost as powerful as saying it out loud daily, so if you do BOTH, you'll be in good shape!

> Got it. What else is there for today?

Not much. I'm glad you talked to your mother yesterday. She will support you as long as she feels you are stable. Seeing you interacting with Aidan, Steve, Shannon, and your friends will reassure her that you are happy and yourself. You can tell her about your new projects—the website, business cards, logo, photography, and plan to start social media. She may not be as excited as you, but it helps you to feel like you are sharing openly about what you are doing, and it helps her to feel included. Yesterday, you started to tell your co-worker your news. You didn't tell her about the website yet, but you will soon. The more people you tell, the more it will get out into the world.

> Yes, I just wanted to wait for it to be PERFECT—for the logo to be added and to make sure my email is set up.

Yes, that is good. Talk to Jane about that today.

> In other news, I'm so happy Aidan made it home safely from Turkey last night. I got to bed a little late waiting for him and had a little wine. You are probably going to tell me to take it easy on the wine. I have been lately, but last night, I felt like I wanted some.

That was the negative energy (your worry) leading you to feel the need to drink. It is OK to drink sometimes for joy and fun. When you drink to self-soothe though, that brings down your energy. So drinking for fun and joy (without overdoing it and losing control) is different from drinking for comfort. Again, drinking is neither good nor bad. We just want you to know how it impacts your energy. "WHY" you drink determines whether it is beneficial to you or not.

> Thank you. That is helpful to understand. I guess if I am feeling like I "need" wine, I ought to stop and maybe breathe and meditate?

That would be good. Or pull some angel cards, or write to us. You just don't want to bring down your vibe. Your vibration is what leads to manifestation and joy.

> Yes, this is where I get worried. I worry I'll do something to bring down my vibe! And, then I'm worrying so my vibe is definitely coming down, and then I feel like I REALLY have something to worry about . . . LOL!
>
> It's not funny, actually, because I do fear that I'll get out of alignment and then I'll be in the predicament that I worry about, like not having enough money, or being cut off, or just having Mama mad or upset with me.

As far as enough money, YOU DO NOT NEED TO WORRY! We tell you this over and over and over again. It should be sinking in by now.

> Actually, it is starting to. I just get a little triggered every time I buy something a little expensive for my new business or things I want for myself. I don't want to be extravagant.

You are not extravagant, my dear. You are doing what you need to do to launch Michelle McCann, Author and Divine Channel, as a BUSINESS! This will be your future career, so it is good to invest in yourself and your future, the way any businessperson does.

I purposely had the photographer talk to you about her "small business package" for photography so you will start to think of yourself as a small business (soon to be BIG BUSINESS) owner. It is important for you to picture yourself this way—like a vision board, only in your mind. Or actually, you could print out your business cards and put them where you will see them to remind you that you are STARTING A BUSINESS!!!

And, as far as extravagant, you are not. But you could be—it is OK to have whatever you wish. You don't want to do anything that would damage the environment, such as having more than you need. But feel free to purchase things that make you happy and joyful. This raises your vibration. In and of itself, purchasing things is not bad.

A lot of the "simplify your life" pages on Facebook espouse minimalism. From a standpoint of not being wasteful, it is a noble pursuit, but it is good to have things (and people) in your life that make you happy and hopeful.

Beautiful artwork, for example, is a splurge that pays dividends of joy every time you see it. Similarly, the makeup and jewelry boost your self-confidence. Try to support local artists and buy from companies with sustainable practices, but it is not "bad" to want to have nice things.

> *This is helpful. Thank you. What else is there for me to know today?*

I think this is enough. Your vibration is back up. You are starting to trust that "It will all work out how it is supposed to," as your mother says. This is EXACTLY RIGHT! Do not doubt. Things are coming together perfectly (and ALWAYS DO). Just go with the flow. 😊

Have a great day, Dear. Enjoy hearing all about Turkey from Aidan. Reach out to us later if you want to connect. And GOOD LUCK with the photographer today. You will like her. We put her in your path for a reason.

> *Sounds good. Thank you! Oh, and I got the "Coming into Power" card from my Guardian angel deck—"I step into my power boldly and confidently."*

YES!

July 18, 2019

> *Happy birthday to Aidan! Such a proud and exciting day for us! What a wonderful life it has been with him. He was such a joyful and loving child and now he's a responsible and thoughtful adult. I'm so proud of him!*

THE NATURE OF GOD

Thunderstorms rolled through last night. Although it is not raining now, drops are dripping from the trees. I'm sitting under the umbrella to keep the laptop dry. The weather channel says there's a 40 percent chance of thunderstorms at 6 a.m. Am I going to get rained on?

NAH!!! YOU'LL BE FINE!!!

Well, good morning, Michael.

GOOODDDD MOOORRRRNING, DEEARRRIEE!!!

To what do I owe this lovely greeting and visit this morning?

I'm here to uplift you. You feel a little down again about not trusting who you are and about going public and what people will think. MY DEAR, IT WILL BE GLORIOUS!!!

It's interesting, Michael. Last night the photographer talked to me about joining the Delaware Small Business and Hockessin chambers of commerce. It felt surreal, as I'm not really a "small business person." And what would those people say about my "business" when I explain that I'm channeling God and the angels and writing about it?

THAT IS EXACTLY WHAT YOU TELL THEM. You can tell them about your history of mental illness, or NOT. It doesn't matter. It is all true and YOU DON'T NEED TO WORRY WHAT OTHER PEOPLE WILL THINK.

How do I trust myself more?

YOU JUST DO! It's that easy. You just choose to. When the thoughts and doubts creep up, remind yourself that you are a child of God and that God has called you to do this work. Indeed, your soul has chosen to do this work and to live this life. It is a beautiful life. Don't spoil it by overthinking it. JUST LIVE IT!

> *I'm going into town today (not working from home) and feel like I should share with my co-workers what has been happening.*

That is a good idea. The more you share and get feedback from people who care about you, the more solid your footing becomes when you engage with those who don't know you. I know it feels like putting it out there to people who don't know you is easier, but you open yourself to more scrutiny that way.

> *Yes, I suppose that's true. If they don't know I'm not really a nutcase, it is easier for them to dismiss me as one.*

THAT'S EXACTLY RIGHT! It's going to sort itself out over time, so JUST TRUST!

> *Jane finished the logo. It looks great, really pretty. I think the angels probably love it, since I know they love pretty.*

WE ALL LOVE IT! All the guides, angels, ancestors, fairies, EVERYONE AND EVERYTHING LOVES IT! We are SO PROUD OF YOU and your creativity in directing Jane with the design, and Jane's creativity in making your vision a reality. It is AMAZING what humans can do! WE LOVE IT!!! 😊

> *Should I post onto the Hay House Writer's Workshop group today?*

If you have time. You have work and Aidan's birthday. So maybe, but it can wait. There is truly no rush, my dear. Soon the time will be right and you will feel called. But you could join those groups the photographer mentioned. Getting the word out locally is a great idea and a good place to begin. That's right—it is going to be BIG, but word of mouth will be the biggest way the GOOD NEWS will be spread.

THE NATURE OF GOD

Put the preface and introduction to your book on your website. You could say this was channeled by God and provide the date. Was it June 10?

I think so, yes.

Why don't you look back now?

Yes, June 10.

It is powerful.

Let me find the preface. That was June 14.

Yes, they were two different dates, so let's do two different blogs. Call one "Preface" and in the body, say "This is the preface to the book *The Nature of God: The Revelation*" by God, as channeled by Michelle McCann on June 14, 2019. Do the same with the introduction, just modifying the date.

Yes, tell me about the date. What is the significance of June 10? Why is that the Day of Reconciliation?

This is not for you to know at this time. There was something specific that happened on June 10 this year, but we will reveal this to you later. Not to worry. It is actually pretty interesting and exciting.

I'm very curious.

Yes, I know, Dear, but as you know, all in divine right timing—DRT, as I like to say . . . LOL. Yes, this is Michael. I LOVE ACRONYMS, especially fun ones. We could pronounce this one "dart" or "dirt" but I don't think either really matches. So, let's just call it D-R-T, Divine Right Timing. I love it! I hope it becomes an expression. People will say, "It must not be DRT if this isn't happening now." It will be cool. They will use this expression to trust, as they do with Everything Happens for a Reason (EHR, I like to call it!) Most times people associate this with tragedy, but it would be nice if they could start to use it in everyday situations, to know and trust all is well and in God's hands!

245

> I will try to remember these acronyms.

Yes, they take a little practice, but once they are in your head, like "LOL," you can use them ALL THE TIME!!!

> That sounds great, Michael.
> I feel like I should send this new writing to Susan.

YOU SHOULD! It would be good for her to read.

> For her or for me?

For both. You will need to adjust how much you are paying her, since this is a LOT more to add, but not to worry. The money situation is FINE! MORE THAN FINE! You are ALL GOOD! This will round out the book. We are nearly done.

> We are? Is this "nearly" in your terms or mine?

In yours.

> Cool. Great! Anything else for today?

Nope, that's all. Enjoy Aidan's birthday. I hope you are excited about almost being finished with the book.

> I am! I'm ready to keep things moving. Well, sort of nervous and excited all at the same time. Nervous about what people will think, but excited for this book and its messages to help people.

YES, DEAR! YOU (WE) WILL HELP MANY PEOPLE!!! It will be GLORIOUS! Now scoot, go, check email, and get ready for work.

> This is me saying toodle-oo! Thinking of you, Michael.

Yes, I put that in your mind, but thanks for thinking of me. Have a great day.

> You too!

You Can Trust That Like a $2 Bill

July 19, 2019

    Good morning! It was 5:22 when I woke up and now it's 5:35. You have woken me up consistently at 4:50 or 5 a.m. for a WHILE now, so I was quite surprised—although I was having a pleasant dream.

You can go back and analyze them later. I have some things to talk to you about.

    That sounds serious. Am I in trouble?

Of course not, Dear. You are never in trouble with me! But I know you want to do this work seriously, and you have much to do to move forward.

    Spill the beans. What do I need to do?

You need to drink less and get up on time.

    I can do that. I just thought it was OK to drink and to let you wake me up.

It is, but I can't wake you up if you are under the influence.

    I don't feel like I drink THAT much. Last night was Aidan's birthday. While we were out, I had a martini and a glass of wine. Then I had a Frangelico liqueur when we came home.

Yes, it was the Frangelico that put you over and made it hard to wake up this morning. I'm not saying for you to NOT drink, but that when you overdo it, your vibration plummets. You didn't hear my call this morning because it was low.

Interesting . . .

I let you sleep in so we could talk about this. You are drinking because you don't feel completely secure in what you are doing. You crave approval, and that drags you down. Tell it like it is and leave it up to them to approve or NOT—and your vibe will remain high and you will feel good about yourself. When that happens, you won't feel the need to drink.

THEN HELP ME!!!! I am REALLY TRYING, but these feelings just bubble up— feelings of unease and worry that maybe I can't actually do what I think I can.

That is your fear talking, which brings down your vibe.

I guess I should listen to the video that came through yesterday from Cristina Aroche about raising your vibration.

That would be a good idea, but talking to me helps raise it. I reassure you that what is happening is real, and that raises your vibration too.

So, what do I need to do?

You need (well, "need" is your word). . . . You can CHOOSE to think differently. You can choose to connect with me when you feel this way. You can tune into how you are feeling. You have taken the first step by starting to notice when the fear bubbles up—like yesterday, not showing your close colleagues your website when you were checking it. IT LOOKS GREAT, BY THE WAY!!! Jane did a FABULOUS job!

Is this you, Michael?

YES, INDDEEEEDDDYYY!!!! The angels LOVE IT! All the pretty colors and flowers and the lovely picture of you! Yes, the new photographs will be BEE-YOU-TI-FUL and blend with the website perfectly, but that picture of you smiling and happy is a great one. Do not wait to put the word out there just for waiting for the photos. You are READY!!!

What about the email?

Wait for that to be set up, but otherwise, you are GOOD TO GO!!!! After you upload your preface and introduction, you can start posting on social media sites.

I don't have my social media set up yet though.

Don't let that stop you. Your vibe and momentum will stay high if you keep putting yourself out there and setting an INTENTION to move forward!

Will you help me set up my social media?

OF COURSE, MY DAAAHHHLLLINNGGG!!! I will help you with whatever you ask. You KNOW that!!!

That is one of the things I want to talk to you about today. You are not reaching out and ASKING for help enough. That is, we know your will is for this new business adventure to be successful and to help millions of people with it. WE CAN MAKE THAT HAPPEN. WAVE OF A WAND, MY DEAR. EASY PEASY!!! TRULY!!! Just trust us and ASK!

Every day, add it as part of your prayer routine to ASK THE ANGELS for help in making your business successful and helpful to people. Specifically, write it down. Say, "Angels, please help me make my business successful so that it can help millions of people." Yep, that will DO THE TRICK! That is all you need do. The inspiration for next steps will come to you with ease. You will be the "doer," but the inspiration for WHAT TO DO will be from us. You can trust that like a two-dollar bill.

What does THAT mean?

Two-dollar bills may seem rare, but they are REAL. When you find one, you know it is the REAL DEAL. Just because you don't see it every day doesn't mean it isn't out there. Of course, that's not an exact analogy, because our miracles are not rare, but many people still don't trust and believe in them. That's why they are like two-dollar bills.

People need to trust that we are out there, READY and WILLING to help make their dreams come true. For that to happen they need to live in the moment, in the NOW. It is not hard to make people's dreams come true. Look at you! You are writing a book now and will write many more. We have helped you find the resources you need—a publisher, an editor, a website designer, the writer's workshop to guide you, the classes you needed to learn to channel, ALL OF IT! It was all DIVINELY GUIDED.

In fact, everyone's lives are DIVINELY GUIDED. We know their will. When their true will (soul's will) is to do something, we can lead them down the path. If they ask, it just goes THAT MUCH FASTER. INTENTION is key. You talked about this with God a little yesterday, but it is an IMPORTANT point. When people share with us what they truly desire, we can help them.

The sharing is part of setting the intention in motion. I encourage people to write down their dreams and ask the angels to help them with those dreams. THAT RIGHT THERE—THE INTENTION SETTING—does AMAZING THINGS! It lets the UNIVERSE KNOW what needs to happen, and IT WILL HAPPEN!

> I'm going to write down my INTENTION RIGHT NOW. Be right back. . . . Done! I wrote, "TO ARCHANGEL MICHAEL AND ALL THE ANGELS: Please help me make my business successful so that it can help MILLIONS of PEOPLE!!!" 😊

GREAT JOB, DEAR!!! We are ON IT!!! I mean, we have been, but it WILL go EVEN FASTER now!!!

> REALLY???

Yes, as long as you do as we guide you to. Free will is still yours. If we inspire you to do something, like starting social media accounts or posting your work, you have to DO IT for this to work. AGAIN, the CHOICE IS UP TO YOU!!! Just know that the magic only happens if you listen and follow our guidance.

> I noticed you used "magic" instead of "manifestation." I'm not sure I like the latter word.

That was me, Michael, sending you a message. I don't like that word AT ALL!

> Again, with the all caps . . . LOL.

Thank you for capturing my essence in the inflection of my voice. I know you don't actually hear my voice as a sound, but you do "hear" it through your heart. Anyway, I digress. SO, nope, "manifestation" is NOT A GOOD TERM. It implies that the human is the doer. The human may be the doer, but we, the ANGELS, MAKE THE MAGIC HAPPEN. I prefer that.

People can say, "Watch this. I'm gonna make some magic happen." Then they ask the angels for what they want or need, and we bring it into their path. They are not actually manifesting ANYTHING. WE, the angels, are bringing it to them.

> You sound like you feel slighted.

Yes, a little. I mean, angels don't have feelings, per se, but we know what feelings are because of our connection to you. We know how you would feel if something like this happened to you.

> Meaning, you are not getting credit where credit is due.

Again, we as angels don't keep scorecards, but like humans, we do love being appreciated and recognized. It is ABSOLUTELY NOT a requirement. We love you and will help you no matter what, but it makes us feel good to know you LOVE and APPRECIATE US!!!

> Michael, I LOVE AND APPRECIATE YOU! I don't think I have communicated that enough. I am SO GRATEFUL for everything you and God and all the angels have done for me. I'm starting to cry.

Yes, Dear, we feel your appreciation. Which goes to say, you don't actually have to say that you are grateful or appreciate us. We know it! Just feeling grateful (appreciative) lets us know and makes us happy.

> This is great. SO what do I need to do today?

Just listen to your heart. I know you want to upload the preface and the introduction to your book, *The Nature of God*, and that sounds great. Work with Jane to get your email and social media stuff set up. That doesn't have to be today, just sometime soon-ish. Up to you how fast you want to move. I know you are on vacation next week, so you may not want to work on these things then. Or you may. Totally cool either way.

Enjoy your time with your mother and sister. Just remember, they love you and want the best for you, but regardless, you do not need their approval. Just put it all out there: THIS IS WHAT IS HAPPENING—I am channeling messages from God and Archangel Michael and writing about them. End of story. I mean, you could add that this is what you have wanted to do since you started down the spiritual path, but you just didn't know exactly at that time. You knew you needed some spirituality in your life and that you wanted to help people.

We knew your heart's true desire was to channel and to write. This is your soul's primary mission, to love and be loved. For you, it will happen through writing and making connections with other souls looking for their meaning and purpose. Your writing will help them connect with that.

> *I just remembered to send the Robert Schwartz link to my therapist and saw the invoice for the web hosting. It makes me think of two things to chat about. One, I have been telling Steve some of what I'm spending, but not everything, because I don't want to worry him.*

It is not good to keep secrets. You run the finances, so let him know you are spending some money now, but it will all come back to you and that you are fine. And, you are thinking about lowering the contribution to Aidan's college fund. DON'T DO IT!

That sends the message that you don't trust us, that you are in fear of lack, and that you think you need to control things. We (God and the angels) are telling you that you will have exactly what you need money-wise, when you need it. No need to worry or fear. Now, if you do worry and fear, that could cause it not to be there.

> *That's what FREAKS ME OUT!!! I do worry, so am I going to cause it not to be there?*

NO! You know in your heart that we are here taking care of you, and since it is deep down your truest belief, the universe sees through the moments here and there when you doubt. YOUR FAITH IS SO STRONG, DEAR! You trust us with your WHOLE HEART. You do as we ask, come when we call, listen when we speak. You are a poster child for working with the angels!

Wow, I don't feel like I'm ALL THAT!

YOU ARE, and that is what you need to work on. YOU ARE ALL THAT and a bag of chips . . . LOL!!!!

I'm not sure where that expression comes from.

We, the angels, find it hysterical!!! But back to my point—you doubt yourself and your abilities and your GREATNESS!!! You ARE GREAT, as are all of God's magnificent children. With our help, you can do ANYTHING you set your mind and intention to do. TRUST THAT!

You trust us to do our part, but you don't trust yourself to do yours. All you have to do is BE YOU! DO YOU!!! Just be your kind, thoughtful, insightful, sincere self and speak how you really feel. You are REALLY good at knowing how you feel and expressing it when you choose to. It's just that sometimes you choose not to, and this is when you are out of alignment. If you feel the call, the nudge to share something about yourself or your work or to challenge someone who is having an unloving belief or action, you are to do that, in your own loving, gentle way.

Wow! Michael, this is really helpful!

Yes, Dear, I know exactly what you need and when you need it. Never fear that your needs will be unmet. I am always with you, as I am always with every child of God EVERYWHERE, AT ALL TIMES!!! So is God. He is there to comfort and I am there to MAKE THE MAGIC HAPPEN.

I feel like you have comforted me today.

Actually, I have given you strength. There is a slight difference. You were not sad, but you were scared. God helps with the sadness. I help when you are afraid. WE ARE A TEAM, always there to help you with whatever you need at the moment. Sometimes you are both sad and scared and you need us both. Sometimes you are one or the other, and whoever is needed will step forward. There are other angels for other feelings, but I won't get into that now. Maybe we can talk about that in your next blog!

> *Yes, that sounds like fun. You are thinking of a title, aren't you?*

Yes! Let me noodle on it for a while.

> *LOL . . . "Noodle" as long as you like.* 😊

Afternoon

> *I feel much FREER today, less burdened by fear of what people will think of me and beginning to share my work with the world! I posted on the Hay House Writer's Workshop, on the Angelic Healing and Support page, and on the Channeling the Divine page. And I shared with a few people from work. The more I talk to people, the more the word will spread. The GOOD NEWS!!! Anything for me to know right now?*

YES!! You are doing EXACTLY as we are inspiring you. You are FEELING the INSPIRATION and acting on it. You are IN THE FLOW!!! Remember what this feels like—joyous and exciting! 😊

> *Yes, and it is fun to make connections with people!*

YES, that is one of the funnest parts of the whole thing, connecting with your brothers and sisters. They are delightful, and the more you get to know them, each one of them, the happier your life will be! These links are what make your soul sing. This is true for all souls, but ESPECIALLY for YOURS! You are the one who wants to make these affiliations for all your brothers and sisters. You want them to KNOW ONE ANOTHER. That was part of the goal of the separation, not just to know our heavenly father and divine mother, but to also know each other as unique SOULS, special individuals with gifts and talents to share.

> WOW! That is AMAZING!!

Yes, we should blog about this. How about tomorrow?

> Sure! What will it be called?

Let me think about it. I want it to be FUN!

> Michael, you are ALWAYS FUN, but I trust you if you want time to consider your options and make it JUST RIGHT!

That's right, Dear! It will be PERFECTO!!! Let's meet tomorrow morning, this bat place, this bat channel.

> LOL . . . OK.

YOU GOT IT!!

Make Your Soul Sing

July 20, 2019

> Good morning! I just got my edited angel book from Susan!!! I'm SO EXCITED!!! I only read the first few pages, but it looks GREAT!

IT'S ALL GOOD!!!!!

> Hi, Michael. Good morning! I'm reading our work together!

Yes, I know, Dear! That is AWESOME!!!

> I'm so excited we will publish soon. There is a little more to add, like our blog from today.

YES!

> Sorry for the distraction. Seeing the edits is exciting.

That process will take some time. For this morning, we are to write our blog.

> I was just rereading.

About connections to God and one another?

Michelle McCann

> Yes, I was getting something like "How to Make Your Soul Sing." Is that right?

YES!!!!!!!!!!!!!!!

I LOVE IT!!!!!!!!!!!!!!!!!!!!!!

Let's write it. Please start typing.

How To Make Your Soul Sing

By Archangel Michael and Mother/Father God, as channeled by Michelle McCann

GOOD MORNING, DAHHHLINGS!!!! Michael here. Just wanted to greet you with a resounding joyfulness and say hello!

There is still so much for you to learn about angels and how we can help you. First, I'd like to talk about CONNECTION. That is right, CONNECTION—how you will relate to me and all the other angels, as well as to one another. Remember that we are all children of God. YES!!! Even angels are children of God. Born before humans, we have always existed in the heavenly realm (the divine state of energy that is love) and have never lived an earthly incarnation. Struggle, fear, pain, and difficulty were unknown to us until our relationship with humans. Though we don't experience anguish or trauma, we have felt it with you and understand how to help people cope.

EXPERIENCE and FEELING are separate concepts. To experience something means to have actually LIVED IT, whereas FEELING means to have sensed what it is like. If friends are suffering or struggling, empathy allows you to step into their shoes and FEEL what it must be like even though you are not going through it yourself.

So it is with us. We are always with you, supporting you, sending you energy filled with love, comfort, compassion, and caring. Even when our vibrations are unfelt, they are always there. You ARE NEVER ALONE!!!! The angels and God are ALWAYS with you. Energy connects us!!! Listen to your heart, and you WILL FEEL our presence even though you cannot touch us, per se.

Michelle does this through writing, her strong suit, but others will CONNECT with us using different senses. A few will hear our voices.

THE NATURE OF GOD

Some will FEEL our presence. Many will just "know" we are there. As Michelle's channeling skill improves, she will "know" what we are trying to tell her just by thinking about us.

Angels and God do not think. We ARE and we FEEL. God created the world for his own and the divine mother's enjoyment as well as for all his children, both angel and human. All of us co-creators, God and the angels inspire and you build, do, create, think. Nothing can be brought into this earthly reality without humans thinking and doing. And, we LOVE YOUR CREATION! Well, most of it anyway.

As of late, people focused on profit and greed have generated some ugly things that damage the environment and dishonor Mother Earth and her creation. At this critical juncture, humankind must PAY ATTENTION to the damage being done and work to repair it. Many realize we have reached a turning point and if the earth is to survive, we (you) need to make drastic changes—better choices that enhance rather than harm our planet or one another. Poverty and devastation abound, though the world has enough resources to take care of all its inhabitants if only greed would not get in the way.

Please note that we do not judge these "sins" as bad, but we know your earthly existence will be happier if you take care of your planet and help others instead of competing. Every soul LONGS to be connected to God and the angels and fellow humans, although not everyone realizes this. Anxiety, depression, and suicide occur when individuals become unlinked from the spirit world and their brothers and sisters.

It is time to bring this to light. We encourage people to share their AUTHENTIC loving selves in order to reconnect with spirit and one another. That's all it takes—simply being loving! Although it may sound like a small thing, TRUST ME, IT IS NOT EASY!!! In a world in which people have undergone judgment, been abused and hurt by rejection, and endured SO MUCH PAIN, it is hard to "put yourself out there" and risk those feelings again. Those are PAINFUL feelings. We know because we have FELT THEM WITH YOU! WOW! Being human is SO HARD sometimes. The grace with which you handle suffering puts God and the angels in awe.

Upon creating the world, we, your divine mother and heavenly father, had NO IDEA how great the suffering would become. We expected a time of revelation (WHICH IS NOW), when the misery would be intense, but knew that when we CALLED EVERYONE BACK to us, you would return to our loving embrace. However, humans brought the level of pain and torment to the breaking point. That was a human creation. You have hurt each other SO MUCH. I don't want to belabor this point, because what is done is done. It needed to happen for you to come to know one another, to know us (God), to know the angels, and to know yourselves. But it is TIME FOR THE PAIN AND SUFFERING TO STOP!!! We are revealing ourselves now so we can RECONNECT.

> *Michelle here. I just realized this is God talking, not Michael.*

That is right. It was Michael earlier, and now us, Mother/Father God, "speaking."

> *I updated the title that this was written by Archangel Michael and Mother/Father God. Is that right?*

Yes, my dear child. That is EXACTLY RIGHT!

This is all for now. Soon we will write more to be shared with the world. For now, post this writing on the pages where you feel so moved. We will continue this important dialogue in the days and weeks to come. In the meantime, we wish you all (Michelle included) much joy and happiness. The time has come to be FREE and to RELEASE the obstacles that hold you back. I know it is HARD TO BELIEVE, but PEACE ON EARTH will come soon. Just wait to see how it unfolds. IT WILL BE GLORIOUS!

Much love and many angel blessings to you all,
Love, God and Michael

July 21, 2019

> *I was a little tired waking up this morning. Thanks for the little "buzz" in my head at 5:05! It was like my spiritual alarm clock. I went to bed at 8 last night after an early supper, and I only had one drink around 6, then watermelon-flavored sparkling water. Thanks for putting that in my path. It is fun to have something a little bubbly sometimes.*

YES, SOMETHING BUBBLY LIKE YOU . . . LOL.

Good morning, Michael! I wasn't sure if I was to write on the angel section of the book or on this one.

It doesn't matter. Remember, they will all be combined.

They will?

Yes, "The Nature of God" is Part I and "The Nature of Angels," Part II.

I thought we decided that it would be better as two books?

No, you thought it would be better to have two books to your name and that two would make you more money. Trust me. This one book is going to make you more than enough money to be more than comfortable! TRUST and HAVE FAITH!

You know I will do whatever you say.

YES!!! There is nothing to hide. The more you "put it out there," the more you can OWN IT and step into your divine, loving self. For others, this is going to be REALLY HARD too. They will have fears and doubts regarding their divine soul purpose, and they need to see that you also struggled with your "coming out."

Back to the book. I'm jumping between your book and Michael's now. I guess I need to create one consolidated document?

YES!!!! Call it the consolidation.

That seems pretty mundane.

I was JUST KIDDING! I knew you wouldn't like that—not COOL enough for you or for me either . . . LOL. WE ARE ON TO PART III: THE RECONCILIATION.

Wow! That is pretty COOL!!!! So, a three-part book!!!

YES, INDDEEEDYY! The main title will be *The Nature of God: The Revelation*, along with Part II: "The Nature of Angels: The Pathway Back to God," and then lastly (yes, this is IT!), Part III: "The Reconciliation."

The Nature of God is Love, Love, Love

This message is from God, as channeled by Michelle McCann on June 26, 2019

As Michelle has said throughout this book, now is the time of reconciliation, which is also the time of Revelation foretold to you in the Bible. All the predictions of doom were true in the sense that you are killing each other and the planet, your home, with all your willful destruction and wanton desire and greed. This is causing massive upheavals in the environment and massive division among you. It is time for Mother/Father God and the angels to intercede.

We beg you to make saner choices to help each other and the planet. Do not be afraid of one another or of the foreboding of doom for the earth. SHE WILL SURVIVE, AS WILL EACH OF YOU! BUT THE TIME HAS COME TO BEHAVE DIFFERENTLY. We know you will, because we have written your life plans. You have free will choices within those plans, but the greater DIVINE PLAN is for the earth to survive and for our children to be reunited with us in heaven. Remember, heaven is not a place, but rather an energetic frequency of love with which you connect. This happens after you die, but can begin to occur while you are living, the proverbial "heaven on earth" scenario.

All it takes is for you to LISTEN to US, LISTEN to your HEARTS, and LOVE ONE ANOTHER AS YOU LOVE YOURSELF. OH, YEAH, AND LOVE YOURSELVES! There is much work to be done to restore each other's faith in humanity and goodness, and to return the earth to her natural wondrous state. Just think of ALL THE PLASTIC polluting your planet. IT HAS TO STOP! NO MORE PLASTIC! Use your great minds to come up with alternatives. We know and trust that you will do this.

I digress. The moral of the story and the BIG IDEA is this: LOVE, LOVE, LOVE. Make choices for yourself and one another (and the planet) out of love. If you do this, you will be free and you will begin to see miracles happen, just like Michelle did. Since she listened to the call to write this book, to get up at 5 a.m. every day to commune with us, she has made AMAZING strides. She still struggles at times to make loving choices and to forgive people who hurt others, but she is working on it. Aren't you, Dear?

> Maybe not hard enough. I am indeed a work in progress... LOL. But I will keep trying! The ol' college try! I don't even know what that means, but you get the point! OK, back to the conclusion for Part I.

That is it, my dear. WE ARE DONE! STICK A FORK IN US, WE ARE FULLY COOKED!!! WE HAVE SAID WHAT WE NEEDED TO SAY. We ask that our children, your readers, review all we have said and take to heart the lessons they have learned. To live with LOVE is to please GOD and make yourselves HAPPY. Just try it out for size and see. YOU WILL BE AMAZED BY THE MIRACLES THAT HAPPEN IN YOUR LIFE WHEN YOU DO!

Wishing you all much love and angel blessings.
PEACE OUT.

Love,
God and Michael

Part II

The Nature of Angels: The Pathway Back to God

By

Archangel Michael
and Michelle McCann

Angels: GPS to God

This message is from God, as channeled by Michelle McCann on March 7, 2020

We are channeling an introduction to this section of the book to help Michelle publish by the launch party we have told her to schedule for June 15, 2020. Since May of last year, we have been toiling away to bring this book to fruition, and we are keen to get it out into the world soon.

Indeed, this is the revelation foretold in the Bible. The time has come for all God's children to "come back into the fold." By that we mean to reconnect with us, God and the angels, and to have a direct connection to us and to all beings that reside in the spiritual realms. THIS IS POSSIBLE. As we have said, Michelle is not special in her ability to do this. She has WORKED HARD to learn this LANGUAGE of communicating with the divine realms. We want to be ABSOLUTELY CLEAR: YOU CAN DO THIS TOO!!! Yes, indeed! You may not believe it now, but if you listen to the words Michelle (and we) have written in these pages, you too will learn to "hear our voices"—the voices from beyond. Please know though, that we are not "beyond" as in some WAY OFF PLACE. We are right here, with you, connected by energy AT ALL TIMES.

Trust that if you call on your angels, specifically your guardian angel, to guide your path, THEY WILL HELP YOU! In whatever way you endeavor to connect with us, they will facilitate the actions you need to take, the books you need to read, the classes that will help you, the prayers you can say. Whatever will help you connect with us, THEY KNOW THE PATH.

It is like plugging an address into a GPS. You may not know all the stops along the way, but you can trust (as long as the GPS is not faulty, you are thinking . . . LOL, but the angels have no DEFECTS!) you will get to your destination—a connection with God, the angels, and the spirit realms. TRUST. Follow our guidance and let the magic unfold! HAPPY READING!

    Love,
    God

June 10, 2019

> Good morning, Michael. I've been feeling you and getting angel messages through oracle cards, but I don't believe we have actually had a "conversation."

That is right, my child. This is our first direct encounter. I am delighted to meet you and get to know you better. Of course, I know all about you, but it will be a new level to have an interaction!

> I'm excited to get to know you too. Thank you for the strength you have given me on this journey. Just thinking about how you have helped me be brave and strong makes me tear up.

My role in the universe is to help everyone be brave and strong. It is hard because of the traumas you all have suffered in this lifetime, in past incarnations, and with the original separation from Mother/Father God.

Despite artistic depictions of me as a warrior angel, my battle is not the kind you imagine. My sword cuts the cords to negative energy you encounter and take in, but I will never harm anyone physically or otherwise. As a source of support, though, I am an indomitable champion. People can call on me anytime when they need strength and courage, and I will help them find it within themselves. They are not to worry that there is a help queue or call waiting. Because I am energy, I can help everyone all at the same time. Appealing to me does not take me away from someone with a greater need. I am here for all of you.

> This almost feels funny, like you think it is amusing that we don't understand this.

THE NATURE OF GOD

Indeed. Since I have always been energy of the heavenly realm, I don't fully grasp time and space. Well, I understand them as concepts but not as experience. I can be everywhere, with everyone, all the time. There is no separation of time and space for me.

> *Good to know. I definitely wouldn't want to take you away from someone who needed you more than me by asking for something trivial in comparison.*

Nothing is trivial in my eyes. Whenever God's children—my children too—are unhappy for any reason, I beg them to ask for help to ease their burdens.

> *If people call on angels, are they in any way disrespecting God by not appealing to him directly?*

Absolutely not. Just as CEOs cannot perform every corporate function themselves, the heavenly father and divine mother created all the angels to be their helpers. They delight when humans call on us. We were created solely for that reason—to help God's children find their joy and their soul's purpose.

That is what this book is about—helping people connect with the angels, so the angels in turn can lead the way back to connection with God. As they said in the introduction to *The Nature of God*, no two paths back to them are the same. Only the angels and God know the plan for each person.

When individuals choose a relationship with angels, they simply call and we lead them every step of the way. We put opportunities and people in their paths to help them accomplish their life missions. They just need to ASK! Remember, angels cannot interfere with free will. Although we regularly arrange advantages and synchronicities, we can do this more often and things move a lot more quickly when we are asked. Plus, as God said, when people look and PAY ATTENTION, they find the gifts and miracles more frequently.

Sometimes patience is required, as the road may seem winding and confusing, but angels know what needs to happen. Part of the process is learning to trust us. We know God's will for each individual, and we know people's hearts' desires as far as their true callings to fulfill on this earth in this lifetime. If they reach out to us, we will help them to be happy, joyful, and connected to us and to God. Their lives will truly be magical. You have seen it.

> Yes, I have! Like my desire to connect with God and to do channeled writing. It's hard to believe this is really happening! And you are right, it did take time, and I had to be patient and work at it, but now that my dreams are coming true, I'm in awe. The angels are AMAZING!

Why, thank you! We think we are pretty good, ourselves!

You will learn about the major angels and some of the minor ones. There is a hierarchy, but we are all here to help. Just like with you, God's children, no angel is more important than another. Each is critical, but some people and angels end up in the spotlight more than others. Remember, that doesn't make anyone better. All are equal in the eyes of God.

This is enough for today. You have to work soon, so please go get some sleep. Our journey is not long, but it will consume a lot of energy in a short period of time. To keep up your stamina, you need to rest often—take breaks, be with your family, ground yourself. Your spiritual task should not be all consuming, but a meaningful avocation (soon to be career) that will bring you much joy. Have a lovely day, my dear.

> Thank you. So nice to be with you. Wishing you a great day too.

I always have great days . . . LOL.

June 11, 2019

> Good morning, Michael. God told me to come and talk with you.

Yes, my child. We agreed it is time for my help.

> That sounds good. It will take strength to move forward in the direction of my dreams. I want to write and speak about what I am receiving from you and God and implement all the metaphysical concepts I am learning, without fear of shame and rejection.

All of this will happen, but not immediately. First, relax and trust. Everything will unfold in divine right timing and only when you are truly ready. Begin telling those you trust about our communications, and their interest and support will bowl you over. Your friends will be ecstatic and eager to read your words. They will be amazed, and this will be a huge confidence boost.

But should I be looking for outside validation?

Not in the future. Only until you get your strong footing.

What about my husband?

It is not time for him to see it yet, although in the future he and your son will both be so very proud of you. Even your family members, who you suspect think you are crazy, will be very impressed and happy at your success.

Sorry to pause for a moment, but is this Michael? The vibration feels like when I'm talking to God or when I talked to Mother.

Yes, my dear, we are in the same vibrational realm, so you perceive us comparably. We will say our names when we connect. When you channel others, ascended masters and ancestors, for example, that will feel different, as each realm has a specific vibration.

So, I will be able to do all this?

You are honing your craft right now. Spirits from all the realms will write through you, and your work will help others learn to unite with them too. Communicating our messages requires no special powers or gifts (well, connecting with us is a gift, but one for all to open).

Ha ha! "Open"—I get the joke.

Isn't that funny? When we talk about opening, we refer to our children opening their gifts, their natural inheritance that is the ability to connect with all divine beings and to know that they themselves are transcendent. This is their truest talent.

> *Pretty cool.*

We thought so when we created the concept!

> *Sorry—had to stop and fix the typos . . . LOL! Sometimes the information is coming in so fast, it is hard to keep up, and you know I'm a stickler for detail.*

Such focus serves you well in this writing, as it will when it comes time to publish. There will be less editing work, so it will go smoothly. You are an excellent writer!

> *Thank you, but I just type what you tell me.*

It is your ability to write and type so well that allows you to unite with us so effectively. Not everyone uses your method. Like you, some people hear voices or have a "knowing," but others see or sense or feel our vibrations. Sometimes they combine several techniques, the way you see us in lights and "know" what we are trying to say. Each person has different psychic senses, and that is what they will use to tune in to our realm.

> *Sorry to get off track a bit, but what do you think about the term "psychic"? I've always preferred "intuition" or "spiritual intuition/connection" because "psychic" makes me think of people with crystal balls or perhaps shysters trying to take people's money.*

That is simply a perception, my dear. When people understand the psychic sciences (Yes, claircognizance[20] is real and will be considered a science in the future!), they will consider them as mainstream as geology or physics. In fact, people will seek out mediums for help dealing with spiritual crises the same way they consult therapists today for emotional ones. Until individuals open their own gifts, plugging into other realms through a psychic is a perfectly healthy and wonderful way for them to resolve trauma and depression that result from feeling separate from the universe. For that is what depression is—a disconnection from

---

[20] Intuitive "clear knowing" about an event or intention without objective evidence.

spirit. You will ease this epidemic by helping people perceive who they truly are and thus restore the link with the divine.

> *Are you happy I'm not saying, "Me? Really?" When I'm with you, it all feels possible, like I am meant to do this. But when I think of others' (for example, my psychiatrist's) reactions, I worry they will think I'm insane and grandiose.*

Your psychiatrist will think so at first but will come to understand when the world recognizes the importance of your work. It will take time for him to realize that all mental illness is related to spiritual connection or lack thereof.

We don't need to talk about all this now. The whole approach to psychiatric care will change dramatically.

> *OK, now I'm saying it—really?!!? WOW! That seems amazing.*

It will be. Many lives will change for the better. There is, as you know, SO MUCH PAIN to process. We are a nation and a world in need of healing. Trauma is in our collective psyche, and we will need to repair it one soul at a time.

> *What a daunting task!*

It will go quickly once the news spreads. What you are writing is the "good news" foretold in the Bible. The time of reconciliation with God—Mother, Father, and Jesus—has come.

The second coming of Christ is not his actual physical return to Earth, as most people expect. Rather, it is his homecoming into the minds of his people to heal them from the separation and trauma they have endured.

No one has to be Christian to experience this. They just need to ask to be restored. Angels will guide them to the right people and resources for the care and renewal they need. For some, this will involve talk therapy, for others music and art therapy, and for many more, just asking and praying for relief and harmony will be enough.

Individuals will be made whole as they begin to connect and start sharing their gifts, who they truly are, and their opening stories. And that will spread like wildfire!

Remember, it is not about money or celebrity. Your heart's desire was and is to help people and to live your own authentic life. This will happen. Just remember—when the fame and fortune come, stay grounded in the earth and only keep what you need. Instead of amassing wealth, use it for good.

We knew your intention before you ever dreamed of it, and your prayers have (or will shortly) come true.

Why don't prayers always come true?

Because God knows what is best for each one of us. Prayer is important because it helps God review all the options available in your life's/soul's "flowchart." Based on people's requests, he makes choices that put them on different paths. So he is indeed listening, and prayer does sometimes change the outcome, but know in your heart that if an appeal is not granted, it is indeed for your highest good. Our heavenly father may answer in other ways, and he is ALWAYS there comforting, even more so when we communicate with him. He comes closer when he knows we really need him, and prayers help him bond more closely to us and our feelings.

Is there anything more to know about this?

Not at this time. I think we have made the point—prayer is good, useful, helps, and also lets those praying feel like they are taking action, which they are. OK, let's move on.

Wow! So much to talk about today.

Yes, indeed. In about thirty more minutes you need to get ready for work, so we will use this time wisely.

What should we write about now?

You asked about "Eve consciousness." Spot on, my darling! The original wounding, known as original sin, was not a mistake, but rather planned by God for your highest good. As we have discussed, your soul's desire was to know your true nature and magnificence. Doing that required separation from God. This bears repeating many times, as it is a foundational concept in the revelation. God put the Adam and Eve story in the Bible so people would feel they made some sort of grand mistake. Of course, that is not true, but knowing disgrace allows appreciation of worthiness and understanding of the difference. The feeling has a STRONGER IMPACT on women.

Why more so for women?

Feeling unworthy is stronger and more prevalent in women because they relate to the feminine energy that was the first to separate, and this was the first imprint on the human consciousness. Men have it too, all humans do, but women are particularly hard on themselves. It was not chosen by us that women should feel this pain more greatly. It is just that women do feel the unworthiness at a very deep level.

It seems like you felt unsure about explaining this.

True. I know most things, but sometimes humans present us with new situations we had not thought about (well, we don't think, we know, but that's another topic for another day!). Humans are creators and come up with products and ideas that sometimes amaze God and me.

Really?

Really! We don't know everything people will create, and that is what makes the partnership between God and humans so amazing. Comprising energy, we do not have minds to think as humans do. So we can inspire an idea, but it is up to an individual to imagine it into reality.

Wow, this is pretty deep!

Yes, it is very complex. The ability to think, a gift from your divine mother, is a double-edged sword. It allows for beautiful creation. Art, music, architecture, science, math, and so much more are all a result of thinking.

So thinking is not to be thought of (LOL) as bad.

It is glorious! Only when it takes over your heart is it problematic. Like the ego (also a gift from Mother) and the mind, it needs to be controlled by the heart. When we do things with love and rest in between, our intellects can benefit us greatly. But when we overwork them or disconnect from spirit (our hearts), we run into trouble.

This is a really important concept for people to understand. Thinking can be good or bad, depending on how it is used. And to clarify, good and bad are not God's or my terms. You are always good regardless of what you think, even when those thoughts are negative or dangerous. That is part of being human and is never judged by God or the angels. We love you unconditionally. However, your judgment of yourselves and others is an obstacle because it interferes with your happiness.

> *Michael, I know it is only 6:10 a.m., but my head is a little cloudy now. I guess it is all the energy?*

Our session has been very productive. You are not physically tired exactly, but exhausted from channeling. It makes the channel less clear when you feel this way, so let's stop for now. Go have your morning coffee and pull some angel cards to start your day. Be productive at work and we will meet back here tomorrow, same bat time, same bat channel.

> *LOL, you like cartoons, eh?*

What a fun human creation. They crack me up.

> *You are funny, Michael.*

Why yes. Yes, I am. I have only learned humor through you, through people. Humor is a human creation. God and I LOVE IT. It is definitely a gift you have given to us.

> *OK. Let's talk tomorrow.*

We will talk throughout the day, but no writing until tomorrow.

> *Will I know it is you?*

Yes, I will provide signs so you know when it is me.

Anything I should look for?

No, you will know.

Thanks! Have a good day too, Michael. Love you.

Love you too, Child.

June 12, 2019

Good morning, Michael. Thank you for sharing your energy with me while I was resting. Thoughts in my head woke me up very early, and I am tired.

Exactly why I came to you, to calm you and allay your fears.

The thoughts weren't terrifying exactly—more worrying about the future.

That is fear, my darling. Preoccupation with future events and being unable to relax is how the fear shows itself. Remember this. When it happens, try to stop thinking. Meditate. Take some deep breaths, and call on me.

Yes, I will do that. Thank you for the comfort. Maybe I should do more to ground myself?

Grounding is always beneficial. Writing outside today will help. Your own backyard chill pill!

Ha! You hinted before that I should chill through yoga, but where will I find the time right now?

Yoga would relieve anxiety, but I don't want to stress you out with too many activities.

> *LOL, you say "stress you out" like we do—such straightforward language!*

It is best to be direct, is it not?

> *Absolutely! Is there anything we need to talk about today?*

No, you are tired. Go back to bed.

> *Really? There is so much to be done.*

True, but there is time. You need a respite. Even if you can't sleep, just rest. Maybe I will come to you again, but we will see. Save and shut down now.

> *Thank you, Michael.*

The God Squad Is Out There Watching

June 13, 2019

Good morning, Michael. I felt you this morning, as if you were merging your energy with mine to give me strength.

That's right, my child. You understood and interpreted correctly.

Then the song "Somebody's Out There Watching" by the Kinleys came to me. I didn't know all the words, just the main part. When I looked it up I found the lyrics. It made me wonder if you are the one watching?

Absolutely. Along with me, God (both your mother and father), all the angels, and the spirits that have gone before (ancestors) form your spiritual team, always watching over you and out for you. We inspired this song, and it would be a good one for people to listen to when they feel alone or like they can't handle something. The words and music will remind them to call on their God Squad to guide their paths to greener pastures.

"God squad"—that's funny! And "greener pastures"? LOL.

One of my favorite expressions, and the grass IS always greener on the other side.

LOL, you mean on your side?

Yes! But it doesn't have to be! People can have "green pastures" in their own lives on earth if they call on us and let us help them. All of us are here to make this earthly sojourn a pleasant and enjoyable one. There have been many necessary trials and tribulations. However, now that people know the truth—the revelation detailed in the first section with God—we hope they are finding peace and feeling more at ease. This will help them to revel in life more fully, as there is SO MUCH to be enjoyed! It can be joyous and glorious!

We in this realm of energy live vicariously through you, as we do not have physical qualities. And while the human experience has often been one of struggle, the tide is turning. Once individuals are "in the flow" of the universe, calling on us, trusting us to guide their way, life will be easier and more satisfying.

> I hope so!

There will be fewer accidents, fewer injuries, less illness and disease, less famine and war—less of all those things that have made the earthly enterprise a difficult one. That torturous time is nearing an end. People will begin to see the changes quickly once they begin to follow what we—God and I—are teaching them, through you.

> Michael. This is going to be a tough question. I have read that people actually can cause their own illnesses, like cancer, and it seems like blaming them for something that is not their fault and kicking them while they are down. What do you say about this?

An undeniably difficult question, my child, for it is true that illness occurs when people bury their feelings and are not living their true life's path. All sickness stems from unprocessed trauma. It is not for us to judge individuals as bad or wrong, but to have compassion as they struggle with how to live their soul's purpose.

People should seek medical intervention while dealing with trauma but be aware that human healthcare focuses heavily on treating somatic symptoms. They should ask us for guidance to find the professionals who can help them physically, emotionally, and spiritually, as each element needs tending. Your friend Kim, who practices functional medicine, looks at the whole person as well as the causes of and connections among symptoms of illness. This field should grow, as it is critical to not divide individuals into the sum of their parts.

THE NATURE OF GOD

> *There you go again with the sayings. I just love them . . . LOL! Way to lighten up a serious topic.*

That's right! The earthly realm can be complicated, but the more people look on the bright side, not covering up their feelings but releasing them and then moving to something joyful, the better off they will be. It is important to be clear. I'm not saying to pretend everything is OK and keep moving. Instead, vent, go to a therapist, talk to a friend or a minister, whoever you feel supported by, to feel heard and LET YOUR FEELINGS OUT! Then, make an effort to do something joyful—be in nature, watch a funny movie, look at clips of babies and kittens on Facebook.

> *LOL, you and God like Facebook, don't you?!?*

It can be a lot of fun!

> *You crack me up!*

Listening to uplifting music is another great way to lift your spirits.

> *What do you mean by that?*

People become conscious of their spiritual selves through music. All music (and art and architecture and all things creative) is inspired by the heavenly realms and executed by human bodies—a productive team. For God and the angels to experience the joys of earthly existence and its imagination, humans must follow their bliss and invent, build, make, dance, sing, draw, and so on and so on.

We love your creations, SO CREATE!!! Dream up new ideas until your heart is full and your passion ignited. Everyone innovates in different ways—some in business, some in the arts, others in the sciences. One is no better than the other. Your creation is this writing (with our help), but it is no more or less important than the banking work some of your peers do. If they love it, that is what they should do. If they don't love it, they should move toward what sets their hearts thumping. This will help them to live fulfilling lives—what we, your spiritual team, so want for you!

> *Wow! Michael, this has been so great! It is*

> reassuring to know that we have so much support from the other side. I have certainly felt it in my life as I have worked more with the angels. Based on what I understand, it was through you that I connected with God?

Yes. You listened in the quiet and could sometimes hear him, but we steered you to the teachers who would enlighten about intuition, the spirit world, and channeling. This was your course. For others, it will be different. They will definitely want to call on the angels to help guide their way and will be amazed at the opportunities that drop into their paths. You are grateful for all the wonderful people you have met and learned from. Now you will teach them too. We all help one another, ultimately.

> How should people call on the angels? What do they need to do?

It is quite simple really—they just need to ASK! As you know, we cannot interfere with anyone's free will, so the more they ASK us for help, the more we can do to grease the wheels . . . LOL. There I go again with the expressions. They are just so fun to use!

> All the flowery language is entertaining me for sure. You like to have fun, eh Michael?

That is indeed the best part of the job, having fun and laughing. Truly, we did not know humor and laughter until you were born of the earth and became human. It is likely the most delightful of the human creations, in my eyes—although there are so many wonderful creations, it is hard to pick a favorite!

> I was also thinking about the song "The Glory of Love" by Peter Cetera. Can you tell me more about why I thought of it?

Eat your lunch while it is hot, and then we will discuss it.

> I'm still snacking but pretty much done.

THE NATURE OF GOD

My darling, God knew your magnificence but you did not comprehend it, and you did not know God apart from his magnificence. Having experienced contrast by agreeing to come to the earthly realm, you now have a new perspective of his all-encompassing love. Your suffering allowed God to become "known" to you in a more meaningful way.

> *So, in a sense, we helped God to be "known" too. We did not understand HIS grandeur just as we did not grasp our own.*

It moves God's heart to know that his children were willing to suffer in order to know him in all his glory . . . the GLORY OF LOVE. Seeing you suffer tormented him. Even more difficult is when people think he could have caused their pain. This is absolutely not true. God loves us more than is imaginable. The nature of suffering is only to understand, never to punish. NEVER TO PUNISH. All people must get this message. Your trials and tribulations were never a result of God not loving you or of him punishing you.

> *What about the story of Job in the Bible?*

That was created by men to help explain their misery. It was not from me. At the time, humans needed such a story to understand the reason for and nature of tribulation. Now it is time for the revelation and for people to know the truth about why they suffer—to know themselves and God as pure, divine love.

> *I feel like I'm talking to God now, not Michael.*

You are, my child. This was important to include in this book, so it is fine to mix me in with Michael. He doesn't mind, do you, Michael?

No, not at all. I love you, God.

I love you too, Michael.

> *Aren't we just having a love fest . . . LOL?*

Yes, and I LOVE IT!

Michelle McCann

> As I reread the lyrics of "The Glory of Love," it comes to me that God was surprised by our strength.

Yes, he has seen what people have endured and the grace by which you bore your pain. Some turned to addictions to help cope, which is understandable, but others remained faithful and believed God would see them through. This touched God's heart. He got to experience what a human father's love feels like for his children. Seeing them persevere through adversity makes him so very proud.

Heaven Is an Energetic Realm

June 14, 2019

Good morning, Michael. God was insistent I talk to you now.

He knows what he wants. Now that it is certain you want to follow his will, he will keep you on track.

LOL, the "WILL"!

That's right! God and I love puns. Another human creation. So funny!

I was telling my friend Elizabeth how funny you two are!

Yes, she (and others) will appreciate our comedy, as do you. Humor is definitely a connection point between humans, and now that has extended to the divine realm. Laughter has almost as high a vibration as love. It is therapeutic. One of your angel notes says, "Laughter is the best medicine." This is so true. Raphael did a happy dance when it was added to his toolbox to help people heal.

Interesting. How does he use it?

He puts funny people in the path of those who are struggling or sick. Treating people with laughter is his favorite therapy. Not that they can use humor alone, as processing the trauma usually takes some releasing and lots of tears, as your friend Lydia knows. But a good belly laugh absolutely speeds up the healing process. Like you on the elevator at work with your colleagues the other day, hee-hawing at Denise screaming at the car.

That was funny! So, you saw and heard that?

I am everywhere, Dear. I see and hear EVERYTHING. There is no place I am ever not present. Folks need to know that I am always there protecting them. In fact, with Denise, it was me who planted the idea for her to call out to the woman in the car. I saw what was about to happen, that the woman was going to go the wrong way down a one-way street, and I intervened.

I thought you couldn't intervene with our free will?

This is important—PAY ATTENTION. I knew it was not the driver's will to go the wrong way and possibly hurt someone. Because of that, I could put Denise in her path to help change her behavior. So, when I KNOW something is not of someone's intent, I am allowed to step in to help. That is why there are so many instances of miracles already—because of the other angels and me interceding to help. WE DO THIS ALL THE TIME. If people think back, they will remember many instances in which they could have been in an accident or something bad could have happened, but another angel or I intruded to stop it.

You are thinking of Aidan's friend from baseball, Zach, when he and Aidan were little and the rebar in the ground almost impaled him . . .

That was so scary—how close he came to being hurt or killed.

I knew no one put that rebar there to injure someone, so we stepped in to move Zach's body just a little. We let the steel scrape him so you would know the rebar was there and could have it moved so no one else got hurt.

That was a good idea.

Yes, we intervene in ways that often help not only the person in danger, but others as well. Like with the car—your colleagues needed a good laugh yesterday, so I gave them the gift of being in the scenario while helping the woman in need. I could have chosen others, but I picked them.

> *Wow, they might like to hear they were chosen by you to help that woman and to laugh.*

Indeed, they would love to hear that. They believe in angels, so they will be excited to know that I was working with them and always do. They are special people, as are all my children.

> *I think Tiffany, Zach's mother, would also like to hear the story about Zach.*

Yes, you could reach out to Tiffany. She also has a strong sense of the spiritual and would be delighted to read your book and support you in "coming out of the spiritual closet." As you have said, in today's world, it is probably harder to say you are channeling God and the angels than to tell people you have a mental illness. You have a lot to be forthcoming about, but do not worry. I will give you the strength to be who you truly are, incorporating both the difficult and loving parts of your history.

Most people have had lots of trauma but lots of love as well. Some have not felt the love as much because they have not allowed themselves to be vulnerable. Genuine love comes when you can be completely yourself—your crazy, weird, fun, messed-up self—with another. As you reveal your authentic self, more loving relationships emerge, and this draws people to love you.

Many people in the world today are lonely because they do not know how to inspire others to love them. I encourage them to be as genuine as possible and do things that evoke joy. This is how they will find their "tribe," those who love them for who they truly are. Truly, I tell you, they need to be themselves and the love will come. I promise. You have noticed that this gets less difficult as you get older. As you learn to laugh at yourself and your mistakes, it is easier to be authentic.

But we need to start teaching our children and young adults and parents to do this as well. When they struggle, they need to describe their fears and be supported. A lot of people call the new generation names because their feelings get hurt easily. TRUST ME—THIS IS PROGRESS!!! People need to feel and express their emotions to be healthy, to feel loved, and to love in return. This is an important step in evolution.

Those doing the name calling are scared, so we must show compassion. Many have never shared their emotions, so they are uncomfortable watching others do so. Fortunately, young people are learning this and will show the older generation how to "let it go."

It is not good or healthy for people to ignore festering pain or emotional wounds. In order to heal, humans need to share their struggles with others. Some may pray and share their angst with God (or me) and that may be enough, but most require human kinship too. As Brené Brown says, we are hardwired for connection and are worthy of love and belonging.

You can tell her we gave her that. The world SO NEEDS to hear this. Brené does a great job of bringing the subjects of shame and vulnerability to the surface. Once people grasp these concepts and adopt them as daily PRACTICE, love will find its way to them.

I feel like this is not quite right. . . . This is a skill?

Yes, my darling, "skill" is accurate. Learning to express your emotions openly is a skill like any other. It takes practice. People should start small, revealing something not too scary, and see how the other person reacts. If that feels safe, they can confess other secrets they consider more embarrassing. The key is building that safety net so there is nothing left that is so shameful it cannot be shared.

This will take time. We have so many defenses built up from years of being hurt that it is hard to expose ourselves and our blemishes.

But in doing so, this is where the healing happens.

Steve just came downstairs and made the coffee. He is up earlier than normal. This is the first time I have been writing with him nearby. It feels a little strange.

You are afraid he will think you are manic and want to stop your writing. But there is no need to be scared. Steve understands that what you are doing is important, even though he doesn't know why or the scope yet.

I was going to go get a cup of coffee. It smells good.

Go right ahead. I'll be right here when you come back!

Thanks!

I'm back. It looks beautiful outside! This morning it felt too cold to sit outside and write, but I might like to head outdoors later with my work and this laptop.

That would be a good idea. As you know, being in nature is good for your soul and helps you to ground, connecting with your divine mother.

Any more to say about her? I am still a little confused about her being "Mother Earth" and also our ego, and whether she is inside of us or around us.

She is all of those things—inside you, around you, of the earth, and of the mind. Your father is in heaven, meaning he is the vibration of love in the heavenly realms, which is a field of energy, not a place.

This is a little confusing.

I know, my dear. Bear with me. Humans are used to the constraints of time and place, so they can't fathom the concept of an "energy realm." It is kind of like when you walk into a room that is buzzing with joy or tension, and you say you felt the energy. We are like that—in the air, sort of, all around you, really.

So, you are in the earthly realm?

We are in every realm. You feel us on the earth, and when you die you will feel us in heaven.

> But again, you are saying it is not a place? I'm still confused . . .

It is an energetic realm that you go to when you die, not in a body, but out of your body.

> My typing is slow now. You are having a hard time explaining this, aren't you?

Human words do not really describe the experience, as your science has not yet found a way to validate it empirically. Einstein started to figure it out, but his work was not finished before he died. It would be nice if one of your fellow humans could continue Einstein's work into exploring the vibrational realms of love, the heavenly father and divine mother, and the angels.

Perhaps this book will inspire some scientists to create vocabulary that will help people understand. I'm going to stop now because I do not have the words.

> This was helpful, but I would love to know more, as I'm sure future readers would too.

Let me think on that . . . LOL. Well, I don't think but I know what others think, so let me find someone who can help me. Let's come back to this.

> We started talking more about Heavenly Father. What about Divine Mother? I keep getting this sense that they are separated and want to be back together.

This is tricky too. They are connected energetically through the vibration of love but have divergent roles. The divine mother is your mind. No, she is not your brain. Thought is its own realm, not of heaven or earth, but an energetic frequency that Mother created for you to be able to build, create, think, draw, sing, dance, and use your mind to make and do things. We cannot do this in the heavenly realms. So Mother is with you and your thoughts at all times. She protects you (via the ego) from feeling the pain of separation from her and your heavenly father. Again, I suspect this is a bit esoteric—is that the right word?

THE NATURE OF GOD

It is hard to follow.

These concepts are hard to explain to someone who is living a human reality. Although you have all had experiences in the heavenly realm, most do not remember what it feels like. You are bound by your minds' limitations now that you are in body.

I just reread. Let's try to do this together, using my mind and thinking to help. Maybe tell me more about the separation.

This is good—thank you for helping me.

Wow, with all you are doing for me, that is the least I can do!

OK, the separation. Before each soul comes to earth, there is a plan for the lifetime. As you learned from Robert Schwartz' work, it is like an elaborate flowchart with many decision points. An important decision point is the time and place of birth. This aligns with the stars and the planets to create your astrological profile and helps to determine your life course. It is all planned out in heaven ahead of time with numerous experiences and outcomes for you to choose from. Not a set "destiny" as some people think, your plan is rather a collection of possible futures based on the decisions you make with your free will.

You have many lifetimes on earth, in which you are to sample all the variations of contrast—love, hate, fear, compassion, joy, sadness, laughter, and so on. Your lives are created to give you the most extensive understanding of all of these feelings and concepts. Some have been painful, VERY painful, and others have been delightful and joyous, and sometimes you undergo both within the same lifetime.

This is as it should be, as God intended to give you the full adventure. It isn't to learn "lessons," as some people say, but rather to sample contrasts that help your soul grow in understanding. Remember, the whole purpose of the earthly realms and all your incarnations is soul growth. When you return to God in the heavenly realm (remember, all humans do, regardless of what "ills" or "evils" they have perpetuated on earth), you bring these memories. Acknowledging the contrasts lets you appreciate the magnificence of who you truly are, a divine child of God, because you have discovered what it is like to NOT be God. Does that make sense?

> Yes, a lot of it does. I still feel a little confused about how the separation actually happens and how Mother fits into it all. I have a better understanding of Father.

That makes sense, as most of your country talks about the heavenly father as part of the Bible. Native Americans and other indigenous cultures recognize the divine feminine and Mother Earth as much as they recognize the heavenly father.

> I'm excited to talk more, but since God woke me up a little later today to let me rest (which I needed), I should go shower and get ready for work now. It is amazing how much we have accomplished in only an hour and a half! It is 7:20 now.

You work fast, my dear!

> No, you work fast, Michael.

No, you work fast . . . LOL.

> You are playing with me now.

Yes, I am. Go get your shower and we will talk later. Have a good day.

> You too!

I always do, Dear.

> Hi, Michael. Me again. Just got the checklist of all that needs to happen for my book. I'm a little overwhelmed and worried it is going to take a long time!

THE NATURE OF GOD

I'm glad you are reaching out to me, Darling. It will not take long, I promise, but will happen in divine right timing. And, remember, you are not doing this alone. Your spiritual team is all here to help you. Remember, in the shower you thought of me as Chief Miracle Officer (CMO)? Tell your friend Meredith that I gave you that nickname for me. I think it is quite creative.

> *I love it too, Michael! Thank you for sharing with me. I was also getting that there are BILLIONS, no TRILLIONS, a multitude of angels to infinity and that their numbers are ever-expanding.*

Correct. For every thought, deed, grain of sand, every hair on everyone's heads, there are angels. Nothing is too small or too great that we cannot perform miracles to assist. As you discuss in your first book, a life experience, or rather this earthly adventure, is indeed *A Course in Miracles*. Now people will truly comprehend what that book is about and what its title means. OK, some will still not get it, but the book was created for you and others to begin the process of the revelation. You are the messenger of the good news, but *A Course* was sent first to open people up to the possibility.

Some of your early readers will be those who study and follow Williamson's teachings. They will visualize almost immediately what you are saying and what is now happening. Others will need more time to absorb and interpret. It is not necessary for folks to go back and study *A Course in Miracles*, although some may want to and it may certainly help them. The information contained in this book and its companion, *The Nature of God: The Revelation*, will comfort people by explaining their purpose and the reason for suffering, as well as reassuring them of a loving God and a spiritual team to assist them. These notions will also benefit the dead, for as more people on earth live their truth, the more easily their ancestors can ascend.

> *Tell me more.*

Ancestors exist in a realm that is divine but not heavenly. They know peace but do not live in the full vibration of love like God. They offer support to loved ones on earth because it helps their souls grow to their ultimate purpose—to be one with God again in the heavenly realm. You can reassure people, as many mediums and others have already, that their loved ones are in a safe place on the "other side," always looking over and helping and loving them.

Ancestors are not constrained by space and time, so they can help all their family members at the same time—nieces and nephews, sons and daughters, fathers and mothers, grandparents (yes, babies look after their parents and grandparents!), and so on. There is no end to ancestors' love, and their earthly connections with you carry over into the spiritual realms. They still feel the same love for you that they felt on earth and want to see you be happy.

> *Wow! That sounds incredible!*

This universe is an amazing place—the heavenly realms, the spiritual realms that are not quite heavenly yet, and the earthly realms. Each has its special place and purpose and all are to be admired and appreciated.

> *I'm thinking about how I am going to get all this great information into the world.*

Your books, my dear.

> *How do I edit* The Nature of God? *It sounds so crazy.*

You do not edit it at all. Write a preface explaining that this was channeled from the heavenly father and divine mother and that because you were a new channel, the information sometimes came through in confusing ways. This is as it should be, for each individual's own awakening will be similarly chaotic. Messages will appear bewildering and disjointed until people learn to sort out the vibrations. Explain this in the preface and then refer readers to this section, which is ever more coherent and concise because you are becoming a clearer channel. Vibration is raised with practice, and you have been training for months (years, really!) to connect with us. You have studied in earnest, taking many classes and reading a lot.

Provide a list of resources—the classes and books—for readers to consult for additional information. As we have said, other people's paths will not be the same as yours, but if they feel drawn to your experience, the citations will help them. Remind them to ask us, and we will guide them to materials and people who will help them on their journey back to God and to connecting with us, the angels.

> Will you help me write the preface?

Talk to God about that. He will dictate for you. It will be very easy, just as the introduction was.

> Wow! That's great. Channeling is so much easier than thinking of what to say.

We are here to make it easy for you. Talk with God now for the preface. It will ease your mind.

> Will do. Thanks, Michael.

You are welcome, my child.

June 14, 2019
Second entry

> I wrote the preface with God. Thank you.

You are welcome.

> I also worked for a while and then lay down over my lunch break. I felt like I was supposed to.

Yes, my child. That was so Raphael and I could give you some healing—me to strengthen and Raphael to calm you. Your energy was out of sorts from so much channeling this morning. That is why you thought for a moment that you were the "messenger of the revelation." You pulled out the Bible to see the reference to Philadelphia and thought this related to the second coming of Christ. It does, in that your first channeling of Jesus back in September of 2007 was in Philadelphia and that the Bible says that one of the places the revelation will start is Philadelphia.

You and others are the first to write about the good news. The others are spread over the globe and you do not know them, nor will you. They will broadcast the message in their parts of the world, just as you will in yours. This is not to say that your writing will not become world famous, because it will, but different personalities are required to bring all the sheep into the fold. So yes, you are A messenger of the revelation but not THE messenger of the revelation. Once people start to read your writing, some of them will take up the mantle and become envoys. They will share the good news of what you have written with God, and the excitement will spread like wildfire.

It is important for you to ground between these lengthy writing sessions. Take breaks and walk in the grass, phone a friend, or do household chores to balance out the energy. Soon you will be able to tell when you need to ground, but for now, just follow our guidance. We will alert you to rest.

Now is a good time to take a break. Look at the link Lois sent you about publishing, but do not work on it yet. Just see what will be coming and then relax. It will all unfold in divine right timing, so you don't need to feel rushed or pressured. WE will help you with each step along the way so it will be easy. No worries, as you like to say!

Guardian Angels Illuminate Our Route

June 15, 2019

>Good morning, Michael.

Good morning, Dear. I asked God to send you my way, as you need me today.

>I do? But I feel OK.

You need to have more love for yourself and for others.

>I guess I could always have more love, but I have been feeling more love for myself and others a lot lately.

True, but you still need to be reconciled.

>What does that mean?

Your ego still takes charge sometimes. It keeps you wrapped up in writing this book and other tasks have fallen aside.

>Steve and I spent time together last night, and I took a break and was outside listening to music. I made some phone calls and ran some errands, and all was good.

But you did not do much work on your job yesterday.

> *I know. I wanted to focus on our writing.*

But you need to also focus on your job for now. It is the right thing to do, and it helps to keep you grounded.

> *I have been doing a lot at work lately, so I didn't think it was a problem to concentrate on writing yesterday.*

I understand. You are a hard worker and accomplish a lot, but some days you get distracted by working on the book when you should be working on work.

> *"Work on work." I will remember this.*

You have a lot to wrap up before you leave your position, and it will be a little while still. Do not get so preoccupied that you let your performance slip. It is important that you continue to do a good job there. I know you want to, but you get distracted with me, and God, and your writing.

> *But that is my primary commitment now.*

It is, but for now you need to maintain balance and do both.

> *Heard and understood. When I get distracted at my job and want to write, I will snap back to the work projects I need to do. I will take my lunch and breaks but make sure I'm concentrating on my tasks when I'm working.*

Good. Now that that is settled, let's talk about what I really want to talk about today—LOVE.

> *That sounds like a great topic. Much better than work.*

It is. By love, I mean not just *eros* (romantic love), but *philia* (love between friends), *storge* (family love), and *agape* (universal love of God

THE NATURE OF GOD

and neighbors). There are lots of people in the world to love, as well as those not on the earthly plane—ancestors and angels, and as I said, God, divine mother and heavenly father.

What would you like us to know?

Philautia—love of self. Self-love may be the most important of all because it is only when you love yourself that you have the CAPACITY to love others. *Philautia* comes first.

How do you love yourself, especially when you may feel unworthy?

You remember your spiritual nature. ALL PEOPLE have the love of God, the spark of the divine, within them. Yes, all caps—EVERY PERSON IS SECURE IN THE LOVE OF GOD. No matter how bad you think you are, the wrongs you have committed, the negative feelings you have of yourself or others have of you, you are still a beloved child of God—NO EXCEPTIONS. This is a point that bears repeating over and over and over again. So often people believe they are unlovable, and this is just not possible. Although they may not feel love for themselves or from others in the earthly realm, it is important to know that they have the unconditional love of God, their divine mother and heavenly father, and the infinite number of angels.

The primary angel humans should begin working with is their guardian angel. Everyone has a guardian angel, a single energetic entity with masculine and feminine qualities. As you know, yours is Jim/Johnetta. You have seen them as beings of light.

I have. It took me months to know their names, and at first I thought they were kind of funny!

Their names are as they should be, and you will learn more about this later. For now, let's help others learn to connect with guardian angels, as that will help them find and stay on their paths. Everyone's guardian angels were created when their souls were incarnated by Mother and Father God. Guardian angels love unconditionally the person they are assigned to. No matter what you say or do, your guardian angel is always there—loving you, cheering you on, working to help you find your path back to who you truly are. They are your champion.

Constantly seeking guidance directly from God, guardian angels make sure to help you in the most effective and beneficial ways. BUT for their efforts to be most meaningful, you need to ask for their help. There is only so much they can do without a person's permission because they can't interfere with free will—that is, your human will, your current desires. They know your SOUL'S desires, but only God . . .

OK, I've stopped typing again.

One moment . . . I am thinking. . . . This is not to be known yet. There will be more on this later, but let's just finish up with the guardian angels' role and the importance of connecting with them. As you have done, people can use oracle cards. The deck you used from Denise Linn, the Gateway Oracle deck, is a great one but certainly not the only one. People can do a Google search for "angel oracle cards," pay attention to what they are drawn to, and use those.

It is hysterical that Archangel Michael is telling people to GOOGLE . . . LOL!

Yes, Dear, we are not antiquated.

I had to spell check this word . . . LOL.

Keeping you on your toes.

You are funny!

I know. Anyway, we angels and God know all the ways of modern life—we created them, in fact. Humans thought them into being, but God and I created the possibility of the world as it is today, with all its technology and advancements. Of these, we are well versed and aware. Even your rocket scientists can pray to us for guidance on a project and we will spark ideas they can implement. It will be phenomenal!

But I digress . . . back to guardian angels. People should begin their connection to the angels by building a relationship with their guardian angels. Yes, everyone CAN and will do this! You can even have a two-way conversation. It starts with "training wheels" like the oracle cards, with you asking a question and the answer coming through the cards. Or people can journal—write down a question and see what answer comes from their guardian angel. You did all of this with Karan. We gave her instructions on exactly what to do, step by step, for you and your classmates in her Angelic Healer certification course to unite with us. She knows how to facilitate these connections and will be doing this for many going forward.

Courses like Karan's will be helpful but not absolutely necessary, as you are going to give enough instructions in this book (manual, really) to enable people do it on their own. Although easy, connecting takes time, as you have experienced. It is like learning a new language, and it requires DESIRE and DEDICATION. If people truly want to connect with the angels and God (which they do whether they know or admit it or not), they will. The dedication will come for people in divine right timing. Some are ready now, and some will need more time, and either way is OK with God, the angels, and me. We know divine right timing is perfect, and we trust that all will be well.

> *So, for connecting with their guardian angels, people should ask for help, then look for signs and synchronicities?*

Feathers may alert them that their angel is there, or they may see a vision or light orb. Some people sense a vibration or just "know" things the angels are saying, although usually this takes a little while, as it did for you, Michelle. When you did the exercise of asking questions and writing what came to mind, you weren't sure at first whether it was real or true. Later these became coherent messages from your guardian angel. You just followed the instructions, and now you pull these notes often as reminders of the love and information I have for you.

By the time this book comes out, Karan will have published the questions others can ask their guardian angels. They can Google her too . . . LOL.

> *OK, Michael. What else?*

That is enough for today. Go work with God to write the description for your first book, *The Nature of God: The Revelation*. People should know that you are working on two volumes concurrently. The first is almost finished, and this one will come soon after. They will be companions, as God and the angels are companions to one another in the heavenly realm.

Have a good day at angel class, my dear. Your classmates will be delighted to hear about your endeavors, and you will be surprised and

Michelle McCann

delighted at what is developing for them as well. SO EXCITING, the work that group will do. Can't wait for things to unfold, although remember, it is all in divine right timing. No need to rush it.

Got it! Have a good day too, Michael.

As I always say, I always do!

June 17, 2019

Good morning, Michael. God asked me to come talk with you.

Yes, my child. I am here to strengthen you with my words and with my energy. Spending this time writing with me means that you are connecting with my energy, and that is healing for you. Although you don't yet feel the difference, this is indeed influencing your energy field. One day soon you will perceive the difference and it will be, as God says, Glorious!

What do I need to do to learn to feel this?

There is nothing to do. As time goes on, you will begin to just feel it, like you felt vibrations from Raphael and me when you were lying in bed. Eventually you will begin to notice even while you are busy with other activities. Trust me, it will be soon. You may even be feeling a little now.

I think I feel something, but it's not clear.

PAY ATTENTION and you will notice. As with the angel lights, it took a while at first to "see" us and to "know" it was us. It came to you gradually, as this will. The process will be this way for all people. They will learn about how it works from reading about your experience.

Michael, I feel sad again. I am crying. I miss you and Father and Mother and am ready to be reunited.

As God said, this is a loss to grieve. It is OK to feel sad and to cry.

I am really crying now.

Yes, my child, that is me helping you to feel your heartache and release it. As your friend and former supervisor Lydia says, "The crying is not the hurt, it is the healing." This is important for all to know. We gave humans the tool of weeping as a mechanism of release. It is an important one. Talking with people about your feelings is one way, but weeping is the easiest way—available to people at any time—to relieve distress. All they need to do is think about the issue and feel their feelings, and cleansing tears will come. It is SO IMPORTANT to teach people it is OK to cry.

Teachers and parents need to STOP telling kids to quit crying. Instead they should say, "You must be sad. Let me sit with you until you feel better," and just let them cry. That is all. There is nothing more anyone need do. Children will ease their own discomfort through crying. They will be relieved when the hurt is released and can then do something joyful. But they cannot return to happiness—true happiness that is, not being faked—until they release the sadness through tears.

Your brother needs to do this—sob out his frustrations and pain over how hard his life has been. His childhood, his period of addiction, losing the mother of his children, the time he was separated from his kids are all traumas he needs to process and release to mend. You can tell him that Archangel Michael is working with him (yes, I am) and says for him to bawl and scream when he is upset. This will help teach his boys that strong men can cry. They need to release their trauma too. Your brother can help them do that by just being with them, showing compassion for them missing their mother, and encouraging them to cry when they are sad.

I know you are thinking: This is helpful, but will I need to remove it from the book? Don't worry about that. We will help with necessary edits when the time comes. And it truly won't be long. For sure, a few months feels like an eternity right now when you just want to relax and BE with us, but I promise it will go quickly. Kind of like your angelic healer class—twenty-two months sounded like a long time when you first started, but you are already halfway through! Just a few more months.

Tell Lois that the price for the combined book will be $11.11, the number of awakening, and as we said before, your future books will be $12.12, the number of the Christ Consciousness.

Good advice, Michael. I do feel calmer now.

That is my energy, my strength, saying, "YOU CAN DO THIS!" You are a hard worker and will persevere when it comes to something important, as this is. I know it is hard getting up early and sometimes you feel tired, but as I work to strengthen you, this will become less burdensome. You will need less sleep and be able to interact with your family, do your work (in the short term), be with God and me, and write. It must feel like a lot, and it is, but it will go quickly, and soon you will have the freedom to rest.

The time is 5:55. Is this a message for me?

Yes! 555 is the number of abundance, along with 444, which you have seen a lot. The only difference is that 555 relates to a sense of accomplishment for bringing about that bounty. You are working hard for your dreams to come true, and the 555 reflects that your time to rest is nearing. All you have toiled for is coming to fruition. Relax and know that good things are in your life now and even better days are ahead.

That sounds great.

Do not focus on what you do not have (freedom from your job). Enjoy the times you do have there for now. Aspects of your job, such as the companionship of your colleagues, are enjoyable, and you will miss them when you have the freedom to write full time. Of course, through your writing you will develop wonderful new colleagues, many of whom you have admired for years and looked to as your guides and mentors. You will be peers and share ideas about how to get God's message out to people so they can heal and "be reconciled."

By reconciled, do you mean be one again, not separate from God?

Yes. People can be reconciled with God's energy in the earthly realms once they learn how. You are reconciled, and through your writing, will show people the way. Actually, it will be the angels who illuminate the route, but people will learn it is possible through you. As we have said before, each person's path is different, but your experience will provide reassurance that it is indeed possible to connect with God in this earthly realm.

> It will be wonderful to see so many people bonding with God and with their ancestors and spirit guides and angels.

It will be GLORIOUS!

> You guys love that word, don't you?

Yes, it is an uplifting word. One of my favorites, after Love, Hope, Faith, and Charity. As God said, we are still learning your words. They are not used in the heavenly realms, but we do find words to be fun and interesting. Kind of like laughter. Words can bring a smile to someone's face and can help support and bring them comfort when they are suffering. Words are beautiful and touching at times. We love when people use words to help others. They are a beautiful co-creation.

> I would love to talk to John Van Auken and Kevin Todeschi at Edgar Cayce's Association for Research and Enlightenment (ARE) about this. That is where I first learned that we are co-creators with God.

You could have many interesting conversations with them in the future, but it is not time yet. Focus on the tasks at hand—your work, family, friends, spiritual development courses, and connection and writing with us. That is enough, don't you think?

> My plate is pretty full.

When you have more free time, you will connect with them and spend time at the ARE, which has a lovely energy. You will delight in being there by the sea in that place founded and created by your spirit guide, Edgar Cayce. You and he are part of the same soul family. His soul was also created to be a "reconciler," bringing people back to God. Edgar will not reincarnate again, as his work, to bring you and others to the reconciliation, is complete. He is here in heaven with me.

> Not in the spirit realms?

No, Edgar is in heaven with us (your divine mother and father), Jesus, and Saint Francis.

Are there others in the heavenly realm?

Not yet. Edgar and Saint Francis just joined us, as their task of leading you to your vocation is now complete. That is how it works—each person plays a part, like you talked about in the "divine play." Every person signed on for a role when their souls were incarnated. Your role, like those of Edgar and Saint Francis, was as "reconciler." Others will need to discover their parts and which soul groups they belong to. Their interactions will manifest these.

Cristina Aroche and Catharine Han are "angelic healers." Along with Karan, they helped reveal your role. Although angelic healing led you to your role, it is not your mission. Of course, you can still use your knowledge to help others, friends and family, with healings, but on a world scale, this is not your calling.

I'm getting a little tired.

This has been a good session. Why don't you go rest for a bit before you have to shower and get ready for work?

That sounds good. Thank you, Michael, as always, for your love and support.

OH, and you are going to love my movie! It is a good depiction of me as not perfect (though I am actually perfect). I am learning the ways of humans, and this shows me as someone who loves the human pleasures, which I do. I get to experience them through you, which I find to be a lot of fun.

Interesting. I'll try to watch it soon. Thanks again.

Thank you, my dear.

Everything Falls Into Place

June 18, 2019

Good morning, Michael. I feel like I am supposed to talk to God this morning, but just wanted to say thank you for coming to me and calming me this morning. I felt a little unsettled and called on you to calm me, and now I feel better.

You are welcome, my child. Yes, please go talk to God. I appreciate you taking the time to write this down and say thank you. We will talk again soon.

June 19, 2019

Good morning, God. Michael sent me to talk to you.

Yes, my child. We are both here to talk to you today. You need more strengthening and calming. The idea of blogging (or rather, adding a blog to your to-do list on top of writing with us each morning) has you feeling a little overwhelmed. Not to worry—we will help you find the time, as we have been working with you on divine right timing for a while now. Trust that we will call you to do whatever you need to do when you need to do it. We will also continue to help you balance our work with your earthly life, being with your friends and family, and doing your job. For example, last night we put the blogging course in your path and it fit perfectly into your schedule.

This will happen more and more. Things will just fall into place, but really, we are placing them there. You found Lois to publish your book because we set up that opportunity. It is magic orchestrated by us, the angels. Not just me, but ALL the angels, whom I have said before are an infinite number. We are there for every moment, every step of the way. If you call on us, you can have whatever you wish (that is, anything for your highest good and your soul's enlightenment).

Once you are on your path and it feels so good to be "in the flow," you will want no other choices. You will leave the decisions up to us and just follow our lead. Remember the song "Queen of the Slipstream" by Van Morrison? This will be you and all our children. Following us, you will slip into the stream of the universe, or as Esther Hicks and Abraham call it, "the flow" or "the vortex." Life becomes truly magical and wondrous. Sometimes it takes time, and there may be some setbacks, as this is part of the process. But caught up in the flow, you won't mind at all because divine guidance will assure you that this is your purpose and place.

We know you want to be free of a nine-to-five job eventually and writing and speaking when you feel ready, but for now you continue, knowing that is what we want for you.

> *Yes, it does feel like I was able to concentrate well yesterday, and I got a lot accomplished.*

That is because you know we want you to do that. Be with your work for now, and continue to put in good effort to keep things in line there. You needed a sort of "come to Jesus" moment . . . LOL. We love that expression!!! But I digress . . . talking with us and writing the book distracted you and made it hard to focus on work. Now that we have told you that you need to do this, it is easier.

> *What else is there to know, Michael?*

Nothing more at this time, Child. That is enough for today. Email your friend Elizabeth, write to Christina now or later if you don't go to the work happy hour. Up to you, depending on how you feel. It will be fun, but it is OK to skip if your body says to rest or if you want to look at your website for updates or order business cards.

> *I don't know what business cards would say.*

They will say, "Michelle McCann, Author and Divine Channel."

> Really? Should I order them?

Sure, pick a design. That will be fun. Include your website and email address.

> I don't know what address to use. Maybe I could talk to Lois or her webmaster about how to set up email on my website, so I could have the address me@michelledmccann.com?

That would be GREAT. Start fresh with a new business email!

> Thank you, Michael. Have a wonderful day. I know you always do!

Yes, indeedy . . . LOL.

June 21, 2019

GOOOOD MOOORRNING! [Michael singing to me.]

> Wow, Michael, you seem very excited this morning.

Darn tootin'.

> Really, "Darn tootin'"?

Come on, it's a funny expression!! I LOVE IT! We're going to have some fun writing your first angel blog this morning. I want people to know that we can be cool, not always so serious. In fact, having fun is our favorite thing to do, much like humans. We will talk about this in the blog. Start a new document for the blog series. Be with you in a sec in that doc!

Michelle McCann

> WOW! That was fun. You are so wacky, Michael. My spirits ARE lifted just by talking with you.

It is my job to lift your spirits, but it doesn't feel like a job. It is FUN!!!! I LOVE IT and I LOVE YOU!

> Awesome! I love you too!!!

June 25, 2019

> Good morning, Michael. I have missed you these last few days!

I have missed you too, my child. You are doing well. I'm proud of you for being so strong yesterday. The old triggers came up at first and fear reared its head, but you worked through that and stood firm, which is EXACTLY what you needed to do. Mama needs to face this, even though it is hard. You are helping her, even though it feels like you are causing her pain. Remember the child with cancer. . . . This is for Mama's highest good. Just be as gentle as possible and let her know you love her even when you disagree.

> I'm thinking about Shan and how her trip out will be.

It will be fine. After thinking about things, she is more open to listening. You will disagree, but she evokes less trauma than your mother, so you will not be triggered so strongly. Tell your side. She will listen and choose to disagree. Then you will laugh and have fun together, talking about your kiddos and how proud you are. Have some drinks and reminisce about your high school days.

Let's get started on the blog. It will be called "Michael's Top 10." Go on over to the blog page.

Thanks. That was quick and easy. I was a little unsure for a bit there.

That is because you have gone several days not connecting with me. But everything is OK. Now that you know how, it is like riding a bike. You always remember how, even if the bike has been in the garage for a decade.

Good analogy. So I got everything right?

Yes, good enough. A few things were a little different from what I was thinking, but I'm happy with the way it all turned out.

What else is there for me to know today?

Nothing from me. Go back to God and he will tell you more about your books.

OK, Michael. Thank you and love you.

Love you too, my child.

[Michael is giving me an image of dancing, like John Travolta in the Michael *movie.]*
LOL. You are so funny, Michael.

Yes, I love to laugh and to make people laugh. Go talk to God.

Thanks!

June 29, 2019

Good morning, Michael. God told me to come and talk to you. My vibration is low due to some things happening in my family.

Yes, I know, Dear. All will be fine. Not to worry. We are working with your mother at the higher levels, and she will come through this OK.

Wow, I feel lighter already.

YOU WILL have a relationship with your mother. TRUST that it will be resolved.

You know this?

I KNOW THIS!!!! It won't be long. She needs to hear that you love her despite all that happened and that it was part of a larger divine purpose. Talk to Steve first, just in case she tries to convince him you are relapsing. Do not worry. Steve may be skeptical, but he knows you are fine.

Sounds like God again…

It was. Back to Michael.

OK, Michael. I'm sensing that you have a joke for me.

Why did the chicken cross the road? To get to the other side.

That's a pretty old joke and not all that funny.

You didn't laugh? I think it is great—so simple. Just "to get to the other side." Maybe it's not that funny, but it is like life. Why do humans go through traumas? To get to the other side, and when you do, life is GLORIOUS!!!

It sorta sucks (OK, TOTALLY SUCKS) enduring ordeals, but now that you know they have a purpose, there's a better chance you can face them with joy (OK, maybe not joy but with acceptance). It's kind of like resigning yourself to labor pains to have a baby. You go into the labor room, knowing the next few hours might be rough but also expecting to come out the other side a changed person—a PARENT! Once you hold that precious infant in your arms, you will admit the pain was all WORTH IT!!!

> You make it sound so easy.

It can be EASIER, depending on your perspective. The process is the same for all, though no two paths are identical. Some people go into labor fearful and scared, making the birth harder and less enjoyable. Others (like you) expect everything will go smoothly, and even if there are complications, they have avoided one source of stress. When people recognize that God and I put struggles in their lives so their souls can grow, they can face those difficulties with grace.

If writing about the challenges with your mother makes you uncomfortable, don't publish those parts. We can write a blog about other family heartbreak. "The Nature of Suffering and Why God Lets Us Suffer" is certainly a worthwhile topic. There is lots to explore regarding your childhood traumas—losing your sister at a young age . . .

> It's funny . . . I don't think about that as much now, but it was a big trauma.

. . . and being diagnosed with and, for a while, HAVING a mental illness.

> Do you want to write it now? I'm interested.

Let's wait. You are back to overworking again and need to take care of yourself. Talk to Steve and tell him what has been going on with both your therapy and the book. Then talk to Mama. Steve can be there or not. If he hears your discussion, he won't question your sanity or wonder what was said that upset your mother.

> I just did the cord pushing meditation.

Glad you followed through on my suggestion. The exercise will help you stay clear-headed and calm with your mother. She needs your love and support now, and it is important that you not let past wounds and triggers provoke your anger. Stay in love and share that you understand this is hard for her.

> I'm thinking this is hard for ME. I fear that people will resist letting me stand in my truth. Because the

> specifics are hazy in my memory, it's hard to know what is true.
> This feels like God again.

It is. I know you need support, my child. I love you and am deeply sorry you had to suffer through such pain as a child. Although necessary so you could connect with me, it was still REALLY traumatic. Just watching you go through this was hard to bear—such an innocent child, all alone. That is your trigger now—if you tell the truth, you will be alone again. But that won't happen. Steve is not going to leave, and while she may be angry, Mama will not stop loving you. Even if you and she stop talking for a while, it doesn't mean that telling the truth wasn't the right thing.

Did Mama repress the memories? Yes. She COMPLETELY repressed the memories. Because she couldn't confront your father, she focused her energy on helping other men to stop abusing. None of this was deliberate, though. Mama's subconscious steered her to take action after her conscious mind refused. Even today, she is not aware of that—but she will be.

> She will?

Yes, my darling. You will tell her.

> Oh my, this is getting harder.

Trust me. This is the path you need to take (and what she needs to hear). Details of the abuse don't matter, and you can tell Mama you don't remember them. God is making sure you don't have to relive them. Bringing that horror back into your conscious memory serves no purpose. The abuse itself is not a trigger for you anymore. The trigger is your mother hiding the truth.

We have done enough for now. Sit with what we have told you. Pull some angel cards, reflect, and process. Distract yourself with email and Facebook for a bit too. But call your mother TODAY—this morning—to clear this anxiety from your energy field.

> OK. Thank you both. Love you and please help me get through this.

THE NATURE OF GOD

Not to worry, we are both right with you, one perched on each shoulder, as your mother says. We never leave you alone. Trust that.

July 8, 2019

> Hi, Michael. Just wanted to reach out. God says my vibration is low because I'm frustrated about wanting the book to move forward so I can leave my job. Plus, I'm upset about Mama. I felt your energy this morning as you reminded me to do all this out of LOVE, not for some outcome. I'm crying, thinking about it.
>
> I want to bring peace to people and be proud of my work. You reminded me to live my purpose, and that is my purpose. I just need to be who I truly am, wherever that takes me. Loving people around me. Having fun. Living in joy. Yes, I will try to get back to that, and your vibes made me feel better immediately.

That is right, my child. I helped "regulate" your energy, which was out of whack.

> LOL. "Out of whack" sounds funny coming from you.

I know! But it's true. It was NOT right. All the NYC negative energy with no grounding and so many people smashed into such a space. It zapped you, but you are recovering now. Your outlook is more positive since we connected this morning.

> I'm sorry I haven't written with you for a while, Michael. I'm not sure why. God hadn't told me to, and I was not myself.

That is OK. We will get back to a regular routine soon and write our next blog. Your energy will return quickly. Having the next few evenings free will help. Maybe we can connect then, depending on how you feel. Totally up to you. So glad to be reunited, and I will come to you again to help balance your energy and get everything back in order. Not to worry, my dear.

Call Steve and make your vacation plans. That will be fun.

> I'm on lunch break now and thought I'd ask if there was anything else you wanted to talk about.

Is there anything you want to talk about?

> Not really, I just wanted to be with you. I'm crying. My thoughts are having a battle in my head. It feels like I'm not channeling correctly. Instead, I'm getting all kinds of weird things about who I am and what has happened in history, spiritually speaking, to make the world the way it is now.

The answers keep eluding you. You want to unravel the mystery of life, but it is intended to be that—a mystery that unfolds. Would you want it to end before you finished reading your story? Sure, some people can't resist peeking at the ending, but not you. You want to savor the story first. You NEVER flip to the end of a book.

> You are right. I do love to be enthralled by the story.

And, so it shall be. A story unfolded. You would be sad to get to the end too soon. Just remember that surprises keep life fun! So yes, we are going to reveal many mysteries of the universe that you will share with the world. This will help LOTS of people. But it will happen in divine right timing. Pushing too hard and fast flummoxes you and your mind starts to make stuff up.

> How do I rein it back?

Do your best to stay in the flow. Let things unfold organically. Be happy. Enjoy life. Take one day at a time. Plan vacations. Big things are coming, but don't get caught up in the hype or you will forget to enjoy and savor the moments in your path now. Remember who you truly are—a person who wants to help others thrive. You can do that in your everyday interactions, whether or not you are famous yet.

I say "yet" because I want you to trust that your work will be disseminated WIDELY in the world and become the solution for many people. This is where you feel the urgency—you want to help people NOW. But it is not time yet. We know the divine right timing for things and the world isn't quite ready for your work. SOON, just not quite yet. Be patient, and in the meantime, enjoy the ride.

Thank you, Michael. This is helpful! It's kind of funny that God hasn't calmed me down about all this. I feel kind of like, why not? Why am I going through this?

My child, you are still going to "go through things" even though you are connected to us. It is part of your life plan. We need to keep challenging you in these ways so you grow. Trust and overcome and reconnect when you don't feel grounded or find yourself stumbling along. Your growth is nowhere near finished! You will grow your whole life! Even after your books are published and you connect more clearly and often with us, growth will dominate your to-do list. Otherwise, you'd be ready to die! And you definitely are a long way from that!

Sometimes, I just feel so "in the flow" and happy, and I would love to have that all the time.

You can, if you set your mind to it. If you let us guide you through your problems, we can help you overcome and CHOOSE to be happy. It is a choice. It sounds harsh sometimes, but it is true. This is not to say you don't need to process negative emotions—you do. Cry or talk or hit a pillow and GET THEM OUT, but then return to love and joy and FUN!

Now I'm wondering about the abuse. . . . Did I make it all up? Was it all confusion in my mind?

No, my child, it was all real. You are simply not remembering because it was too painful.

Will I remember?

Michelle McCann

That remains to be seen. In the meantime, just as with your book, let the memories unfold. Live your life, love your mother and your family, and see where the path leads.

> I will try. Thank you for your guidance and support. I am very grateful!!!

I know, Dear. Smooches.

> Love you!

3 p.m.

> Hi, Michael. Just talked with my friend whom I think of as pretty religious and was dismayed that she dismissed my writing. I thought she would be excited to read it.

You must expect that some people are not going to "get it" at first, or maybe ever, and that is OK. What you are sharing will touch a LOT of people and help them, just as Marianne Williamson's work did and does. Your religious friend couldn't get into her either. Some entrenched Christians will have a hard time facing that things are different from what they were taught. That is all right. Go forth and put this out into the universe and wait for the reverberation. Do not be discouraged. Change takes time.

> Got it. Thank you!

July 9, 2019

> Good morning, Michael. God told me to come talk to you. I have been worried about spending too much money. In my writing/channeling, God tells me everything is under control, but I wonder if I am confused. I have misinterpreted other things. Actually, I thought God was misleading me, but now I think it is my own stumble.

THE NATURE OF GOD

That is right, my child. God would never lie to you. It is your own mind that has caused the confusion and mixed messages. Your ego and your dark side sometimes get ideas that overshadow what God is communicating.

What do I do about this?

Practice, practice, practice. Listen for the word of God and see what resonates. If it doesn't make sense, know that your own ego is getting in the way.

What about other negative energies?

White light helps, so as God said, practice it several times a day.

What about the money?

Do not worry. You are well protected. It is not in your life plan to struggle financially. No matter what you do, money will not be a problem because that is not part of the flowchart laid out before you were born. Even when you had lower-paying jobs, finances were never a problem. Budgets always worked out. So it will be with this. Some of your savings will be depleted in the short run, which will make you nervous, but trust that the replenishment is on its way. You are not meant to be destitute or unable to afford to do and have the things you enjoy.

Relax and appreciate the scenery. Focus on being in the flow. Enjoy your day-to-day life. Walk with friends. Have an occasional glass of wine. Read. Write. Listen to music. Spend time with Steve cooking, going to the farm, visiting new restaurants and wineries, all of that.

Will we get back to the blogs? I was so excited about how those were going.

Soon. Those will be our focus while Jane works on your website and Susan edits your book. Continue to write daily with God and me, and we will add in the blogs here and there. They will become more regular soon. When your energy dissipated, we took a break to focus on getting you back to a higher vibration. You are almost there, but still have some things to work out with your mother. Talk to your therapist today about ways you can forgive Mama without judging.

So was I confused about being the first and last soul? The one who had the idea to separate from Mother and Father and go on this adventure? Or was I tapping into the collective?

No, you were not wrong on that point. Indeed, you were the soul who sparked the original separation and the one who will be the last to reconcile with God. In that sense, you ARE the alpha and omega. In reality, though, all souls are alpha and omega because we have endured the beginning of the severance and will experience the reconciliation. You are just the first and the last soul to do that in time and space.

So, I was the first human?

No, humanity evolved as the scientists describe. There was no Garden of Eden, ever, with any soul. Your mind made up the story that you were in the garden with Mother and Father God. But you were God's first child in the sense that you were the first to express the desire to know him, to be separate from him so you could understand his (rather, their—Mother and Father's) magnificence.

Yes, we keep forgetting to use "they" language. It is difficult even for us because currently they are separate—Father is still in heaven and Mother is of the earthly realm. But, THEY are one in the sense that their energy is intertwined.

I feel a little confused again.

OK, let's take a break. Just know that you are the soul who started the journey and will be the soul who ends it. That is why your numerology chart has so many 1s and 9s—the beginning and the end.

What else is there to know?

Nothing right now. You need to go soon to get ready to take Steve to the train. Back up your work, check your email, and POWER DOWN!

OK . . . LOL. You love the ALL CAPS!

YES. YES, I DO.

Love you, Michael.

Love you!

Breaking the Trauma Chain

July 9, 2019
Second entry

    Michael, should I do these empower activation calls?[21]

    YES! YES! YES! Both the coaching and this program will be helpful. In addition to Jamie, you will connect with others on the same path, awakening the collective unconscious. We want to bring it into the light. The ancient wisdom, secrets, history, and trauma all need to come to the surface and this will help.

    OK! I signed up. First call tonight.

    YIPPEE!!! You are gonna LOVE it! You will feel your vibration rise very quickly. That will help you release your judgment of Mama and of others who have different, destructive beliefs. Even though they are not heart-centered, you will generate more compassion for the pain they must be in to espouse such malignance.

    I hope so. I don't like having these feelings of judgment, but such hateful things cut to my core.

    It does hurt you. You feel it.

    I'm crying now.

---

[21] Small group conference calls in which participants connect energetically to amplify one another's light to heal and manifest intentions.

I know.

> This is God now, right?

Yes, my child. I am with you, providing comfort for the trauma you have witnessed and experienced in this lifetime and all the others. As the first soul, you have borne it ALL. You have seen it from every side, endured the highest highs and the lowest lows. Incarnated next after you, people with bipolar disorder have experienced similar highs and lows throughout their lifetimes.

> Tell me more about what you mean by incarnated, because you are not talking about being human.

No, the soul separated first before the human incarnation began. Souls existed in the earthly realm even though not yet in human bodies. They inhabited the earth first, then humans evolved from the . . .

> My typing has stopped.

This is not important. Just know that you were the first soul, and this is why your joy and your pain are so great. You felt the same suffering Jesus felt when he was persecuted.

> I'm trying but not quite comprehending this.

It's good that you are making the effort. You did not feel Jesus's pain until this lifetime when you thought you were Jesus and merged with his energy.

> I'm going to stop again. I'm getting out of sorts.

You are. Good! We are trying to help you distinguish what is and is not real, in the sense of our energy versus the energy of the collective. The collective felt the pain of Jesus's death, but you as an individual soul did not. Neither did we, your Mother and Father, feel it. We do not feel pain, per se, although we understand the pain you feel, if that makes sense.

> Not exactly.

THE NATURE OF GOD

Not important. Just know that we do not feel pain. We understand that it is difficult for you, but we don't "feel" it.

> *Another question—was I the first soul as part of the collective, or was it me as an individual?*

Both. You are an individual and collective soul, as is every soul. All felt the separation, but as the first, you suffered alone before your brothers and sisters were created.

> *OK. Trying to keep up again . . .*

That's not necessary here. Except for Jesus's, your suffering was the greatest because as the first, you experienced it by yourself. You paved the way for the others. It was difficult for them too, but because your soul was already in the collective unconscious, they had comfort and support. You were the only one to bear it alone.

6 p.m.

> *Had a good therapy session today. At first we weren't sure where to go with things. I just knew from earlier that I felt the pain of the collective and really struggled when Mama and others posted hateful things on Facebook. EMDR helped me realize that I want to feel loving and compassionate toward them, knowing that they are good at their cores, their cruelty coming from a place of pain. However, my emotional reactions are judgment and fear of speaking up. These stem from my childhood, of being afraid to tell my mother when Daddy was violent and worried that Mama wouldn't love me if I "disagreed" with her.*
>
> *During the session, I figured out that my fear was making me unlovable, and I confronted my tendency to judge myself harshly for negative reactions. I discovered that I can see people as good and disagree with their stances on subjects. They can still love me*

> and disapprove of my positions. Both can coexist. Also, I believed that asking for my soul to be separated had been a mistake but concluded that this was not true.

It is interesting how memories come together.

> Michael, is there anything you would like to share?

No, just to say GOOD WORK, Dear. You are doing a great job of assessing what needs to be addressed, and your therapist is doing an AWESOME job of helping you negotiate these issues. The worst is not over yet, but you have come far.

> Oh! I'm not happy to hear the worst is not over yet. It has been difficult!

I know. But you will get through it with support, both divine and earthly, and everything will be fine. You are safe in God's loving embrace at all times, and they never give you more than you can handle. And remember, you agreed to this as part of your soul plan when signing up for this lifetime. Knowing the process would be rough (but also delightful at times), you asked a lot of questions but still WANTED to do it. "NOW IS THE TIME," you said. You were ready for the reconciliation to begin and knew there would be some HEAVY LIFTING to advance it in this lifetime. You are doing GREAT! It is pushing forward. All the souls who signed up to "pioneer" the revelation/reconciliation are marching ahead and moving things quickly.

Although the current state of the world might seem to belie this, TRUST ME! Consciousness is rising at a RAPID pace. Even the surge of vegan and gluten-free foods is an example. The more conscious people become, the more they want to take care of themselves, each other, the animals, and the planet. Eating this way is just one method of doing that.

> You still have me a little worried over "the worst is not over yet."

I shouldn't really tease, but I couldn't resist. You were bound to ask about it.

THE NATURE OF GOD

The WORST IS OVER?!

Yes! You have processed so much and MOVED MOUNTAINS. Soon it will be time to reap the rewards. But first you must understand energetic boundaries and learn to clean and clear your energy regularly so it doesn't get confused with the collective. Being so plugged into that field, you have difficulty distinguishing what is self and what is not. Once this is resolved, it will be much easier to channel clearly. You are starting to, just not quite there yet.

Revisit Karan's teachings on cleansing and clearing, and YES, you NEED to do this. It sounds a little "out there" and "hokey," but Karan knows what she is talking about. Review your notes and start practicing—pulling white light, incense, salt baths, the house/space clearing, the whole nine yards. This IS A MUST!

And grounding. Spending time outside in nature is critical. Writing outdoors today is invaluable. I know you can't yet differentiate among the energies of different environments. But just as you don't notice negative vibrations entering your energy field, neither do you perceive the positive power of nature and how a natural environment bathes you in uplifting light. Birds singing, the wind caressing your skin—even if you aren't paying attention, it surrounds and permeates you.

> This all sounds good. So the never-ending question—What about the book? It seems nowhere near finished and is disjointed with stuff I'm not sure I should share.

Don't worry about it. Let Susan work her magic and see what transpires. It will be wonderful—TRUST ME! You will want to do some tweaking, but the finished product will be GREAT!

> Is there much more writing to be done?

Not much, but some. Just continue to get up and write every morning and periodically add it to what Susan is working on. You will know when the time is right to bring it to a close. IT IS CLOSE . . . LOL. CLOSE TO A CLOSE. Love words that have two meanings. Language is SO FUN!

> So you are a writer too, Michael???

Why, YES! YES, I AM! I have written all of this, haven't I???

> Why, YES! YES, YOU HAVE . . . LOL. Good thing you had me to type it all up for you, slacker.

HA!!! You are funny.

> No, YOU are funny!!!

OK. Now take a break and RELAX. You have worked hard today and for months now. Try to glide "in the flow." Let the magic transpire. IT WILL HAPPEN, and SOON!

> OK. Good night, Michael.

Good night, Dear. Talk to you soon!

July 17, 2019

> Hi, Michael. It has been several days since I wrote to you directly, although you joined in while I was writing with God for The Nature of God. I pulled an angel card from the oracle deck I use to receive messages from you. "Break the Chain" concerns ancestral patterns, healing, and rewriting the future. I definitely am bumping up against some negative energy about standing firm for what I know to be true and right.

Yes, Dear, this is true. You are the one who will break the cycle of abuse and silence (ancestral and present) in your family.

> How do I do this?

Continue to speak up about what you know to be true.

> Is this God?

THE NATURE OF GOD

Yes, Dear, this is a conversation for me. You will need to talk with your family about some of the truths they are not facing.

I was planning to just have fun on vacation.

You need to discuss it. Don't belabor it, but at least don't avoid it entirely.

What do I need to address?

It's up to you. There is no need for rancor, but at least share what you are doing.

Anything else?

NOPE, not at the moment.

OK, that is Michael.

YEPPERS. I'm jumping in to give you a little lift, a BOOST, a HIP HIP HOORAY! YOU CAN DO THIS!!!! Don't back down or be afraid. It is the fear that brings down your vibe. Just tell it like it is. You are an AUTHOR and DIVINE CHANNEL and others can think WHATEVER they want. You just need to communicate your truth and how you feel. TELL EVERYONE, ANYONE WHO WILL LISTEN!

You don't have to broadcast on the street . . . LOL.

But I do! As you talk to folks, SHARE! SHARE what is happening with you. Trust that you will be OK, even if they don't believe or think you are out of your gourd. Look to Laurie as an example. When she first came out as a psychic and channel, people weren't sure what to do with her either. Now she has the admiration of LOTS of people for the love and support she has given them in connecting with the spiritual realms. It might be helpful to talk to her about her "coming out" story.

I would love to talk with Laurie. You know what? Kind of a random thought . . . but I'm wondering—are you and God inside me? Or outside?

INSIDE!

Really? In my body?

Yes, as ENERGY in and around your body. We are not across the room, up in the heavens or the sky. Our vibrations enfold and encompass human bodies.

Are you other places?

We are EVERYWHERE and in EVERYTHING!

Interesting. I'm not sure how that works, and maybe I'm not supposed to know now, but I was curious.

Yes, that was me who planted that seed of curiosity. I wanted you to start to think about it, but let's not go into too much detail now. Just know we are definitely "inside" you. All the love and strength you need are within!!!!

Thank you!

July 20, 2019

Good evening, Michael! My angel class, all about Archangel Uriel, just ended. Though I felt OK in class, I've been a little unsettled all day.

Yes, Dear, you are still anxious about "coming out" to your family, to your angel friends, to your psychic development friends, TO THE WORLD!!! Keeping that secret limits everyone's soul growth and needs to come to light.

Oh boy. I have one foot in the closet and one out.

Yes, Dear, we are letting you take your time, as we know this is difficult given your diagnosis. Of course, your mental illness was actually you connecting with spirit as you processed trauma. Besides Jesus and Mary, you also integrated with the "Eve energy" (we call it

THE NATURE OF GOD

this since Eve did not really exist). Belief in the banishment of Eve from the Garden of Eden is strong in your culture, so it was easy to tap into.

The notion that you did something "bad" or are "bad" was perpetuated in the Bible, and people have believed the story. This is as intended. Although God was one divine energy then, they disunited so Mother could be in the earthly realm and Father in the heavenly one. When the reconciliation is complete they will reunite. All souls will return to their loving embrace before the earthly realm no longer exists.

Again, remember, this world was created as your "playground," your place to experiment with feelings, experiences, and relationships, and to appreciate the universal law of cause and effect (karma). You have learned much. All humans have learned MUCH! Now it is time for the learning to end and for the reconciliation to begin. Each soul has a special and crucial role to play in the reconciliation. The puzzle will not be complete until all the souls stand in their rightful places. You must START the trend by standing in yours.

> *I'm not sure I understand exactly what this means or how it happened, as much as I have written about it.*

Let me explain. As pure energy, you were intertwined with Mother and Father God. Then God cut the energetic cord that connected you to the heavenly realm. You found yourself a spirit, all alone in the earthly realm, searching and searching for someone to find you, join you, be with you. Through telepathy you "knew" it was because you had done something wrong. This was NOT TRUE but put into your mind to begin the process for all the souls to separate.

It wasn't long before Mary joined you. Apart from God, you were like a child, inconsolable. It was as if you lost your favorite teddy bear and could not get it back. Mary comforted and consoled you as any mother would. Even though it helped having that nurturing mother figure with you, the feeling of having done something catastrophically horrific was unbearable. You did not stay a spirit for long, choosing instead to incarnate on earth, where there were other humans.

> *This is so confusing.*

It is not important to get caught up in the details of human incarnation but rather to understand the energetic separation and the feelings it caused. This explains your hesitance to come forth about who you truly are. You don't want to feel the shame and anguish again. Your subconscious remembers (and now your conscious mind is beginning to, as well) the TRAUMA and the PAIN.

Is this still Michael?

It is both of us, Dear. We are working together (tag-teaming . . . ha ha) to help you sort this all out.

So how do we sort it all out?

We will help you, a step at a time. You have come this far, haven't you?

Yes, I have come a long way, but boy, this just seems HUGE. I am afraid.

Of course you are, but have FAITH in us. TRUST US. We will make sure everything is OK. It is not in your life plan to suffer any longer. The time for joy and peace is here, and you are ALMOST ready. While in human form you will have doubts and fears, but call on us—as you most certainly will because you LOVE and TRUST us—and we will come running! Actually, we don't run, but you get the gist! FASTER THAN LIGHTNING! WE will be there to comfort, support, and guide your path.

I'm feeling a little tired and overwhelmed. I think I need to shut down and just sit with this. Maybe go to bed and just rest.

Good idea. You are taking in a lot right now and thinking about next steps. Try not to think about the future and instead focus on what an amazing thing you have done. You have returned to us from your separation. This has been a LLLONNNGGG time coming!!! Ages and ages—in the earthly realm, anyway. In the heavenly realm there is no time, but for you and all the other souls, it feels like FOREVER. But not to fear, the waiting (and the pain) will soon be over! Now, go rest and we'll talk tomorrow. Pay attention to your dreams tonight. We will visit.

OK. Roger that.

Night-night.

July 21, 2019

> *I was just rereading your suggestion to pay attention to my dreams. Was there a special message?*

No, we just wanted you to go to sleep. Since you love dreams and their interpretation, we gave you something to look forward to. All dreams have significance, and experiencing them helps process trauma. Analyzing them is helpful and fun but not necessary. It is simply the act of dreaming that helps people to reunite with God. The work is done automatically while you sleep. Though the true reconciliation has not yet occurred, REM sleep is a moment of reconciliation each night. It keeps the energetic cord tied to the heavenly realm.

We wanted you to ask about this so we could make it clear that it is as Mother and Father God intended. You are connected to Divine Mother when you are awake and to Heavenly Father when asleep. In addition, you maintain a constant bond with both, but at those times you feel the energetic cord in your subconscious, rather than your conscious mind. The soul knows that you are united, and that is what is important.

> *So, is our subconscious our soul?*

In a way. It is where the imprint of your soul's plan is housed. We are working on bringing it to light now for all souls. There is so much darkness at the moment, so much hate. The darkness needs to be transmuted into light to make room for the love. Enlightened individuals are already doing this. For example, hate speech abounds, but so do people (like yourself) standing up in love and protection for those who are being denounced. That is the love vibration stepping forward, coming to light to "fight" the darkness.

For all of us to be reconciled, we have to look at our ugly, dark parts. No part of my children is actually "ugly," but people judge it as such. You are beautiful souls in human form who make "wrong" choices sometimes. And by wrong, I simply mean choices that are not for the highest good of yourself and others.

Just Ask the Angels

This message is from God and Archangel Michael, as channeled by Michelle McCann on March 13, 2020

Thank you again for joining us on this journey! You now know how to connect with your guardian angel and other angels and how to make the most of those relationships. Angels are like your very own personal assistants, whom you can call on to protect you, help you live your best life, and guide you to God. Remember, all you have to do is ASK.

We hope you received ideas to comfort your head and your heart, given the current trials and tribulations of your lives and the world around you. There is SO MUCH JOY TO BE FELT and experienced in the earthly realms, and we hope that the "Angels" part of this book has given you some nuggets of wisdom to help you as you navigate this tough terrain. Yes, there are struggles and losses that often seem difficult to bear, but as the Bible says, God never gives you more than you can handle. It is important to note here that what Michelle is saying does not go against the Bible, but that the Bible is incomplete. There are references that should have been stricken from the record and stories that were never told, such as the Gospel of Mary Magdalene.

As subsequent reading, we recommend the book *Mary Magdalene Revealed* by Meggan Watterson. Michelle has not yet read this book, but she will, and will detail more from us on this subject (and much more) in future writings. Stay tuned to this bat place and this bat channel for more to come from Michelle. May you take pleasure and comfort in our words, and may you have joy in your hearts knowing that soon, each of you, and the world, will be at PEACE.

Love, God and Michael

P.S. YES! You can picture me as John Travolta in my movie *Michael*. I love that image!

Part III

The Reconciliation

By

God, Archangel Michael, and Michelle McCann

Wrap It Up with a Bow

This is it! You are nearing the end (at least of this book!). Michelle will continue to write much more to help you strengthen your connection to us—your divine mother, your heavenly father, the angels, and all the beings in the spirit realms, including loved ones and ancestors. This section is primarily to bring some closure to the ideas presented thus far. There will be nothing new and "earth-shattering," but you will find that these words will "tie a bow" on what you have learned so far. Read CAREFULLY and DILIGENTLY, as these words are IMPORTANT. They are the final "keys in the lock" to reveal what you need to do to connect with us, live a truly happy and peaceful existence, and find joy and magic in everyday life. This life here on earth may seem mundane compared to the spirit realms, but TRUST US, it is not. Earth is a "divine playground" where you learn SO MUCH to help your soul grow and to build loving and AMAZING connections to us and to one another.

This is no small potatoes . . . LOL. We love your phrases! OK, this is Michael jumping in here! God is just humoring me. Proceed, Michelle.

God: Actually that is all, Michael. We are done here. Stick a fork in me!

Michael: Ha ha! Yes, I know you love my humor too!

God: We all do. I can't wait for all our children to HEAR YOUR VOICE and to experience the humor and delight you can bring to their lives.

Michael: OK, peeps! Get ON IT! I have so much to teach and share with you! READ ON! That is all for now. Keep calm and carry on!

The Freedom of Embracing My Truth

July 21, 2019

I'm starting a new section per your request! I'm not sure where to start.

There is still MUCH work to be done. OK, not THAT MUCH!! But some. 😊 Not to worry—we will make it easy for you. We are helping Susan with the editing, inspiring her words and her organization of the writing so it will be just as we want it to be. We've got it all under control!

Now I'm wondering how to tell Steve.

JUST TELL HIM! It will be TOTALLY FINE. He won't be worried. It is YOU who is worried about everyone's reactions. You are stable and fully grounded. There is no need for concern that Steve or others will doubt what you write. Remember that this is a defense mechanism to avoid accepting the TRUTH.

The truth shall set you free. It will set all my children free. When my children live in their TRUTH, the TRUTH of WHO THEY TRULY ARE, they will experience total FREEDOM—freedom from pain, suffering, doubt, all of it. FREEDOM to be full of FAITH. Of course, there will be no need for FAITH anymore because everyone will know, as you do, that we are real, we are here, and we are connected to you and DIRECTLY supporting you.

All you need to do is ask to receive answers or guidance. You KNOW what we want you to do and how to be in alignment with our will. It is being your authentic self that opens your connection with Mother/Father God and to the angels (who guide you back to this connection and help you to open up to who you truly are). This is why your angel classes with Karan have been so powerful for you and the others in the group. You are opening up to help and guidance from the angels so we can MAKE MIRACLES HAPPEN!

Just look at you! You're talking with and writing about us, and you have a website, an editor, a publisher, a photographer, and a tribe of people who support you fully! You are truly blessed! All because you opened yourself up to be blessed.

Now, if you could just stop worrying about MONEY! TRUST US!!! You have plenty to get you by until your book sales take off. It won't be long.

> How long? Can I know?

It remains to be seen. You have plenty of money to get you through until then, when all this REALLY TAKES OFF! It will take time to finish the writing, editing, and publishing. In the meantime, you will set up email and social media and people will FLOCK to get your book! You just wait!

> Please continue to guide me in setting up social media and what to do with email.

Jane is all ready to help you. Pay her to help you! You will be fine financially, and she will do a great job.

July 22, 2019

> Good morning, God and Michael. Guessing you will both be "talking" to me today?

Yes, Dear. You will know when each of us is talking. It is not important to distinguish unless you feel the need to speak to one of us specifically.

> I just wanted to say it is still dark out. It is 5:05 a.m. but I can see the moon through the trees.

This is as it should be. We want you to feel the moon's energy today.

> What is that for or what does that mean?

You will meet with your family today but still harbor negative energy related to trusting that they will support you in your new spiritual endeavors. THEY WILL SUPPORT YOU! It is only your worry getting in the way. The moon's energy helps cleanse and clear old energies or vibrations that no longer serve you, and this idea that you are "at odds" with your mother and sister is an OLD IDEA THAT NO LONGER SERVES YOU!!!

> Is this Michael?

Yes, Dear. I am here to build your strength to LET GO! Reflect on the love and support your mother and sister give you and look forward to sharing your EXCITEMENT about your new endeavor. At first they may not understand, but you will TEACH THEM! Being a natural-born teacher and leader is part of your soul imprint. You love to help others learn (and just to help others, period). And you are VERY GOOD AT IT!

> I am? I guess I do feel like that sometimes. Thank you for saying that. I'm actually getting a little tearful.

Yes, my dear child, this is you coming into who you are, REMEMBERING YOUR GIFTS!!! They have been long forgotten or buried, but now they are coming into the light. You got a glimpse when you taught and supervised students at Widener and more recently with onboarding new colleagues to the email channel role. You are an EXCELLENT teacher—kind, caring, loving, patient, and inquisitive. These traits allow you to share your knowledge in a way that helps people understand. You teach the way you would want to learn, with an open and fun and interesting approach.

This TEACHING ABILITY is what is going to help you help others to know us, God and the angels. While you feel most comfortable with writing, soon you will speak and offer classes, along with a variety of services to provide help and relief to others. Interaction through these kinds of teachings will support your soul. The writing does too, but it will be too isolating for you long-term.

Interacting with people makes your soul sing. Yes, the Gibraltar Center[22] will be a reality, but that will not be for several years. In the

---

[22] I received messages that I, along with a team of friends, mentors, and professionals, will open the Gibraltar Center for Soul Rejuvenation in Wilmington, Delaware, converting a beautiful but run-down mansion into a wellness center.

meantime, focus on your writing and offer one-on-one coaching and other courses.

You are wondering who will record everything, how to navigate the technology, what is involved with marketing, etc., etc. There is no need to worry about the "how" yet. This will all be given to you as inspiration from us. It will be FUN and EASY!!! Although it will not happen right away, it will be fairly soon in your time. We will help you transition from your banking position to your new role as a spiritual mentor, teacher, and healer.

> *I am thinking about Karan. She will not want me to share what I have learned about the angels through her until I am certified.*

That is just fine, Dear. You can teach what she has made public through her books and not release the specifics you have learned in class. That information is trademarked, or private, in Karan's eyes. Next summer when you finish the certification, you'll be ready to share the rest. There is still much to learn from Karan, so yes, you should continue. The door of channeled writing has opened to you, but the angels have more to teach you. Plus you need experience connecting closely with other angels. For example, you made a nice connection with Uriel in the class on Saturday. Like all angels, "he" has masculine and female energy. You see "him" as female because "he" is currently sharing with you more of "his" feminine energy.

> *If Uriel is masculine and feminine, why are we not saying "they" instead of "him"?*

Because Uriel's primary energy IS masculine, but "he" presents to you as feminine. You don't need more details—it is not for you to understand right now. Just know that all angels have masculine and feminine energy, usually with one manifesting more strongly than the other.

Gibraltar means "strong one of God" and will be a place where people who are recovering from mental breakdowns or trauma or longing for healing of mind, body, and spirit can participate in EMDR or talk therapy, EFT tapping, Reiki, acupuncture, astrology, massage, hypnosis, yoga, Zumba, meditation, cooking, gardening, walks in the gardens, bird watching, jewelry making, angelic healings, psychic readings, sessions with mediums, spirituality classes, and other services yet to be determined.

What else is there to know today?

That is it for today. We want you to enjoy the start to your vacation. Write in your gratitude journal, pull some angel cards, go back to bed if you like, surf Facebook—whatever feels good and right and makes you happy! You will have a lovely vacation. It is not necessary to take the laptop with you, although we have a feeling you will WANT TO!

Yes, now that I'm into the routine of connecting with you both, I don't want to take a break. It is not a burden—not something I WANT a vacation from. I LOVE connecting with you both!

That is great, Dear. We will not write as much while you are on vacation because you do need to rest. You have been working HARD and need a break from working full time and writing so much. Susan has noticed. Others aren't aware, and you don't realize it yourself because you love doing this now. But you will deplete your energy if you don't get time to relax and just "chill," as Aidan might say! We think you should go back to bed.

I don't feel tired.

Maybe not, but you have a busy week ahead doing fun things with family, so you want to be rested even if you don't sleep. Just RELAX!!! ENJOY!!! HAVE FUNNNN!!!!

OK, sounds really great. Thanks to you both. Love you.

AND, WE LOOOOVVVVVEEE YOU!!!!

Thanks, Michael. 😊

July 23, 2019

Good morning fellas! 😊 *I got my first real comment on my new website! Someone said my post*

> touched her heart. SO EXCITING!!! No idea how she found me, but I'm glad she did. It makes me realize that soon others will too!

Before you know it, they will come in DROVES. Your Facebook presence and email list will help. You have some subscribers already—ask Jane to show you.

> Sounds great! As you know, my psychiatrist called yesterday to say he had gotten an email from my sister. She saw my website and thought I was suicidal. My psychiatrist said my website was beautiful. He wasn't concerned about my mental state and knows I'm happy right now. He will not respond to my sister but just wanted to make sure there are no secrets.
>
> It is dragging me down not to be able to talk about it. There is a piece of me that doesn't want to deal with it and would rather let my family think what they want. But of course, I don't want them to worry, and I would like to have their support. I'm thinking about talking with them on the ride to the beach today, although I wonder if Steve should be present.

NAAAHHHH!! YOU GOT THIS!!! It will be fine. Avoiding it perpetuates the family pattern you are working so hard to break. It is in everyone's best interests to bring your feelings and needs into the open. Your family members have needs too, which are different from yours. They need to make sure you are stable and accept that your feelings about your childhood do not come from insanity. Even if they don't want to examine that, your willingness to bring it up breaks the chains of bondage that have held your family back for years, generations—for a VERY LONG TIME.

> Any thoughts on what to say?

Just speak from your heart, Love. You know how you feel and what to say. When you stay in touch with your feelings, you are very eloquent. That is your divine connection—God speaking through you.

Actually, God is within you, so you are just letting his and your light out, which are one and the same, by the way.

> Is this Michael?

Yes, Dear, helping you to understand that when you are YOU, you shine your light, which is God's light on and in the world. This is why, when you respond to Facebook posts or write to Julie or talk with Lori, you feel so GREAT! It is because you are shining your/God's light and feeling it in return. That's the great thing—when you shine your light, others can do the same.

It is contagious—not like a disease, LOL, but like JOY, the way laughter and fun spread through a room or how love begets love. Maybe we need to come up with a better word so people don't associate it with disease. . . . ANYHOO, it's all good. You and the readers will catch my drift. HA! Another expression. I don't even know exactly what CATCH MY DRIFT means, other than for someone to understand what you mean.

> It is also a boating term, I think.

Not to digress, but I love this term. When someone catches someone's drift, they are in the flow. I LOVE when people are in the flow, just going with the current, living their lives as their true selves. It is BEE-YOU-TI-FUL!!!

> I'm feeling a little distracted this morning. I don't want my typing to wake Aidan.

No worries, Dear. He is fine. But you can go out onto the porch and say your prayers, write in your gratitude journal, and pull some angel cards. You went to bed later than usual, so if you just want to go back to bed, that would be fine. You are tired.

> Yes, I am. Sounds good. Love you guys.

Love you too, Deary, Darling, sweet one.

Vacation—But Not from God

July 24, 2019

Good morning, God and Michael. How are you guys doing today?

We are GGGREEEAAATTT!!!!!

Oh, yeah? Tell me more.

We are excited that you are on VAAACCAATION!!!

Yes, it is nice to have a break from work. I drank a little too much yesterday but had a nice day overall. Talked with Shan and Mama and cleared the air a bit.

YES! That was FAANNNTTTAASSTICC!!! You still have work to do on expressing your views, like when someone makes racist comments or rather, doesn't understand the suffering that African Americans have endured in our country. People can't absolve themselves by saying they had no part in it. Sure, oppression and discrimination may not have been at their hands, but it is up to everyone to be part of the solution to ending racism. That can never happen until the story/history is brought into light. Every person plays a part. Though many like to say, "There is not a racist bone in my body," in our culture and society it's IMPOSSIBLE not to harbor racism.

Kind of funny—you sound like a social worker talking (or me if I would speak up!).

I know you have a problem challenging your mother, but you did start a little last night just raising the idea that history has been hard on people of color. It is fine that you stopped there. You are learning to stand up for what you believe in, and it takes time to become comfortable with a new behavior. We are PROUD of HOW FAR you have come!

In the past, you likely would have said nothing, but this time you injected your point of view. Your opinion is important because it is aligned with God's. The more you think about sharing the will of God with others, the more you will be inclined to stand up for what is right. As you know, God doesn't judge "right" or "wrong" in the sense that he thinks his children are bad if they make "right" or "wrong" choices. It is true, however, that God does want us to make choices that are for our highest good and in alignment with his will.

You know God's will most of the time because of your experience writing and talking with them, along with your own personality, knowledge gained in past lives, and social work training in this life. God loves social workers. Of course, they love all their children, but social workers have a special place, just as the LGBTQ+ children are special. Social workers try to "do his (their) will" or help others, and LGBTQ+ individuals are most like God because they are suffering.

> This was interesting. Love that God has a "special place" for social workers and LGBTQ+ individuals! And we haven't talked about race before.

Yes, it is an interesting discussion, as there is much to be said about how to make the world a better place for our LGBTQ+ children and people of color. But let's pause that subject and talk about you.

> LOL, I was just thinking I feel like you have something to tell me.

Yes, Dear, you need to leave your job.

> Oh my! It is not quite time yet. I need to be bringing income in before I can leave.

YES, I'm ONLY KIDDING!!!!

> Oh, Michael, you REALLY SCARED ME!!!!

Just wanted to keep you on your toes . . . LOL.

GEEZ, please try to not FREAK ME OUT! You know I have all these fears about money. Actually, I have been trusting more that it will all be OK, but I'm DEFINITELY NOT ready to leave my job until I have a source of income.

Income will come soon, and you will be able to leave your job, but you need to stay a little longer. We will try to make it easy for you so your focus can be on your writing and social media platform building. The writing is almost complete.

What do we need to do to finish up?

We have a few more tweaks to put on this section and then Susan can edit it.

I feel like this section is not very robust.

IT IS, my dear! It may not be long, but it communicates the important messages. Readers will see you in communion with us, talking with us daily, sharing your life struggles and joys, getting support from us DIRECTLY, and knowing our will for you. They will understand that they can do the same.

It is SO SIMPLE really. OK, it is not THAT easy, but it is not THAT HARD. Once people understand God's will for them and start to LIVE in alignment with that will—following their passions, asking us (the angels) for help, having FUN, and communing with us—LIFE WILL BE EASY AND GRAND!!!! That is the end of the RECONCILIATION. THAT IS IT!!! You can keep writing to us every day, but the book is pretty much done.

Don't you want to write some sort of conclusion?

NAH, we can just leave it here hangin' a little bit so people will want to read more. We DO have much more to say, but we have covered enough ground. It is time to publish so you can earn an income and focus on writing and speaking.

OH, GEEZ. Here we go again—SPEAKING???

Yes, my child. We will help you, but you WILL BE SPEAKING.

I feel like I only know your voice when I'm writing.

You know it more clearly when you are writing. You can bring your laptop and write when you talk, communicating questions to us from the audience.

That seems a little awkward.

HA! GOTCHA!!! No, Dear, you will HEAR OUR VOICES!!!! Indeed, you do already but just don't trust it is real. You feel safer and surer when you are writing. BUT if you LISTEN, you know how to hear our VOICES in everyday life. Starting today, let's practice that. If you have a question for us or want to talk to us, just ask it or think about it in your mind. Then wait for your "knowing" to take over and you will get your answer. We can even have a dialogue like we do now. JUST PRACTICE. START NOW. Stop typing for a bit, take some deep breaths, and ask us a question.

I asked about the speaking engagements. You said I will do PowerPoint presentations to help me with talking points, and those will be channeled through you guys to make it easy (and accurate). The presentations will be called "The Nature of God: The Revelation Discussion Groups."

YES, EXACTLY. You got exactly what we were telling you without having to write. It will get easier the more you practice. Throughout today and in the coming days, just reach out to us, ask us what we think or want you to know. Ask what meal to pick on a menu ... LOL. (Really, you can pick what you want!) But if you have ANY QUESTIONS or DOUBTS or FEARS, just ASK us for help, support, or guidance. WE are here for you as we are for ALL SOULS. They don't know it yet, but they will learn through this book and through you! GREAT JOB, DEAR!

THE NATURE OF GOD

Thank you, but for what exactly?

For LISTENING! You are a good listener WHEN YOU SET YOUR MIND TO IT!!! Sometimes you get distracted and don't listen to our call. Like last night—we tried to tell you to stop drinking because you would not feel so great today, but you did it anyway.

I didn't hear that call AT ALL.

That is because your will to have another drink drowned out our call. When people have such a strong will, it is not for us to interfere. Today you are on VACATION, but when you are in your regular routine, drinking too much brings down your vibration and makes it harder to hear us. We know you want to hear us loud and clear, so just remember that. Although you are not "addicted," per se, it is an old habit to drink to relax.

You really are quite happy and relaxed most of the time now, so you don't need it anymore. Once in a while you may want to enjoy the taste, but there is no need for you to drink daily. The sparkling waters we put in your path will help you transition to a lifestyle of drinking very little.

Again, this is not to say we "judge" drinking or that you should never do it. That is not truth. When it is done for flavor and fun, it is all good. However, most people drink to dull their emotions, and they don't even realize they do it. It can be hard to break the habit, but it is not THAT HARD if you put your attention on it and remember God wants you to be HAPPY! Burying your emotions makes you unhappy, but feeling and then releasing them returns you to JOY! You can do it! Indeed, you already have done much of this work.

I am a little distracted.

You are tired. Go back to bed.

I really want to pull some angel cards and do my gratitude journal.

Well, then do those, and THEN go back to bed. This is enough writing for today, although we want you to remember to "talk" to us today.

Michelle McCann

Will do. I hope I remember.

Not to worry. We will remind you!

Great. All righty. Have a good day.

You too, Dear. Enjoy the beach and lunch and SHOPPING!

The Divinely-Guided Life Plan

July 25, 2019

     Hi and good morning! I slept really well last night. Even though I went to bed later, I feel good getting up early.

    Yes, my darling, GOOOODDD MORNIN'!!!! Glad to connect with you. We didn't hear from you yesterday.

     I sort of forgot to do my practice! I'm so sorry.

    No need to be sorry, but focus on remembering. Practicing how to talk with us will be important. You hear us sometimes, but your skills need to improve for you to do the things we've planned.

     OK, I will be sure to practice more today.

    Let's practice now. Stop and close your eyes and see what comes to you.

     Thank you. I started to cry as feelings welled up about how things are with my family. They are better, and I am proud of myself (and know you are proud of me!) for standing up and speaking my truth. It is still sad for me because they don't see my perspective, but I can't change that. The only thing I can change is my

> own actions, thoughts, and behavior—and I HAVE DONE THAT! Others, including my family, don't have to accept my truth or my perspective, but I NEED TO SHARE THOSE! I guess you are letting me know this because it will be true with my writing as well.

THAT IS RIGHT, MY DAAAHHHLINGG!!! For you to be in the public eye and receive criticism and yes, sometimes even hatred, you need to be comfortable in your own skin and able to stand up for what you believe and for what you know is "right" in terms of aligning yourself and others to the will of God.

> I'm a little nervous that I will get "hatred."

Unfortunately, there will be haters. They will know deep down that you are telling the truth but do not believe it is possible (or right) to connect with God. They will be afraid. When the hate comes, remember that it is fear talking, the way your mother is afraid to face the truth of the past for you and for herself. To her, acknowledging all that happened would mean to hear that she was a bad person and bad mother, and she doesn't want to feel that. It is better to "put on a happy face," she believes, than to dredge up the past. She doesn't realize that releasing feelings is an important part of being happy. If you don't release the sadness, the grief, the trauma, it comes out in health problems, addictions, negative behavior, or possibly even hatred for others.

> Yes, I know and understand this now. I realize that my mental illness was a result of unprocessed trauma. Well, actually, I know it was part of my life plan to bring me to this point, as were the love and the trauma of my childhood. It was all part of the master plan. The mental illness was the path I needed to walk to "remember" and connect with you. It has helped me have compassion for others, learn to reveal myself and parts of my history that feel shameful, and become who I truly am.
>
> My social work training helped me understand trauma. It gave me skills to be empathetic and put

myself in others' shoes, especially those who have been oppressed in our culture. My banking experience taught me how to be a good business person, how to manage email, and how digital marketing works. It also connected me to many wonderful people, for which I am truly grateful!

You guys did a good job with my life plan. Even though it has been rocky at times, it has been wonderful. How could I not mention Steve and Aidan—the biggest blessings I ever could have received! I couldn't ask for a better family! And I have friends, too many to name here, with whom I connect and have fun and who love me. When I was younger, I wished I had more close friends. Now I realize they have come to me—my tribe is finding me—because I'm being who I really am! It is GLORIOUS, as you like to say.

I've been talking a lot. What else would you like to say today?

You have done a good job covering it. We wanted to talk about your life plan and how you came to be where you are today. It has been a wild and AHHH-MMAAAAZZZ-IIIINNNGGG ride. We have been right there alongside you, supporting you, cheering you on, nurturing you, guiding you, opening up doors for you, laughing with you. We have been partners in crime . . . LOL, not in crime. Thick as thieves—but, oh my, we were not stealing.

Funny, there are a lot of sayings for people who steal together! How about two peas in a pod?

Truly, we have been many peas in a pod because you have had God, ALL the angels, your spirit guides, your ancestors, and your earthly family all supporting you.

Stick a Fork in It: Done!

This is the end of this section and the book. We want all our readers to remember this—your life plan is AS IT SHOULD BE. Have faith and do not doubt that the path you are on is the one intended just for you.

Even though it is difficult at times, you agreed to this life plan before you came to earth, and you have not been alone in living it. TREMENDOUS amounts of support from the spirit and earthly realms have helped you get through. WE LOVE YOU and WOULD NEVER LEAVE YOU to struggle and fight your battles alone.

Your SPIRIT TEAM, which includes Mother and Father God, the angels, the ascended masters and spirit guides, and your ancestors, is ALWAYS HERE WITH YOU. We are all up in heaven and in the spirit realms supporting you, nurturing you, cheering you on, doing for you the same things we did for Michelle. She is not unique to have this going for her. YOU ALL have our love, grace, and support. All you need to do is REMEMBER to reach out for help when you need it. WE ARE HERE!

This concludes this book. May it bring you peace and joy and love. WE LOVE YOU!!!

With much joy and many angel blessings, we bid you ADIEU!
God, Michael, and Your Spirit Team

A Message from Michelle

"Be patient toward all that is unsolved in your heart and try to love the questions themselves, like locked rooms and like books that are now written in a very foreign tongue. Do not now seek the answers, which cannot be given you because you would not be able to live them. And the point is, to live everything. Live the questions now. Perhaps you will then gradually, without noticing it, live along some distant day into the answer."

~ Rainer Maria Rilke

I have SO. MANY. QUESTIONS. in my heart: Why are we here? How does a loving God allow suffering? How can we help each other cope? How can I be the person God—and I—want me to be? What happens when we die? Will suffering end? Was it necessary? Was it worth it?

Channeling messages from God and Archangel Michael has given me a greater understanding of many of these issues, but it seems that each answer leads to more questions. Of my readers, I ask, What are your questions? Have they been answered? What new things do you want to ask?

This process has been an amazing journey. Like a butterfly emerging from a chrysalis, the sometimes arduous process has transformed me. After experiencing childhood trauma and living with mental illness, I discovered the spiritual realms. I tried to make sense of it all while trying to live a normal life, be a good wife and mother, have fun with family and friends, and enjoy simple pleasures like a delicious meal, a good night's rest, and a beautiful sunny day.

For years I longed to live a spiritually-centered life in which I felt a personal connection to God, the angels, my spirit guides, and my ancestors. When this started to come true, I was in awe. WOW! I can actually talk with God and Archangel Michael. At the same time, I wanted to maintain a loving connection with my family and friends. I worried that my husband would not support my "traversing the spiritual realms," given my history of a mental illness diagnosis. Although he doesn't read my writing or ask about messages I receive, Steve shows steadfast support in simple ways.

One night, I couldn't sleep, so I tried to converse with him, which I often do. He JUST LOVES IT (not!). Steve rolled over and said, "Talk to your guides and angels, will ya?"

Even as my connection strengthened, sometimes I forgot to call in spiritual support. But my husband had seen me get up at 5 a.m. EVERY SINGLE DAY for months, channeling messages from God and Archangel Michael. When I asked Steve for advice about a difficult situation, he said, "Why don't you ask Michael?" "Who's Michael?" I said . . . LOL. It didn't dawn on me to ask the archangel for help, but that solution occurred immediately to Steve! My husband hitchhiking on my spiritual adventure—that is true love!

I felt "called" to write *The Nature of God*. Technically, having free will means I had a choice, but the pull was so strong I couldn't ignore it. Funny thing . . . I used to hear people talk about being called to a vocation (like pastors saying they were called to a new congregation), but I had no idea what that meant. Now I know—you feel so moved to do something, there is no way to say no!

THE NATURE OF GOD

During our sessions, God and I discussed so many remarkable ideas, including:

- We separated from God's energy of love and will reunite once we discover our true natures.
- Hell does not exist, God does not judge, and karma balances our negative actions.
- We co-create with Mother/Father God.
- Angels guide and protect us.
- There will be peace on earth!

But perhaps the most encouraging inspiration is that our human lives are not random or purposeless. There is a reason for everything that happens, and all is as it should be. While we struggle and suffer, we also feel joy, laughter, and love. We chose—longed for, actually—our life challenges to gain greater understanding of ourselves and God.

My hope is that each reader will find comfort and joy in these pages. God and the angels help us navigate life's trials and quell our fears by reminding us that everything is part of a grand plan. They also guide us to be who we truly are—God's divine children—so we can share in the universal love and celebration that is meant to be ours.

As you "live" your questions, let the answers here direct your journey toward hope and peace. I may be moving along a different path, but our destination is the same. Remember that everyone in the spirit realm—God, the angels, guides, ancestors, and loved ones—supports all of us, all the time. You just have to ask.

Resources

Teachers, Healers, and Mentors on My Journey

Cristina Aroche
Archangel Channel
https://cristinaaroche.com

Sean Blackwell
Bipolar Awakenings
https://www.bipolarawakenings.com

Laurie Blomer
Psychic, Channel, and Animal Communicator
http://www.laurieblomer.com

Emma Bragdon
Psycho-Spiritual Counseling
https://www.emmabragdon.com/

Brené Brown
Author and Professor Researching Courage, Vulnerability, Shame, and Empathy
https://brenebrown.com

Janet Brown
Advanced Practice Nurse in Psychiatry
https://serenemindsllc.com/providers

Michelle McCann

Meryl Brownstein
Nationally Certified Counselor
https://merylbrownstein.com/

Dr. Joseph Bryer
Psychiatrist
https://josephbryer.com/

Glen Cooper, Kent Hoffman, and Bert Powell
Co-Originators, Circle of Security International
https://www.circleofsecurityinternational.com/

Ellen DeGeneres
American Comedian
https://www.ellentube.com/

Glennon Doyle
Author, Activist, Thought Leader
https://momastery.com/

Christina Goetz
Intuitive Relationship Coach
https://www.christinagoetz.me/

Janet Fongheiser
Angelic and Pranic Healer
janetfongheiser@gmail.com

Jackie Fox
Astrologer
Jackie.fox3@gmail.com

Tracey Gazel
Mentor for Emerging Healers, Spirit Guide, and Angel Intuitive
www.litupsoul.com

Kyle Gray
Author and Angel Expert
https://www.kylegray.co.uk/

Catharine Han
Angelic Energy Healer and Spiritual Coach
https://linktr.ee/compassionatelighthealing

Thich Nhat Hanh
Spiritual Leader, Poet, and Peace Activist
https://plumvillage.org/about/thich-nhat-hanh/

Esther Hicks/Abraham
Inspirational Speaker and Author,
Interpreter of Infinite Intelligence
https://www.abraham-hicks.com

Lois Hoffman
Author and Self-Publishing Coach, The Happy Self-Publisher
http://happyselfpublisher.com

Andrea Bosbach Largent, MSW
Ancestral and Spirit Realms Therapist
www.AncestralRealms.net

Dr. Alice Lee
Holistic Psychiatrist
https://www.holisticpsychiatrist.com/

Tamara Levitt
Author/Mindfulness Instructor
https://www.tamaralevitt.com/

Alice Miller
Researcher on Childhood, Author
https://www.alice-miller.com/en/

Doreen Moore
Reiki Master, EFT Tapping Practitioner
metamorphosiswellnesscenter@gmail.com

Anita Moorjani
Author and Speaker
https://anitamoorjani.com/

Kelly Notaras
Writer, Editor, Author and Self-Publishing Coach, kn literary arts
https://knliterary.com

Tammy Petruccelli
Medium
https://www.tammypetruccelli.com/

Susan Robinson
Writer and Editor, Creative Power Writing
https://www.creativepowerwriting.com
susan@creativepowerwriting.com

Robert Schwartz
Spiritual Teacher and Regression Therapist
https://www.yoursoulsplan.com

Kevin Todeschi
Executive Director and CEO
Edgar Cayce's Association for Research and Enlightenment
https://www.edgarcayce.org/events/event-listings/event-speakers/kevin-j-todeschi/

Reid Tracy
President and CEO, Hay House Publishing
https://www.hayhouse.com

Karan Tumasz
Channel, Soul Coach, Healer
https://karanangel.com

John Van Auken
Author and Speaker
https://www.johnvanauken.com/

Sara Wiseman
Teacher of Spiritual Intuition
www.sarawiseman.com

Jamie Marie Wey
Intuitive Empowerment Coach and Numerologist
https://www.instagram.com/jamiemariewey/

Books

A Course in Miracles Made Easy, Alan Cohen
A Return to Love, Marianne Williamson
Angels in My Hair, Lorna Byrne
Ask Your Guides, Sonia Choquette
Bridging Two Realms, John Holland
Conversations with God, Neale Donald Walsch
Daring Greatly, Brené Brown
Dying to be Me, Anita Moorjani
Edgar Cayce and the Kabbalah, John Van Auken
Edgar Cayce on Auras and Colors, Kevin Todeschi and Carol Ann Liaros
From Karma to Grace, John Van Auken
Getting in the Gap, Wayne Dyer
Gorilla and the Bird, Zack McDermott

Michelle McCann

Healing Through the Akashic Records, Linda Howe
KaranAngel's Guardian Angel Guidebook and *Guided Meditations,* Karan Tumasz
Lost Connections, Johann Hari
The Magic Mala, Bob Olson
Many Lives, Many Masters, Brian Weiss, MD
Mary Magdalene Revealed, Meggan Watterson
Miracles Through Pranic Healing, Master Choa Kok Sui
Opening to Channel, Sanaya Roman
The Power of Now, Eckhart Tolle
Psychosis or Spiritual Emergence? Dr. Nicki Crowley
The Secret, Rhonda Byrne
The Universe Has Your Back and *Spirit Junkie,* Gabrielle Bernstein
The Velveteen Rabbit, Margery Williams
Untamed, Glennon Doyle
What Color is Your Parachute? Nelson Bolles
Writing the Divine and *You Are Enough,* Sara Wiseman
Your Soul's Plan, Robert Schwartz

Music

"Closer to Fine," *Indigo Girls,* Indigo Girls
    https://www.youtube.com/watch?v=HUgwM1Ky228
"The Glory of Love," *Solitude/Solitaire,* Peter Cetera
    https://www.youtube.com/watch?v=yQHhqDRn4_c
"Have a Little Faith in Me," *Bring the Family,* John Hiatt
    https://www.youtube.com/watch?v=7aYxMuLb3h8
"Prayer of St. Francis," *Surfacing,* Sarah McLachlan
    https://www.youtube.com/watch?v=agPnMxp5Occ

"Queen of the Slipstream," *Poetic Champions Compose*, Van Morrison https://www.youtube.com/watch?v=LLIYiL-UOnA
"The Rainbow Connection," *The Muppet Movie*, Kermit the Frog https://www.youtube.com/watch?v=WS3Lkc6Gzlk
"Somebody's Out There Watching," *Touched by an Angel: The Album*, The Kinleys https://www.youtube.com/watch?v=piPRJc6-MO0
"Trouble Me," *10,000 Maniacs*, Natalie Merchant https://www.youtube.com/watch?v=gXnDGEM2oOg
"Wind Beneath My Wings," *Beaches*, Bette Midler https://www.youtube.com/watch?v=0iAzMRKFX3c

Films/Video

Crazywise (trailer)
https://www.youtube.com/watch?v=YDM5_nyla9A
"Lessons from the Mental Hospital," Glennon Doyle,
https://www.youtube.com/watch?v=NHHPNMIK-fY
Michael (trailer)
https://www.youtube.com/watch?v=Tw1jwFTDrSU
Miracles from Heaven (trailer)
https://www.youtube.com/watch?v=CldGTG6iVrU
"The Power of Vulnerability," *TED Talk*, Brené Brown
https://www.ted.com/talks/brene_brown_the_power_of_vulnerability?language=en
"Shame is Lethal," *Supersoul*, OWN, Brené Brown
http://www.oprah.com/own-super-soul-sunday/dr-brene-brown-shame-is-lethal-video

Toy Story 2, All Zurg Parts
    https://www.youtube.com/watch?v=wRxY7KzkoGg

Articles/Websites

A Course In Miracles https://acim.org/

"Akashic Records," Edgar Cayce's A.R.E.
    https://www.edgarcayce.org/the-readings/akashic-records/

Anne Cooke, ed., "Understanding Psychosis and
    Schizophrenia," The British Psychological Society (2017),
    https://www.bps.org.uk/sites/www.bps.org.uk/files/Page%
    20'%20Files/Understanding%20Psychosis%20and%20Schiz
    ophrenia.pdf

Daily OM https://www.dailyom.com/

Edgar Cayce's Association for Research and Enlightenment
    https://www.edgarcayce.org/

Ellen DeGeneres, Ellen Tube https://www.ellentube.com

EMDR Institute, Inc.: Eye Movement Desensitization and
    Reprocessing (EMDR) https://www.emdr.com/what-is-
    emdr/

Mad in America: Science, Psychiatry and Social Justice
    https://www.madinamerica.com

"Martin Luther King Jr. Quotes," Goodreads
    https://www.goodreads.com/quotes/21045-if-a-man-is-
    called-to-be-a-street-sweeper

The Mighty: Making Health About People
    https://themighty.com

Mt. Cuba Center https://mtcubacenter.org/about/

National Alliance on Mental Illness (NAMI)
https://www.nami.org
Pranic Healing https://pranichealing.com/about-us
Sacred Scribes, Joanne Walmsley
http://sacredscribesangelnumbers.blogspot.com/2011/11/angel-number-717.html
Sara Wiseman https://www.sarawiseman.com

Facebook

Fred Rogers Center
https://www.facebook.com/FredRogersCenter/posts/anything-thats-human-is-mentionable-and-anything-that-is-mentionable-can-be-more/10155842127808069/
Hay House Online Writer's Workshop
https://www.facebook.com/HHWritersWorkshop/

Oracle Decks

Angel Prayers Oracle Cards, Kyle Gray
https://www.kylegray.co.uk/store/angel-prayers-oracle
Gateway Oracle Cards, Denise Linn, Hay House
https://www.hayhouse.com/gateway-oracle-card-deck
Magical Times Empowerment Cards, Jody Bergsma
https://www.amazon.com/jody-bergsma-Magical-Times-Empowerment/dp/B01DPV3HO6
Work Your Light Oracle Cards, Rebecca Campbell
https://rebeccacampbell.me/oracledeck/

Michelle D McCann
Divine Channel

https://michelledmccann.com
https://www.facebook.com/MichelleDMcCannAuthor/
https://www.linkedin.com/in/michelledmccann/
https://www.instagram.com/michelledmccann/

Acknowledgments

I would like to thank the teachers, mentors, and healers along my journey, without whom this "revelation" would not have been possible. These individuals are included in the resources section above. I would like to extend a special thank you to my current therapist, Meryl Brownstein, for working her EMDR "magic" and for sharing her gifts and light with those who are aiming to heal from trauma. Dr. Joseph Bryer, my psychiatrist for many years, has also been a special person on my road to recovery. While he and I may not see eye to eye (yet!) on the root causes of my diagnosis, he was an invaluable partner in keeping me stable and fully functioning in the world while I sorted out my truth. Much love and appreciation to Emma Bragdon and Andrea Bosbach Largent for their clinical expertise and wisdom in the ways of the spirit world, helping me to learn about spiritual emergence and my role as a "sensitive."

I am forever indebted to the dear friends who have supported me throughout my life and through my time of mental illness and self-discovery. Please accept my deepest gratitude for loving me for who I am and for helping me learn to accept myself. It has been a long road, but I am closer than ever before to my destination of feeling worthy of love and belonging.

To Lori and Julie, my dear high school friends, for your faith in God and me, for listening to my fears on this journey, and for being my biggest cheerleaders, encouraging me to share this work with the world. To Michele and Donna, my college roomies, for the never-ending laughs and the Skype conversations about our lives, families, and the joys and tribulations of parenthood. To Nedda "in the know," for your listening ear, loving heart, and wise counsel. To my social work friends, Cheryl, Pat, Lydia, Karen, and Barb, for years of friendship and mentorship, for opening my eyes to the importance of sharing my feelings in order to heal, and for being role models inspiring social justice. To all the incredible Social Work Counseling Services (SWCS) crew of staff and students, especially Regina and Michelle, for your genuine and kind spirits, always helping others and sharing your light with the world.

To my Mt. Cuba Center family, especially Urszula, Marty, Duncan, and Jackie, for humor, friendship, memes, and group texts that make me laugh out loud.

To my German friends, Wilfried, Klaudia, Dietmar, Piet, Luc, and Julia, for some wonderful adventures and for giving me and my family the gift of a beautiful friendship across language and culture that has been a treasure in our lives. To Michelle, for letting me be part of your German adventure all those years ago and for the bonds that formed as a result. To my other high school friends, Lisa, Sandy, Ginny, Jon, Craig, Doug, and Katrina, who, even though we are not in touch as much these days, will forever be remembered for the good times and positive (and sometimes crazy . . . LOL) influence on my life.

To Karan, Janet, and Nicole, my angelic healing community, for teaching me about the angels and sharing this path toward a personal relationship with them. To my psychic development soul sisters, Laurie, Elizabeth, Nancy, Jackie, and Jenn, for sharing your gifts with me and for nurturing my own gifts with kindness and love. To Tammy, for offering knowledge, time, and a space for me and others to learn and grow spiritually.

To my incredible corporate world friends and colleagues, the incomparable PEOPLE of MBNA, who helped me learn and grow personally and professionally. Very special thanks to my Consumer Finance teammates and to these great souls:

Jacqueline, for your genuine spirit and for seeing strengths in me that I didn't always see in myself; Lisa and Cheryl, for helping me learn to laugh at myself and not take life too seriously; Benaifer, Rushad, Denise, and Joe, for your friendship, mutual sharing, and our fun dinner gatherings; Amy, for always keeping it real and being a role model on how to be brave and stand up for what is true and right; Meredith, Feif, and Katya, for the laughs and for being such strong female leaders; Patty, whom I think of as an honorary social worker, for sharing of yourself and always listening and offering insights about my struggles and celebrating my triumphs.

To my wonderful Bank of America and email channel teammates, especially Abby, for offering a space for me to be myself and for teaching me what it means to be a real team player; Chris, for your humor and acceptance of my "out there" ways; Grace, for good thinking about how to handle challenging situations; and Denise, for being the "rock," offering steadfast guidance and support.

To my "new age" friends, Doreen, Maureen, and Kim, for your openness to the spirit world and for supporting me on the journey of my own opening. To my writing soul sister, Christina, for encouraging words of wisdom and insights as I wrestled with this book-writing adventure.

Many thanks to my editor, Susan Robinson. Words cannot begin to describe what a gift and blessing she has been in my life. It was no easy task to take this jumble of channeled writing and create a cohesive body of work that would contribute meaningfully to the world and be of service to others. While working her magic on this manuscript, she spent countless hours offering professional and personal guidance, counsel, love, and support. My gratitude for her generosity with her time and wisdom spans far and wide.

I would also like to acknowledge Lois Hoffman, The Happy Self-Publisher, for her patience, kindness, and in-depth knowledge, helping me on this publishing journey and turning

Michelle McCann

this dream into a reality. My appreciation also goes to Jane Clark and her staff at Teakettica, for their creativity and expertise in creating my beautiful website, business cards, email template, and Facebook page, and for having the patience to teach me how to use them! Warm thoughts of gratitude go to Ana Yevonishon for her encouragement and genuine nature, and for capturing my essence with her photography talents. Thank you to Nevena Knezevic at Graphic3D Design for my beautiful and symbolic book cover.

This journey would not have been complete without my birth family, Mama, Daddy, Vicky, Shannon, Duke, and Will, and their spouses and children, as well as all my aunts, uncles, and cousins; and my in-law family, Joe, Terri, Cathi, and Pat, and their spouses and children along with Uncle Len and Aunt Camille. I love you all dearly and thank you for the blessings you have been in my life. Things have not always been easy, but we have shared a lot of love and laughter, for which I have immense gratitude. A very special shout out to my loving and crazy (in a good way!) mama. You are an inspiration and a role model for how to love kids unconditionally with patience and kindness and to help us feel special and proud of ourselves. Like George Bailey in *It's a Wonderful Life*, your positive impact on those whose lives you have touched has been remarkable.

Lastly, but absolutely not least, I wish to thank my dear husband, Steve, and my wonderful son, Aidan, for being my joy and my motivation every day. You have stood by me through thick and thin, through lots of love and laughter and the hard times, steadfast in your love and respect. For this I will forever be grateful. I love you more than words can ever express.

Above all, I thank my creator and my angels for bringing me into the world and guiding me through this glorious and wild ride called life! Much love to all!

Peace and angel blessings! ☺

About the Author

Michelle McCann's background and personal experiences make her uniquely qualified to help individuals connect to God and understand the true causes of mental illness and trauma. The holder of a Master of Social Work (MSW) degree, she practiced as a social worker (LCSW) for eleven years in various roles with women, children, and families. At Widener University (PA), she directed a welfare-to-work program, supervised graduate students, and taught in the MSW program. Michelle also spent many years in the corporate world, primarily in marketing roles.

In 2007, Michelle was hospitalized following an acute psychotic episode and later diagnosed with bipolar disorder. During this and subsequent episodes, she believed she was Jesus. Through psychiatric care, Michelle has lived a "normal" life as a wife and mother of one really terrific son, as well as a daughter, sister, friend, and successful working professional. She recently discovered the concept of spiritual emergence and has come to believe that some of her unusual experiences involved her connecting with the divine. She has taken a wide array of coursework and participated in numerous groups on spirituality, intuition, psychic development, and angelic communication and healing.

Although Michelle was exposed to Christianity throughout her life and honors the love and compassion Christ symbolizes, she has no religious affiliation. Through her experiences and the teachings of many spiritual mentors, Michelle now understands that it is truly possible to make direct connection with God,

Source, Creator, Higher Power—whatever you choose to call that mystery of the universe that is greater than we are. Her hope is that by sharing her story, others affected by the challenges of mental illness, as well as those seeking their spiritual path, will find peace.

A true Delawarean now, Michelle lives in a heavenly garden oasis with her husband, Steve, and son, Aidan. Michelle's southern roots (Mississippi) and small-town Midwestern upbringing (Illinois) help to keep her grounded as she traverses the spiritual realms.

Visit www.michelledmccann.com for informational blog posts, including channeling, and to sign up for Michelle's email list.

About the Book Cover

The cover spoke to me as soon as I saw it, although I couldn't tell you why! When it first popped up in my email, I told my husband, Steve, that I LOVED it and thought it was beautiful. As with all things, I knew it had been divinely inspired to be just what it needed to be. Because I always look deeply at things (never judging a book by its cover . . . LOL), I said the squares were a little curious. Steve suggested I look up the symbolism of the square, and I found some amazing meanings. Reaching out to Susan Robinson, my visionary editor, I asked what she gleaned from the cover art. She said she saw the squares as representing the Holy Trinity—God, Jesus, and the Holy Ghost—and that the swash portrayed souls moving toward heaven.

My spirit team suggested I ask Susan to write more about the semiotics of the cover features and to include her further insights. Her initial draft said the design elements were carefully chosen for their symbolism. I laughed because I didn't actually "choose" anything. I emailed the designer, Nevena Knezevic, to ask what sparked her idea for the cover, knowing it was divine inspiration but wondering if there was more to the story. She indicated that she couldn't really say why she chose the image, except that she loves rose gold. When she saw the title of the book, she just knew that color would be perfect.

I asked Susan to Google the design's symbols and share her findings about the depth and complexity of the piece of art that is the cover of this book. Here is what she discovered, along with her personal interpretations:

To the ancient Chinese, the square symbolized the earth. A square's straight lines suggest stasis and immutability, and the shape itself embodies structure, foundation, and balance. Four sides and corners signify grounding through the four cardinal directions, four seasons, four earth elements (fire, earth, air, water), four cosmic elements (sun, moon, planet, star), and four phases of life (birth, childhood, adulthood, death).

Thus the cover's squares represent the synergistic blend of earth and heaven and the solid foundation for an authentic life that we build by connecting with God. That the squares are tilted into diamonds promises clarity and wisdom that transcend the earthly realm. Gold symbolizes the achievement, abundance, and enlightenment that come when we have a relationship with God.

The rose gold color of the swash is a nod to God's feminine aspect, our divine mother, who created the earth and all nature. Her influence nurtures and protects us, helping us to infuse all situations with love and light. No single hue, the swash seems to contain particles, suggesting several meanings: the earth, the multitude of angels, and human souls. The upward brush stroke implies our striving to raise our energetic vibration to become one with Mother and Father God.

On the back cover, the flourish underlines the infinity of the universe and that individual souls are all part of the larger collective soul.

Surely Nevena's design was divinely inspired, as it perfectly illustrates and connects all the concepts I have channeled in the text.

Does the cover design evoke other meanings for you? Please share your thoughts with Susan and me!